Annabelle Sreberny is Emeritus Professor of Global Media and Communications in the Centre for Media Studies at the School of Oriental and African Studies (SOAS), University of London. She is the co-author of *Blogistan: The Internet and Politics in Iran* (I.B.Tauris, 2010) and, also with Massoumeh Torfeh, *Persian Service: The BBC and British Interests in Iran* (I.B.Tauris, 2014).

Massoumeh Torfeh is the former UN Director of Strategic Communication in Afghanistan, now a research associate at the London School of Economics (LSE), and SOAS. She was previously a senior producer at the BBC World Service.

CULTURAL REVOLUTION IN IRAN

Contemporary Popular Culture
in the Islamic Republic

Edited by Annabelle Sreberny
and Massoumeh Torfeh

New paperback edition published in 2017 by
I.B.Tauris & Co. Ltd
London • New York
www.ibtauris.com

First published in hardback in 2013 by I.B.Tauris & Co. Ltd

Copyright © 2014, 2017 Annabelle Sreberny and Massoumeh Torfeh

The right of Annabelle Sreberny and Massoumeh Torfeh to be identified as the editors of this work has been asserted by them in accordance with the Copyright, Designs and Patents Act 1988.

Copyright Preface © 2017 Annabelle Sreberny and Massoumeh Torfeh.

Copyright Individual Chapters © 2013 Liliane Anjo, Mahmoud Arghavan, Alice Bombardier, Katja Föllmer, Mehri Honarbin-Holliday, Azadeh Kian, Pardis Mahdavi, Amin Moghadam, Parmis Mozafari, Bronwen Robertson, Naghmeh Samini, Nahid Siamdoust, Vit Šisler, Annabelle Sreberny, Anna Vanzan and Saeed Zeydabadi-Nejad.

All rights reserved. Except for brief quotations in a review, this book, or any part thereof, may not be reproduced, stored in or introduced into a retrieval system, or transmitted, in any form or by any means, electronic, mechanical, photocopying, recording or otherwise, without the prior written permission of the publisher.

Every attempt has been made to gain permission for the use of the images in this book. Any omissions will be rectified in future editions.

References to websites were correct at the time of writing.

ISBN: 978 1 78453 513 1
eISBN: 978 0 85773 440 2
ePDF: 978 0 85772 297 3

A full CIP record for this book is available from the British Library
A full CIP record is available from the Library of Congress

Library of Congress Catalog Card Number: available

Typeset by OKS

CONTENTS

List of Illustrations   vii
Preface to the Paperback Edition of *Cultural Revolution in Iran*   viii

1. Thirty-plus Years of the Iranian Revolution:
   Culture in Contestation   1
   Annabelle Sreberny and Massoumeh Torfeh

Part I. Social Context and Sexuality

2. Iran's Green Movement in Context   13
   Pardis Mahdavi

3. Tehrani Cultural Bricolage: Local Traditions and Global
   Styles of Tehran's Non-Conformist Youth   27
   Mahmoud Arghavan

4. Social and Cultural Change and the Women's
   Rights Movement in Iran   43
   Azadeh Kian

5. Emerging Forms of Masculinity in the Islamic
   Republic of Iran   59
   Mehri Honarbin-Holliday

Part II. Performing Arts and Cinema

6. Contemporary Iranian Theatre: The Emergence of
   an Autonomous Space   81
   Liliane Anjo

7. Dance and the Borders of Public and Private Life
   in Post-Revolution Iran   95
   Parmis Mozafari

8. Beyond Gender: Women Filmmakers and
   Sociopolitical Critique   109
   Saeed Zeydabadi-Nejad

Part III. Music

9. 'I am an Original Iranian Man': Identity and Expression
   in Tehran's Unofficial Rock Music   133
   Bronwen Robertson

10. Neither 'Islamic' nor a 'Republic:' Discourses in Music   151
    Nahid Siamdoust

Part IV. Representation

11. Digital Heroes: Identity Construction in Iranian
    Video Games   171
    Vit Šisler

12. Satire in the Iranian Media: Development and Diversity   193
    Katja Föllmer

13. Gendered Taboos in Iran's Text Message Jokes   209
    Naghmeh Samini

14. Iranian Mural Painting: New Trends   217
    Alice Bombardier

15. From the Pen to the Rotary Press: Women Book
    Publishers in Post-Revolutionary Iran   231
    Anna Vanzan

Part V. Beyond Borders

16. The Other Shore: Iranians in the United Arab
    Emirates Between Visibility and Invisibility   247
    Amin Moghadam

List of Contributors   267
Index   273

LIST OF ILLUSTRATIONS

Fig. 1.1	Basiji poster, Tehran	2
Fig. 1.2	'Death to America' wall painting, Tehran	3
Fig. 1.3	Religious mural, Modares Highway, Tehran	4
Fig. 1.4	Biscuits, Armenian bakery, Tehran	9
Fig. 5.1	Hooshyar and Ashraf, Iranian men	66
Fig. 5.2	Joljota in performance	69
Fig. 5.3	Winged man	71
Fig. 5.4	Hojat and Lorestan rock	72
Fig. 5.5	Billboard in Tehran	73
Fig. 5.6	Poster of Imam Hussein	74
Fig. 7.1	Mural of Safavid entertainers, Chehel Sotoon Palace, Isfahan	98
Fig. 9.1	Zina and his band Yellow Dogs in their rehearsal studio	134
Fig. 9.2	Marcus, Mehran and Shervin of Audioflows rehearsing in a disused sauna	135
Fig. 11.1	*Resistance* video game	176
Fig. 11.2	*Valfajr 8* video game	177
Fig. 11.3	*Lotfali Khan Zand* video game	181
Fig. 11.4	*Age of Pahlevans* video game	182
Fig. 14.1	Mural, Tehran	221
Fig. 14.2	Mural, Tehran	222
Fig. 14.3	Mural reform, Tehran	223
Fig. 14.4	Mural, new genre, Tehran	225
Fig. 14.5	Inhabitants of Tehran mural	226
Fig. 14.6	Pre-urban Idyll	227

All images courtesy of the individual authors of the chapters unless otherwise specified.

PREFACE TO THE PAPERBACK EDITION OF *CULTURAL REVOLUTION IN IRAN*

Annabelle Sreberny and Massoumeh Torfeh, 2016

The publication of this volume in paperback could not be more timely.

While considerable attention in 2015–6 has been focused on the diplomatic resolution of the nuclear issue and the development of the Iranian economy, issues around cultural expression and human rights have been sidelined. Yet they remain as urgent as ever and constitute a key emerging political struggle for Iranians.

In June 2013, Hassan Rouhani was elected president of Iran. Between November 2015 and spring 2016, negotiations were held that lead to an agreement signed between the Islamic Republic of Iran and the P5+1 group of world powers constraining Iran's nuclear programme and heralding a new mood of peaceful diplomacy.

Yet throughout the negotiations, Ayatollah Khamenei, the Supreme leader, repeatedly warned that the US goal was to gain 'political, cultural, security, ideological and economic influence'.[1] With ensuing uncertainties about the future of the nuclear deal and statements by the two main candidates in the forthcoming US presidential elections indicating a tougher US line, Khamenei has also reverted to his more hardline stance. In April 2016, he compared the danger of a cultural invasion by the West to a real war: 'You can liken this soft war to a hard war and the front line of a war, just like the conditions that exists [*sic*] in Syria, Iraq, Yemen.'[2] Later, on 26 May in a major speech on "soft war" to the Assembly of Experts, he called for stronger measures, saying 'this is the time when we should engage in the great jihad.'[3]

In February 2016, peaceful elections in Iran meant that the reformists could regain much of their lost influence in the Parliament, especially in the capital, Tehran. After the late April runoff elections an unprecedented number of 18 women were elected, making up 6 percent of the new cohort of 290 MPs. This meant that for the first time the number of women superseded the number of clerics, who had 16 seats, the lowest figure in all the parliaments of the Islamic Republic. Yet, despite such successes by the reform/moderate camps, in the elections to the Assembly of Experts the conservative cleric Ayatollah Ahmad Jannati – who had the lowest number of votes – was elected leader, indicating that hardliners are still in control of the assembly.[4]

These harbingers of an emergent new politics have as yet made little positive difference to the cultural field and the many forms of expression and practice with which this book is concerned. The creativity seems just as vibrant but the controls seem just as tough or even tougher, while the protests against censorship have taken on a strong international dimension and there is more consistent monitoring and documentation of abuses.

Some brief updates through to September 2016:

Journalists and Writers

The organisation Journalism is not a Crime monitors the censorship of journalists, with a 'wall of shame' on their website that documents all journalists arrested since the 2009 election.[5] It shows three deaths (Sattar Beheshti, Hoda Reza-Zadeh Saber and Alireza Eftekhari), the photographs of 150 journalists arrested and 25 imprisoned, and many more names without images attached.

Four journalists (Afarin Chitsaz, Ehsan Mazandarani, Saman Safarzaei and Davoud Asadi) accused in November 2015 of being part of an 'infiltration network' that colludes with hostile Western governments, were sentenced in April 2016 for a total of 27 years. Isa Saharkhiz, also arrested in November, who has gone on several hunger strikes since his incarceration, once wrote '... now newspapers and magazines can do whatever they want except professional journalism, and journalists can write anything except the truth.'[6] Jason Rezaian, the dual-national *Washington Post* journalist, was imprisoned for more than a year before being released in January 2016 along with six other dual nationals, in a move widely seen as linked to the nuclear negotiations.[7]

Other kinds of writers have also faced difficulties. The blogger Hossein Ronahi-Maleki was given a 15-year sentence for writing critical blogs and founding an anti-censorship group. Poets and lyricists Fatemeh Ekhtesari and Mehdi Moosavi were held in Evin without formal charge, because their lyrics had been performed by Shahin Najafi, the exiled singer; they were later released on bail.

Not every publisher is allowed in to the Tehran Book Fair. For the first time a number of independent Iranian publishers across Europe held an uncensored Tehran Book Fair in London in early May.[8]

Cartooning

Cartooning has a long tradition in Iran but cartoonists have had a very difficult time recently. In a case that began in August 2014, Atena Farghadani was sentenced to 12 years for depicting members of the Majles as animals, a cartoon she drew in protest against two proposed bills that would outlaw voluntary sterilization, restrict access to contraceptives and tighten divorce laws. When she spoke out on social media about her prison treatment she was targeted further, being accused of 'indecent conduct' because she shook hands with her lawyer in jail and subjected to a virginity test in prison. In January 2015 she went on hunger strike. A campaign was organised by cartoonists around the world, under the hashtag #Draw4Atena.[9] She was released on 3 May 2016.

Hadi Heydari was jailed for a cartoon called "blindfolding" that depicted Iranian soldiers having their eyes covered as they were marched off to the Iraq War. The Revolutionary Guards built up a substantial case against him, accusing him of 'spreading propaganda against the regime' and also closed down *Shargh* newspaper, not for the first time. He was released in April 2016.

Touka Nayestani, now living abroad, has written a biting piece about how he learned to cope with the censors who pointed to familiar symbols to find fault with his cartoons.

> The most important symbol was the beard, which is the exclusive domain of the clergy. Then we have walking canes and keffiyeh, which are symbols of the Supreme Leader. Drawing handkerchiefs over the eyes or the mouth was dangerous because it offends the paramilitary Basij. Drawing a few old men who are dozing off is a direct insult to the members of the Assembly of Experts. Drawing monkeys angers members of the parliament. Drawing a shark was dangerous for a few years (under Hashemi Rafsanjani) but it is one of those rare banned symbols that are now permitted.[10]

The Islamic Republic received global condemnation for an international Holocaust cartoon competition in 2006, yet a second one was organised in May 2016. Foreign Minister Zarif ran into considerable controversy as he claimed the organisers behind the competition were independent NGOs, while both Owj Cultural Center and Sarsheshmeh Cultural Center are funded by the IRGC and the cartoons were shown at Iran's Cartoon Biennale, which is funded and organised by the Ministry of Culture and Islamic Guidance. There was significant international denouncement of the exhibition.

Women

One of the best-known activist campaigns is *My Stealthy Freedom*, a Facebook page where Iranian women dare to post photos of themselves without hejab. The campaign was started by Masih Alinejad, a journalist who now lives in London and who has won international awards for this initiative.

There has also been the first FEMEN-type action of naked protest.[11] On 31 March, Iranian theatre actor and director Moujan Mohammad Taher staged a nude protest near Tehran's Milad Tower. Soon after, the protest attracted widespread attention, with videos and photographs being posted across social media, views of Tehran clearly visible in the background. 'I am not a slave,' the 36-year-old wrote across her body. She modelled her protest on public acts by FEMEN activists, known for their topless demonstrations against religion, authoritarianism and the sex industry.[12] According to Mohammad Taher, this is the first nude protest in Iran, a defiant 'no' to the Islamic Republic's anti-women laws.

Access to sporting venues remains an issue for women. In June 2014, Ghoncheh Ghavami, an Iranian student based in London, was arrested with others for trying to gain access to the Vozara sporting complex to see an international volleyball match. She was released but later returned to retrieve her belongings, was rearrested and put in solitary confinement in Evin prison. She was released on bail in November 2014.

In May 2016, there was a crackdown on eight models for posting 'vulgar' photographs on Instagram, with Javad Babaei, the Iranian government's prosecutor for cybercrimes, saying that "Sterilizing popular cyberspaces is on our agenda."[13] At the same time, Kim Kardashian was lambasted as a secret agent for Instagram who was working to corrupt the women of Iran.

Indeed, the summer of 2016 saw more pressure placed on dual-nationals and on women, so that Hoda Hodfar, the sociologist, had a particularly brutal time.[14]

Music and Dance

Music has a complicated place in the Islamic Republic. Much of it has been developed and performed literally underground but some individuals have been allowed to perform in public spaces such as the many new shopping malls. Yet in a 2015 trial that lasted no longer than three minutes, Mehdi and Hossein Rajabian and their friend Yousef Emadi were found guilty of 'insulting Islamic sanctities', 'spreading propaganda against the system' and 'illegal audio-visual activities'. Mehdi was the founder of the now-blocked website Barg Music, which distributed unlicensed music, while Hossein made a feature film *Inverted Triangle* that touched on women's right to divorce. They were sentenced to six years' imprisonment and a fine of 200m rials, around £4,000.[15] In June 2016, their appeal was rejected and they were summoned to start their sentences.[16]

Other areas of cultural concern include architecture where much old housing stock is being torn down in Tehran, Isfahan and elsewhere – although there is also new interest in the conservation of old properties as well as some cutting-edge new architectural design. The state-sanctioned public art, which includes huge murals of rural life, is often naïve and clichéd. Nazgol Ansarinia shows these parallel dynamics well in her art.[17]

In May 2014, seven young Iranians were put on trial for having made a video of themselves on a Tehran rooftop dancing to Pharrell Williams' pop hit 'Happy' and putting it on YouTube. They were put on trial in September 2014 and sentenced to jail time of between six months to a year plus 91 lashes each; the sentences were suspended, so will not be carried out if the defendants are not found guilty of other crimes in the subsequent three years.

Minorities

Minorities in Iran face language and other forms of discrimination, processes which are increasingly well-documented.[18] Baha'i are not allowed to enter higher education, so have set up a sophisticated Baha'i Institute of Higher Education (BIHE) online, to provide university courses for those in Iran. In September 2014, a number of Gonabadi Sufi adherents were arrested and their attorney went on hunger strike.

Internet Developments

The "post-sanctions" Iran is trumpeted as a crucible for new digital start-ups, where the role of women is much vaunted, while at the same time there is increasing control of cyberspace and growing arrests for cybercrimes of various kinds.

New tools such as Telegram, which offers end-to-end encryption for its secret chats, were important mobilizing tools for the spring 2016 election process, although it was subsequently found to offer poorer encryption and thus to be less secure than WhatsApp.[19] Gershad, an app that crowd-sources data to inform people about the patrols and checkpoints of *Gashte Ershad*, Guidance Control or the morality police, proved instantly popular but was also blocked by the authorities within twenty-four hours of its release.

Going Forward

Cultural rights are a key component of broader human rights which look to be the next site of political struggle. More organisations have sprung up to provide better monitoring and international campaigns are better organised, as many have realised that silence does not help those victimised for any reason by the regime. It is often unclear of what the regime is frightened. Is it a specific message, the manner in which a message is presented or the messenger him or herself, simply the daring to speak up and out?

Culture and politics are inextricably linked. Iran is re-entering the global market and Western companies talk expectantly of the untapped buying potential of a population of over 70 million. Yet ironically, the very tight controls on internal expression and cultural production make Iran vulnerable to foreign cultural goods in exactly the way that concerns Khamenei. Supporting internal cultural production – from books to films to software – could make Iran a serious global player and not just a consumer. Acceptance of copyright laws and developing new mechanisms to encourage and finance creativity would benefit Iranians and the Islamic Republic far more than aggressive yet random censorship. Economic development without the parallel spaces of expression would be very thin indeed.

All societies make determinations about what is culturally acceptable, but suspending the Iranian goalkeeper for six months for wearing SpongeBob trousers does not suggest a serious or viable policy.[20] The cultural revolution continues.

Notes

1 cited in Ganji, Akbar, 'A new wave of repression is imminent in Iran', Tehran Bureau for The *Guardian*, 2 November, 2015 (http://bit.ly/20ohxRw)
2 http://english.khamenei.ir/news/3676/Hezbollah-is-shining-like-a-sun
3 http://english.khamenei.ir/news/3871/Without-a-doubt-Islam-is-a-demolisher-of-oppression-and-arrogance

4 http://www.bbc.co.uk/news/world-middle-east-36366595
5 (https://journalismisnotacrime.com/en/wall/
6 Saharkhiz, Isa, 'Censorship, Iranian Style: "The Working Journalist in an Atmosphere of Terror"', 27 April, 2016 (http://en.iranwire.com/features/7209/)
7 http://www.theguardian.com/world/2016/jan/16/iran-releases-washington-post-journalist-jason-rezaian
8 (https://www.freewordcentre.com/events/detail/tehran-book-fair). See also the visualization by Small Media on censorship in Iran (https://smallmedia.org.uk/writersblock/#section1)
9 Walsh, James, "#Draw4Atena: add your cartoons in support of the jailed Iranian artist", The *Guardian*, 12 June 2015 (http://bit.ly/1Uvlh1X)
10 Nayestani, Touka, on IranWire: 25 April 2016 (http://en.iranwire.com/features/7203/)
11 http://en.iranwire.com/features/7183/
12 <http://www.theguardian.com/world/2013/mar/20/naked-female-warrior-femen-topless-protesters>
13 http://petapixel.com/2016/05/17/iran-arrests-8-instagram-models-says-kim-kardashian-secret-agent/
14 See the excellent article by Ziba Mir-Hosseini in *Foreign Policy* (http://foreignpolicy.com/2016/08/29/the-islamic-republics-war-on-women-iran-feminism/
15 http://www.theguardian.com/world/2016/mar/24/filmmaker-two-musicians-three-years-prison-iran
16 https://www.theguardian.com/world/2016/jun/06/iran-mehdi-hossein-rajabian-yousef-emadi-jailed-distributing-underground-music?CMP=share_btn_fb
17 http://www.theguardian.com/cities/video/2016/jun/07/tehran-iran-artist-nazgol-ansarinia-murals-bureau-beautification
18 Article 19/PEN, International Joint submission to the UN Universal Periodic Review of the Islamic Republic of Iran, 15 March, 2014 (http://www.pen-international.org/wp-content/uploads/2013/05/Iran-submission.pdf.)
19 Bajoghli, Narges, 'How women, the Green Movement and an app shaped Iran's election', *Washington Post*, 1 March, 2016
20 https://www.theguardian.com/world/2016/jun/08/spongebob-squarepants-trousers-iranian-footballer-sosha-makani-suspended

CHAPTER 1

THIRTY-PLUS YEARS OF THE IRANIAN REVOLUTION
Culture in Contestation

*Annabelle Sreberny**

The relationship between culture and politics is endlessly fascinating and perhaps nowhere as tantalising recently as inside the Islamic Republic of Iran. Despite, or even because of, a draconian system of surveillance and control, an extremely lively cultural milieu of practice and representation exists in Tehran and elsewhere in the country that utilises many different forms of expression.

Iranians are used to state interference in their cultural lives and censorship. Under the Pahlavi regime the state controlled broadcasting, the privately-owned press was censored and SAVAK was active in universities and work-places. Satire and film that raised social issues or questioned the direction of the White Revolution were proscribed and the regicide histories of Shakespeare were prohibited from being performed.

From its establishment in 1979, the Islamic Republic has engaged in a totalising project of cultural hegemony that dictates what counts as acceptable 'cultural expression' and the forms this may take. The state spends a big budget on ideological maintenance and its public presence. Islamic Republic of Iran (IRIB), the state broadcaster, is an extensive organisation with multiple radio and television channels, including foreign language channels and extensive holdings in publishing and film. State-supported events are publicised with street posters; colourful flags that denote significant events line major roadways and are changed regularly; and religious figures, war martyrs and others receive due recognition in wall paintings and other imagery. The

---

* All photographs in this Introduction by Annabelle Sreberny, Tehran, November 2008.

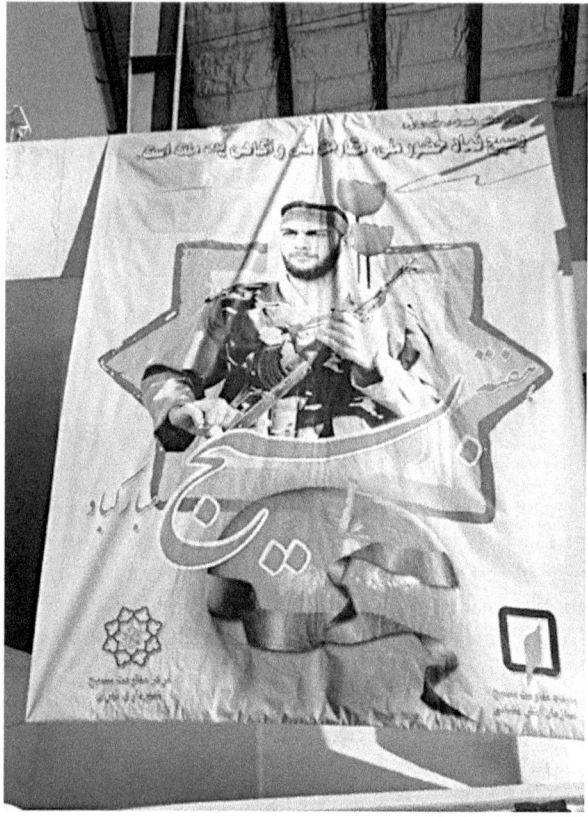

Figure 1.1 Basiji poster, Tehran, November 2008.

anti-Western murals of decades past remain, if fading, on city walls while new muralists are encouraged to produce life-enhancing visions of religious promise and anodyne public art (see figures 1.1–1.4). The state in various forms is thus a huge producer of material and immaterial cultural content.

The state is also a powerful inhibitor of expression. The arrest and imprisonment of film directors, journalists and bloggers accused of 'endangering national security' has been widespread (Sreberny and Khiabany, 2010), while there is extensive harassment of artists, musicians and singers (Robertson, 2012). Arguments about Islamic values, sexual modesty, the threat of western cultural imperialism are variously invoked to justify these incursions.

Abbas, the internationally-recognised photographer, argues (2012) that censorship corrupts all walks of life in Iran: 'politics and journalism, the internet and the cinema, visual arts and literature, dress code and women's

Figure 1.2 'Death to America', wall painting, Tehran, November 2008.

voices – even children's stories'. There have been periods of greater 'openness', most notably under the presidency of Khatami (1997–2005) who promoted a 'dialogue of civilisations' as a discursive counterpoint to Huntington's 'clash of civilisations', although this did not produce any significant results. Indeed, his presidency ended with considerable censorship of the press and violence against university students (Khiabany and Sreberny, 2001). However, the period under Ahmadinejad (from 2005 on) has seen a profound return to political and religious conservatism. Strict rules about public comportment include mandatory *hijab* (Islamic covering for women), clothing rules for men and the prohibition of displays of public affection. There is a ban on the recording of the female voice, women have been excluded from over 70 degree subjects in the 2012 academic year and control over the travel of single women up to age 40 is being imposed.

Figure 1.3 Religious mural, Modares Highway, Tehran, November 2008.

Limitations are imposed on any and all imaginable forms of cultural expression. There are arcane and complex systems of vetting and approval to make a film or stage a play (Zeydabadi-Nejad, 2008) Askhar Farhadi, director of the very successful film The Separation, acknowledges the creativity demanded of cultural producers as well as the fickleness of the controls: "The restrictions and censorship in Iran are a bit like the British weather: one day it's sunny, the next day it's raining. You just have to hope you walk out into the sunshine." (2011).

The Ministry of Culture and Islamic Guidance (*Ershad*) vets all books before publication. Kamali-Deghan (2012) describes the detailed and elaborate process:

> Three censors read each book to make sure it conforms to Islamic values. Censorship might apply to only a word, a sentence, a paragraph or sometimes a text as long as a dozen pages and the result would be given to the publisher after a long procedure that might last a year or two. Censors, who sometime use computer software to look up 'unIslamic words', go as far as advising writers to substitute certain words with other 'appropriate' phrases, should they wish their book to be approved. Publishing houses will be given negative points if they persist in sending too many books to the ministry which they deem to be unsuitable, encouraging self-censorship.

This complex process of book editing is wonderfully exposed in Mandanipour's humorous novel *Censoring an Iranian Love Story* (2011).

In the summer of 2011, Ayatollah Khamenei made a comment about 'harmful' books, which he likened to 'poisonous' drugs that should be removed from public consumption. Ata'ollah Mohajerani – who was culture minister until 2000, favoured greater cultural openness and removed thousands of titles from the lists of banned books – argued against this; Mohajerani now lives in exile in London. The subsequent crackdown on Iranian writers and publishers triggered a petition signed by 160 acclaimed Iranian writers and translators addressed to the *Ershad* complaining about the new restrictions. In 2012, many prominent publishing houses saw their licences revoked and were banned from the Tehran book fair. This included *Cheshmeh*, a prominent Tehran publishing house that specialises in translations of global literature and poetry, including Katherine Mansfield, Mario Vargas Llosa, Toni Morrison, Paul Auster and Kazuo Ishiguro.

Cartoonists have had a difficult time. In late September 2012, the Iranian authorities closed down *Shargh* newspaper because of a cartoon they believed was an 'insult to warriors'. In November, the Kayhan Caricature magazine, affiliated with the hardline *Kayhan* newspaper, published a cartoon depicting a young man in a fashion show surrounded by a group of women who accidently cut themselves after seeing him. This alludes to a story in the Qur'an in which women cut their hands after seeing Joseph, who was known for his beauty and attractiveness. The popular and prolific cartoonists Mana Nayestani and Nikohang Kowsar now live in Paris.

And the attempts at control reach beyond borders; not only does censorship by the Islamic Republic have a long history but also an extensive reach. Salman Rushdie, the British author, is the best-known victim of a fatwa against him, triggered by the publication of *The Satanic Verses*. More recently, in April 2012, Naghi, a rap artist based in Germany, was accorded the same recognition of a *fatwa* for a song he wrote and performed – perhaps an elevation in artistic status even as it puts his life in danger. The live performing arts, including theatre, dance and music, all face particularly severe obstacles and especially when they involve women's bodies.

The farce of the 2009 presidential election, immediately and widely discredited as 'stolen', triggered a wave of digital responses, from videos of demonstrations to music videos that reversioned Ahmadinejad's comments about the demonstrators being nothing but '*khas o khashak*' ('dirt and dust') with satirical effect (See Sreberny and Khiabany, 2010). The contemporary responses often echoed older Iranian poetic traditions and previous moments of political resistance, as in Kiosk's track *Morgh e Sahar* (morning bid) that related the 2009 protests to the quest for freedom and justice in the Constitutional revolution of 1906 using the poetry of Malek o-Sho'ara Bahar.

But even as diverse forms of expression are blocked as 'political' and the social environment appears hostile toward artistic expression and cultural creativity (see also Khalaji et al, 2011), so in wonderfully contradictory fashion, the arts and cultural expression are booming in Iran like never before.

Creativity and digital adepts

Cinema production is high, and women directors and female actors have come to the fore, making both popular but also prize-winning films. The film *No-one knows about Persian Cats* showed the dynamic underground music scene and gave particular prominence to Hichkas development of Iranian rap as one voice for a voiceless generation.

Iranians travel in and out of the country and are keenly aware of international trends, helped by the range of new television channels such as BBC Persian Television, Farsi One and Manoto TV and their culture and technology programmes, soap operas and films. Iran has a highly youthful population (approximately 70 per cent of the population is under 35) but comparatively limited leisure facilities. Hence many of the approximately 30 per cent who have access to the internet and to global cultural production have also become digitally adept, sourcing, producing and distributing content across a range of platforms and avoiding regime surveillance by hacking, filter-breaking and using personal privacy systems like TOR.

There are of course long and rich traditions of musical and artistic creativity from which contemporary artists can draw. Their work is increasingly recognised by global gallerists in Dubai, London and New York and by the global art market. For example, in 2008, the first piece of Iranian art was sold for over $1 million. Of course, Iranian expressivity might be valued as much for an 'orientalist' surprise at its vibrancy as for serious engagement with the work.

On the other hand, Iranian audiences are well-versed in 'reading between the lines' of film or theatre to comprehend the second-level resonances of political resistance that many contain (for just such a discussion of reading *Caligula* in Tehran, see Dokouhaki, 2011). Much music happens literally 'underground', in private basements, as illegal activity (see Robertson, 2012). Sometimes an audience has to wait patiently in the auditorium for the start of a public performances while the organisers continued to debate with the authorities as to whether the performance could go ahead or not – for example, Morteza Shafiei conducting the Isfahan Symphony Orchestra.

Even the much vaunted 'red lines' of journalistic regulation have come to mean little; the Committee to Protect Journalists (2011) cites Iran as 'the world's worst jailer' of journalists, with 42 journalists behind bars, as authorities kept up a campaign of anti-press intimidation that began after the country's disputed presidential election Citizen journalists are also heavily monitored and numerous bloggers are in jail. In November 2012, Sattar Beheshti, arrested for his Facebook activism, died in custody.

If much cultural expression contains coded inflections, social and civil disobedience is more overt and widespread. Many young people frequent certain areas of Tehran in their cars, eyeing up the sexual talent on display and throwing their telephone numbers into passing cars. The performance of both consumption and resistance can be seen in some extreme hairstyles and fashion sported by both men and women, while a more profound 'sexual revolution' is seen to represent a widespread rejection of traditional sexual mores. Much of this urban activity has been captured in striking photographic images. (See Halasa and Bahari, eds, n.d.; *Urban Iran* Reshid, K and Araghi, S (2008)). These behaviours, attitudes and expressions of identity herald new subject positions for both men and women. A new phenomenon called *Gandbazi* developed over the summer of 2011, a particularly Iranian version of a flashmob. Organised via social media, these were fun activities to cope with boredom as well as a rejection of the regime's stifling social regulations. Iran's Prosecutor-General, Gholam Hossein Mohsen Ejei, actually called the water fights 'a campaign orchestrated from abroad' and some of the 'conspirators' were detained along with their toy guns.

The regime has developed the notion of *Jang-e narm*, literally 'soft war' and a play on Joseph Nye's idea of 'soft power', as a pretext and useful way to discredit Iranian creative actors by associating them with external forces, especially 'western powers'. For example, after BBC Persian Television showed a documentary about Ayatollah Khamenei in the autumn of 2011, six more film directors were imprisoned on suspicion of collaborating with the BBC, although they had *no* connection to the programme. Panahi remains under house arrest and is prohibited from making films for 20 years. His last film, made with Morteza Mirtamasb, *This is Not a Film*, was smuggled out of the country on a USB buried in a cake. It was shown at the London International Film Festival 2012. In October 2012 Panahi, along with Nasrin Sotoudeh, an imprisoned lawyer, were awarded the EU's prestigious Sakharov Prize for the defence of human rights and freedom of thought.

Cultural diplomacy brings people together and Britain does currently have an appetite for Iranian works: from the inclusion of Iranian artists in the Saatchi, Janet Radi and Rose Issa galleries, to big concerts in the Barbican and Royal Festival Hall respectively for Mohsen Namjoo and

Mohammad Shajarian. Yet at the formal diplomatic level, things have not been so bad in a long time, with Basiji forces storming the British Embassy in Tehran and, in response, all Iranian diplomats being thrown out of Britain in November 2011.

As the country embarks upon the long crescendo to the next presidential election in June 2013, there are already ominous signs of a regime in full repressive mode. Forty-one people were killed in the first 35 days of the year with a public hanging staged at the House of Artists (*Khaneh Honarmandan*) in Tehran, a vile interruption of its urban calm. More journalists, not only from reformist but from conservative papers, have been arrested and titles closed. 2013 will be an interesting year for culture and politics.

This volume

This volume explores some of the cultural production currently popular and available inside the Islamic Republic as well as various novel forms of social resistance to the attempted imposition of a tough Islamic code. The conference 'Thirty Years On: The Cultural and Social Impacts of the Islamic Republic' held at SOAS[1] provided an exciting initial opportunity to explore what Iranian youth were trying to communicate to the people of Iran and to us in the West. Since this event was held just before the 2009 election, many speakers did not join us from Iran because they felt the situation was too volatile and that their energy was needed inside the country. The backdrop of the election provided the event with an extra dimension of urgency.

The political and cultural crackdown that has ensued has brought this multi-dimensional cultural contestation to the fore once again and gives extra urgency to these issues. Other chapters have been added to extend the range of cultural phenomena explored. But this is by no means intended to be a comprehensive analysis of cultural production; indeed, it is not clear what that would or could be. Topics such as photography and contemporary art fell away for practical reasons. The book does not include the activities of the many Iranian cultural producers living and working outside Iran – which would be a fascinating project in its own right, although a hint of the impact of the Iranian diaspora on cultural life is provided by Moghadam's chapter on Dubai. And while many of the chapters discuss the nature of cultural controls and censorship, there is much more to be done in this area, including the need to try to systematically

Figure 1.4 Biscuits, Armenian bakery, Tehran, November 2008.

map the complex, overlapping and changing state organisations involved in articulating and enforcing such controls.

Nor does this volume attempt to understand the economics of cultural production and the financing of artistic performance and expression. The Islamic Republic does not adhere to copyright regulation, so that pirated computer software and global films are available at a fraction of their costs in the West. Yet without copyright and royalties regimes, it is not clear how recording artists and software developers among others can make a living. This is yet another area where serious research is badly needed.

We do hope to show across many different forms of expression two important and contradictory dynamics: the control exerted by the state *and* the remarkable creativity that exists despite such constraints. The contributions in this volume explore this contradiction. The book contains work by Iranian and non-Iranian authors, and by those living in Iran and those outside. It is important to note the huge difficulties under which work in this general field operates. Many authors inside Iran feel constrained as to how critically they can write. Others feel constrained by their limited access to Iran, which is currently a hostile environment for serious social research. The volume also celebrates the emergence of the next generation of Iran scholars, with many chapters written by newly- and nearly-minted doctoral students.

We hope that the volume acknowledges the endlessly creative ways that Iranians find to express themselves despite the obstacles they confront and to reinvent fascinating lives in a culture that some would make monotone. Many hope that the election of Hassan Rouhani as President in June 2013 may presage some relaxation in the cultural environment. The contradiction of the work, and of contemporary Iranian life, is nicely captured by Iranian biscuits, both happy and sad.

Note

1   The conference was held on June 5, 2009: www.soas.ac.uk/centresoffice/events/iranian-revolution/.

References

Abbas (2012) 'The art of censorship'. *Index on Censorship* 41: 72.
Committee to Protect Journalists (2011) 'Journalist imprisonments jump worldwide, and Iran is worst' 8 December 2011 (http://cpj.org/reports/2011/12/journalist-imprisonments-jump-worldwide-and-iran-i.php).
Dokouhaki, P (2011) 'Tasting blood: "Caligula" in Tehran'. *The Middle East in London* 7, 7, 15.
Farhadi, A (2011) Interview with David Jenkins, *Time Out*, June, http://www.timeout.com/london/film/asghar-farhadi-censorship-in-iran-is-like-the-british-weather-1
Halasa, M, Bahari, M, eds (n.d.) *Transit Tehran*, London: Garnet Publishing.
Kamali-Deghan, S. 'Iran's supreme leader attacks "harmful" books', The Guardian, Thursday, 21 July 2011; http://www.guardian.co.uk/world/2011/jul/21/iran-supreme-leader-attacks-books
Khalaji, M, Robertson, B, Aghdami, A (2011) *Cultural Censorship in Iran*. London: Small Media Foundation (smallmediafoundation.com/#).
Khiabany, G and Sreberny, A (2001) "The Iranian Press and the Continuing Struggle over Civil Society 1998–2000". *International Communication Gazette*, May 2001 63, 2–3, pp. 203–223.
Mandanipour, S (2011) *Censoring an Iranian Love Story*, London: Abacus.
Robertson, B (2012) *Reverberations of Dissent*, London: Continuum.
Sreberny, A and Khiabany, G (2010) *Blogistan*. London: I.B.Tauris.
Reshid, K and Araghi, S (2008) *Urban Iran*. New York: Mark Batty.
Zeydabadi-Nejad, S (2009) *The Politics of Iranian Cinema*, London: Routledge.

PART I

SOCIAL CONTEXT AND SEXUALITY

CHAPTER 2

IRAN'S GREEN MOVEMENT IN CONTEXT

Pardis Mahdavi

In December 2009, I visited an exhibition of works by a prominent American photographer who had spent time in Iran in the days leading up to the Iranian revolution (1979). As I walked the halls of the exhibition space, drawn in by the powerful and haunting images of clashes between students and the Shah's militia, large-scale protests, and young people taking to the streets in defiant styles of dress, I was momentarily lost in time. 'Wait,' I said to my husband who had accompanied me to the gallery. 'Are these pictures of this past summer, or are they from 30 years ago?' We both leaned in to take a closer look at the photographs. 'It looks just like this summer', he said, referring to the images of the mass street demonstrations that had flooded the press following the controversial re-election of President Mahmoud Ahmadinejad. 'In fact, it could be this summer, if it were not for the 1970s style clothing worn by some of the student protesters', I added, pointing to dark-rimmed glasses and suede vests and bellbottoms that characterised the era.

The mass demonstrations that followed the announcement of the controversial election result in 2009 closely resembled those that led to the Iranian revolution 30 years ago. Some young people, disenchanted and frustrated with a regime that does not embody their hopes and dreams for Iran, have taken to the streets and are coalescing behind the opposition candidate Mir-Hossein Mousavi and the movement referred to by themselves and in the press as *Jonbesh-e Sabz* or the Green Movement. Green was the colour of Mousavi's campaign and has become the symbolic hue of their protest movement. This movement was not created overnight; it was an amalgamation of a series of processes and movements that had been taking shape over the last two decades. The Green Movement was most prominently spurred on by multiple women's movements (religious and secular), civil and political reform movements, and a movement referred to by many young Iranians as Iran's 'sexual revolution' (*enghelab-e jensi*), which had been growing in momentum since the late 1990s (Mahdavi, 2008). But the Green Movement was about more than a demand for a new president, just as the Iranian revolution was about more than taking down the Shah. This movement was a call for a change of state apparatus. This movement was about Iranians communicating to the global public that they are not happy, that they wanted a change in their political system and to reclaim their full rights as citizens. People were taking to the streets, flagging their resistance in their comportment, in the slogans they chanted and the types of civil disobedience they have operationalised. These young Iranians have signalled their message to the regime that they wish to overthrow, as well as to the rest of the world.

Inspired by the women's movements and reform movements (movements pushing for a reform of principles of Islamic law), the sexual revolution started to take hold as a social movement and led some young people to begin to move from activism toward sexuality to a larger push for social justice and equality. 'For me, well it started out about looking good, having fun, and dating' began Azar, a 23-year-old student at Azad University in Tehran. 'But then I saw the politics behind what we were doing. I saw that it meant something, that it was threatening [to the regime]. I began to see things differently. I began to view my actions as my rights, and that's how I got involved in pushing for social change', she explained, echoing at least a dozen other interviewees who narrated a similar trajectory. In the protests following the controversial announcement of the presidential election result in the June of 2009, these movements began to coalesce in the Green Movement.

But what has led to the building of this powerful force of momentum? How did this group of young Iranians reach this juncture? Much has changed since the June 2009 elections, and it is important to recognise the various types of activism that have laid the foundation for what we are witnessing in Iran today. As was the case 30 years ago, young people, and students in particular, are at the heart of this political movement. It is rooted in and has taken many cues from the historical memory of student protests and youth movements leading up to the Iranian revolution. This movement also resembles social movements across the globe in different cultures and different times whereby youth engagement in promoting sexual and social change has led to a civil rights type movement (such as that which occurred in the USA in the 1960s).

Much attention (Asef Bayat (2007), Roxanne Varzi (2006), Shahram Khosravi (2009)) has recently been turned toward youth habitus, consumerism, appearance and 'reckless' behaviour in Iran. Documentaries about everything from the number of nose jobs in Iran to upper class obsessions with consumer culture abound. This may have all been part of a larger discourse about panic over urban Iranian youth going astray. However, it is perhaps more productive to read these behaviours in context and to note that for many of these 'unruly' young people there was an intellectual architecture behind what might seem to be flippant social choices. In fact, many of the young people involved in the Green Movement have articulated their comportment as an active part of their resistance.

Between 2000 and 2007 I made several extended ethnographic trips to Tehran to explore what young people referred to as their 'sexual revolution' (Mahdavi, 2008). During this time I was able to document the ways in which some young people oppose the regime through their bodily practices. More specifically, my interlocutors showed me that youth practices of resisting Islamist rules about sexuality and consumption in Iran must be read as political statement. Those who break the rules of the Islamic Republic are demonstrating an intrinsic resentment to the regime they are trying to resist and those who cooperate with the regime demonstrate their support by behaving in a 'model' sexually constrained manner. During my time in the field, I spoke to 187 young people mostly living in Tehran, Mashad or Shiraz. My interviewees were typically between the ages of 18 and 25, and had all lived in urban areas for at least a year. Roughly three-quarters of my sample were university educated, and I attempted to draw from a cross-section of socioeconomic strata by employing targetted sampling in various neighbourhoods in town. I also relied on the helpful assistance of three Iranian–American students from my home colleges (the Claremont Colleges) as well as one Tehran University student and two Tehran University professors. Overall, the young people with whom I spoke were very adamant that many of their behaviours, which had been read as examples of a downward spiralling youth culture, were actually part of demonstrating their opposition to the regime. 'We act and dress this way because these are the signals this regime can hear', said one young woman in 2004. Another young man echoed her sentiments a year later in 2005 and added:

> This is a regime that is so overly focused on our bodies, all their attention, all their rules, all of it. It's all about regulating what we wear, what we do, and who we do it with. So we use these same things, push the boundaries and speak back to the regime.

In other words, these young people use their bodies, their habitus and their comportment to subvert the fabric of morality woven by the regime. This subversion was intended to weaken the foundations upon which the authorities operationalised their power, and was seen as politicised action by many young people. In 2009, the world witnessed the further politicisation of a number of young Iranians in the aftermath of the election. These young Iranians, who had up until that point been comporting their resistance simply through their habitus, for example by wearing clothes that alluded to their liberal reformist tendencies and disdain of the *hijab* or through listening to music the government deemed immoral, became overtly political and started to take to the streets in a more organised form of political activism. For many youth, their involvement in what they called the 'sexual revolution' paved the way for their involvement in the Green Movement.

In this chapter, I focus on the Green Movement, placing it in a historical, social and global context. I argue that we must understand youth activism within the historical framework of the groundwork laid by the student activism of the 1970s and show how this youth movement is similar to other global youth movements that have sought to deploy the same types of resistance in achieving social and political change.

Iran's sexual revolution

Today, 70 per cent of Iran's population is under the age of 30. Many of these young people were born during or right after the Iranian revolution, and are thus, very literally, *children of the revolution*. Urban young adults who comprise almost two-thirds of Iran's population are highly mobile, highly educated (84 per cent of young Tehranis are currently enrolled in university or are university graduates with 65 per cent of these graduates being women) and underemployed (there is a 35 per cent unemployment rate among this age group). Many of these young people are highly dissatisfied with the current regime and are using their social behaviours and comportment to resist what they view as a repressive government.

Young Iranians have been engaging in various types of social movements over the course of the past decade and thus their involvement in the Green Movement should not be surprising. Following the election of President Khatami, and the social reforms that characterised his two terms, reform-minded young people have become increasingly involved in pushing for social and political change with varying degrees of success. What we witnessed in the streets of Tehran following the controversial 2009 presidential elections is the combination of a series of movements that have been building since the revolution.

As mentioned in the introduction to this chapter, many types of youth movements and many facets of each faction have contributed to recent uprisings. The youth movement I became most interested in while conducting research in Tehran was a specific group of young people's involvement in what they were calling their 'sexual revolution', and it is important to highlight the fact that the terminology came organically from my interlocutors. A departure from overt civil and political activism, the sexual revolution was about changing discourse and views about sexuality. While it did have political undertones for some, Iran's sexual revolution was a movement that began, as have other sexual revolutions in other parts of the world at various points in history, among the middle and upper middle classes in the most urban of centres – in this case Tehran – and then moved to other socioeconomic groups in other parts of the country. What began as a small movement seeking to shift attitudes towards morality, comportment and sexuality in Tehran, quickly broadened to a larger focus on the body, sociality, and habitus in the face of what many young people viewed as a repressive regime.

This sexual revolution, led by educated and restless youth, aimed to change sexual and social discourses, habitus and comportment, and has played an integral role in leading some young people to become involved in a larger movement pushing for social change. Having fun and carving out spaces for recreation are politicised by the policies of the ruling authorities, who have, since the establishment of the Islamic Republic in 1979, sought to regulate social activities and cleanse the public sphere of 'morally questionable' behaviour. In 2006 President Ahmadinejad rolled out a new 'morality plan' that sought to re-enforce the ultra-conservative vision of Islamically-approved behaviour and comportment. Although behaviours deemed 'morally questionable' differ based on interpretation, they range from something as small as wearing excessive makeup or bright colours to public displays of affection, drug use and sex work (see Bayat, 2007).

The young Iranians with whom I spoke have been using their bodies and social behaviours to challenge and subvert the fabric of morality woven by the Islamic regime in post-revolutionary Iran. Their methods include sexual activity, recreational drug use, and the creation of an underground music scene (sex, drugs and rock-n-roll).[1] By not responding to Islamic laws (of dress, comportment, modesty and lack of heterosociality) some young people are rejecting the notion of being Islamic subjects.[2] Policymakers in Iran are increasingly trying to find ways of inspiring belief in Islamic ideology, especially among the youth. State television and the standardised school curriculum are two of their most relied-upon mediums. However, as Roxanne Varzi notes (2006: 147), at play in Iran's understanding of its own world is the notion of a public secret. Everyone in Iran knows that religion does not exist on the level or in the form that it appears to exist on the surface. Even Islamic policymakers know this, which is why it is crucial that the surface remain untouched and unquestioned, and the secret never voiced.

However, as young people embody their subversion and seek to change social discourses, the smooth surface covering the secret is being broken.

Behaviours of young people are indicative of the success of the sexual and social revolution and show that their resistance is threatening the entire social and moral order of the Islamic Republic. The Islamic government has adapted by no longer punishing young people on the level they once did. Whether this is because young Iranians have become more adept at not getting caught or the government and police force no longer have the resources to deal with an overwhelmingly subversive youth population or because they are simply becoming more 'light-hearted' is not clear, and neither are the rules of the republic. Although the rules have never been clear, those who crossed the invisible red line in years gone by received the harshest of punishments: lashing, imprisonment and hefty fines. Over the last decade the momentum of social reform has pushed up from beneath the regime. Indicative of the success of the sexual and social revolution, the fact that the state has adapted to the demands of Iranian youth shows that their resistance is threatening the entire social and moral order of the Islamic Republic. Young and old alike indicate that they no longer fear the state, that they are ready to stand up to the authorities and that it is time for the state to start listening to its people. One young woman articulated this sentiment most clearly to me in a conversation I had with her in 2007.

> There was a time when my heart would sink seeing members of the morality police. I would sweat, I would be afraid. But now I see it as an invitation. A challenge. An opportunity for me to speak back, to tell them how I feel about my home.

Several months later I spoke with her mother who interestingly had similar views as her daughter:

> Yes, we all used to be afraid that maybe the doorbell would ring and it would be a morality police, maybe they would be coming to round us up and take us in. But not anymore, now I think to myself, let them come, I'll give them a piece of my mind.

Many of the young people I spoke with view these sexual and social changes as an integral part of delegitimising a regime that claims to have restored the country's 'morality'. The behaviours I observed while conducting research in Tehran (specifically the sexual activities as well as changing comportment among youth) are viewed as dissent by members of the regime as well as by the young people I interviewed. They are consciously making behaviour choices *against* the regime, thereby decisively engaging in 'transgressive' sexual and social behaviours. Without a doubt, it is possible that young people could possibly engage in these behaviours even if they were permitted to, it is also possible that some young people respond to peer pressure. However, it is important to note that while the act of wearing red lipstick might be read as trying to look good or just desire, because it *could* be punishable, and because it is read as political by members of the regime, it has political ramifications. For a Euro–American example, the wearing one's hair in an alternative way ('rocking an Afro' or long hair) in the 1960s and 1970s in the USA was read as a political statement, regardless of whether the person him or herself was intending it as such. Transgression is in the reading as well as the intent. One conversation I had with a young woman from Azad University in 2004 demonstrates this most clearly:

> Yes, I wear lipstick, I wear tight outer clothes. Yes, it's about looking good, but it also means something. Maybe it's a signal. Maybe it tells likeminded people where I stand. Maybe it marks me as available. Maybe it marks me as a revolutionary. But it definitely means something.

These young people choose to reject the regime's morality injections by flouting the Islamic dress code, playing illegal music loudly, passing phone numbers between cars, creating impromptu dance parties in the middle of the street or parks, holding hands with boyfriends or girlfriends, and wearing large amounts of makeup. Although those who are this overt are in the minority, they are gradually chipping away at the moral cement of the Islamic Republic. As Khomeini said repeatedly, 'the Islamic revolution is a revolution of values'.[3] The young Tehranis I interviewed spoke of enacting a 'counter-revolution of values' through a cultural revolution or *enghelab-e farhangi*, by challenging current state morality codes and creating an alternative value through sexual and social behaviours. When it eventually becomes clear that the regime has failed to instill a certain moral code or to make young people obey it, it will no longer have a defined platform on which to stand. Both the regime and the young people who oppose it view social and sexual behaviours as political.

Youth movements in historical context

The use of comportment, style and youth habitus as a mechanism for expressing identity and resistance is neither unique to Iran, nor is it a new phenomenon that has surfaced recently. Rather, the use of street protests, fashion and outward comportment have historical roots that can be observed in the years leading up to the Iranian revolution of 1979. During the 1970s, many of the young people who were disenchanted by the Shah's policies began expressing their frustration in public protests. Some women began taking on the veil as a symbol of defiance, making a visual symbol of their disapproval of the Shah's attempts to Westernise the country. The veil had been banned from public spaces in 1936 and as a result women from religious families had retreated into the private domain. The Shah's 'Westoxification' (al-Ahmad, 1984) was considered by many to be a betrayal of Iran's rich cultural heritage. It was therefore a return to 'Iranian-ness' that fuelled much of the activism during that time.

In addition, during the years leading up to the Iranian revolution, universities became a major centre for organising the enactment of social and political change. Students were perceived as a major threat by the monarchist regime (as they are by the Islamic regime today) and young people played an integral part in the staging of public protests and were active in producing the anti-monarchical sentiment that swept the country. Beyond appearance and style, young people came together to work with other emerging social movements in an effort to push for regime change. Inspired by the experiences and narratives of their parents, many of whom took part in the revolution, a number of the young people with whom I spoke draw on the historical memory of the 1970s when articulating their own youth movement.

'Our parents did it in the 70s, we can do it today', said one young woman from Shiraz who is very active in the Green Movement. Another young man added, 'Students and universities have always been at the heart of the most important changes in our country. So it was in the 70s, so it is today.' Many young people with whom I spoke articulated similar sentiments. Student organisers of the Green Movement, studying at Tehran University and Shahid Beheshti University in Tehran, were all very adamant that, as students, they could and should build on the experiences of the preceding generations and turn the university into a political space. Inspired by the activism of their parents, many young people said they have recently shifted from pushing for social change in the form of their own social and sexual revolution, to coalescing behind the Green Movement to push for regime change.

Youth movements in global context

While it is difficult to identify whether the young urban Iranians I have studied are constructing a new sexual and social culture or are a part of a broader subculture within Iran, it is useful to look at literature describing the creation of subcultures as well as frameworks for understanding and describing emerging sexual cultures. Hebdige (1991: 76) defines the subculture as,

> [A] set of people with a distinct set of behaviors and beliefs from a larger culture of which they are a part. The subculture may be distinctive because of the age of its members, or by their race, ethnicity, class and/or gender, and the qualities that determine a subculture as distinct may be aesthetic, religious, political, sexual or a combination of these factors. Subcultures are often defined via their opposition to the values of the larger culture to which they belong, although this definition is not universally agreed on by theorists

Literature on subcultures and ways in which they use style and comportment provide some tools with which to analyse the emerging shift in sexual discourse amongst this particular population of Iranian young adults.

Dick Hebdige's *Subculture and the Meaning of Style* (1991) and Stuart Hall's *Resistance Through Rituals: Youth Subculture in Postwar Britain* (1993), both originally written in the 1970s, analyse how countercultures and subcultures form and shape themselves as unique and distinct to the dominant culture through style of dress, music, and demeanour. Hebdige and Hall both explore the status and meaning of revolt within youth subcultures, the idea of style as a form of refusal, and the elevation of 'crime' into art. The repurposing of crime as an artform translates to the Iranian context where criminal behaviour can, in many cases, be read as subversion against the ruling regime.

Hebdige notes that within some subcultures (punks, mods, rockers, hippies, beats and teddy boys in England during the 1960s and 1970s), the core values of the 'straight world' – for example sobriety, ambition, conformity, etc – are replaced by their opposites such as hedonism, defiance of authority, and the quest for 'kicks' (1991: 76). He notes that the young people he observed were trying to elicit an outraged response from their parents, teachers, and employers, who repressed them through their positions of power. I found remarkable similarities among the young people I studied in Iran.

Many Iranian young people appear to be experimenting with some of the characteristics that defined various subcultures in Europe and America in the 1960s and 1970s, specifically characteristics of rebellion, resistance, and the desire to be separated from the Islamic ideology that the regime has sought to inject into society. Hebdige also discusses ways in which style becomes intentional communication. Many young urban Iranians are also seeking to make social and political statements through their style. Choosing to wear Islamic dress in defiant ways (for women: head scarves pushed back to reveal dyed bouffant hairstyles, high heeled shoes, shorter pants that reveal ankles, and open-toed shoes during the summer time; for men: hair grease and long locks, smoothly shaven faces, tight pants, and chunky jewellry), these youth are using their style to make a public statement *and* to communicate political dissent. Their style becomes both a code and means of communication in much the same way as in many of the subcultures studied by the Birmingham school.

Sex, drugs, and rock-n-roll were seen as the main components of the counterculture of the sexual revolution in the USA and Europe in the 1960s and 1970s (Escoffier, 2003; Allyn, 2001). The sexual revolution that took place in the USA in the 1960s, and similar versions of social movements taking place in parts of Europe around the same time, set the stage and were a major part of larger social movements which culminated in changes in attitudes towards social justice, equality, and the self.

In the USA, the 1960s were a time marked by shifting views towards sexuality, gender relations and social recreation. This was a time marked by profound social and societal changes. The sexual revolution in the USA was about more than changing views towards sexuality and intimacies; it was about a search for authenticity and claiming autonomy and resisting authority. During this time, youth experimented with sexual relations outside of traditional familial arrangements and heteronormativity, which set the stage for larger and deeper self and societal exploration. In the years following the sexual revolution, a series of interconnected movements emerged, which included the struggle for civil rights, women's rights, minority rights, the rights of the disabled, lesbian and gay liberation and so on. These movements were often connected to broader social justice issues such as anti-poverty, lower income housing, unionisation and so on.

The backdrop to this sexual revolution and its accompanying social movements (often captured under the umbrella phrase 'counter-culture') was a profound distrust of authority, and a resistance to 'The Establishment'. This social movement was fueled by a series of events including President Eisenhower's 1960 deception about the U-2 incident, the botched Bay of Pigs invasion in 1961, distrust of the investigation into the assassination of President Kennedy in 1963, the resistance to the Vietnam War, and a number of clashes between activists/protesters and the police. Activists in the counterculture movement began pointing towards the shortcomings of the government, while simultaneously seeking to marginalise members of law enforcement (this was a time when words like 'pigs' and 'fuzz' entered into the vernacular to refer to policemen). Similarly, activists in the Green Movement point towards the shortcomings of the Iranian regime, profoundly distrust authority, and resist the rules of the Islamic Republic.

The counterculture movement had a series of defining characteristics, which set it apart from its predecessors. First, and perhaps most importantly, was that young people were the leaders of these movements. They were headed by the 'baby boomers' and students were at the very heart of counterculture. University campuses were the primary home to many of the major events. The baby boomers sought to break free from the repression of the 1950s and looked to transform notions of social justice, tolerance and equality. Furthermore, resistance to authority and fighting 'The Establishment' through civil disobedience was a centrepiece of this movement. A culture of experimentation, which extended from the body and gender roles to dress and drugs, were a major hallmark of the counterculture. The societal shifts that were set in motion in the 1960s are still being felt to this day.

Outside the USA, the counterculture movement was spreading rapidly in western Europe as well as parts of eastern Europe and the harsh authoritarian regimes of the Soviet Union spurred on a series of social movements. The Hungarian revolution of 1956 was perhaps the first instance of a civil rights type social movement in Europe; it was met with harsh resistance by the Soviet government. This was followed in 1968 by Czechoslovakia's Prague Spring, which embodied many of the characteristics of the counterculture movements and laid the groundwork for the Velvet Revolution to take place in the Czech Republic in the late 1980s.

In western Europe, counterculture spread rapidly to major European centres such as Amsterdam, Berlin, London and Paris. The German student movements of the 1960s and the French general strikes of 1968 are examples of the many manifestations of counterculture that continued to build upon social movements in the region. In England, the emergence of the 'new left' (also coming to fruition in the USA at the same time) was a move from leftist activism that centred on labour unions, to a broader movement seeking out social justice, tolerance and equality for all populations. Like the USA, the UK was also home to the experimental side of the counterculture, giving birth to The Beatles, Pink Floyd and many other types of counterculture styling such as the mods, the rockers, the teddy boys and the punks.

These social movements were about challenging established views on politics, gender, the body and the self; they were broad movements of social justice and cultural change. These movements relied on activism in the street, but also cultural productions such as the music of Bob Dylan or Joan Baez, and the 'body politics' of the hippies and the beats. Civil disobedience and opposition to 'The Establishment' was manifested through dress, music, lifestyle, experimentation, and, in later years, as public protests. The various aspects of the counterculture combined in the USA and parts of Europe to push for major sociopolitical change.

The 'Personal is Political' was the phrase echoed across the USA during nationwide civil rights protests. Just as involvement in pushing for discourse shifts and social change led many young people down the path of political involvement in the USA and Europe, so too has involvement in the sexual revolution paved the path toward more overt political activism for many urban young Iranians. And just as civil disobedience was the primary strategy in the counterculture of the USA and Europe four decades ago, so too is this the strategy employed by members of the Green Movement in Iran today.

It is important to recognise that both the sexual revolution in Iran as well as the Green Movement are absolutely not attempts to mimic similar movements in the Western world, but rather are organic movements that have been building inside the country over the past few decades. Some of my interlocutors indicated that they had read widely on the topic of sexual revolutions in the USA and Europe and that, while their movement was similar, they felt the contours and what they were up against differed. 'We read Foucault, we read about sexuality, discipline and power', began one young man in a conversation I had with him in 2007. 'So I think maybe what is happening in Iran is similar to the US, but we are not copying, we are trying to change things our own way. Also, for us, the stakes feel higher.' Although many parallels can be drawn and the movements can most certainly be read in the context of one another, it is of utmost importance to highlight that each movement has specific characteristics and has been built within a particular space, a particular geo-political location, at a very particular moment in time. The young people with whom I spoke were adamant that the 'sexual revolution' and concurrent social movements such as the Green Movement were very much about them trying to express their identities and their resistance to the regime and the restrictive world around them.

Concluding thoughts

The Green Movement has captured the attention of people around the world, but it is important to recognise the many predecessors to the Green Movement that form the foundation of this push for regime change. The young woman who took to the streets in protest of the 2009 election result, ready to clash with members of the riot police, is the younger sister of the young woman who fought in previous years with the morality police about the length of her *manteau* (regime-approved outerwear) or the young man who fought for his right to listen to the type of music he enjoyed.

While none of these drives towards social and cultural change have resulted in changes to the rules and regulations of the Islamic Republic, the authorities have become more relaxed as to their interpretation of them. Music and clothing are still very heavily regulated in the Islamic Republic of Iran and while Iranian men and women do not have absolute freedom of choice in what clothes they wear or what music they listen to, many police will nowadays turn a blind eye to minor infringements. What started out as subtle changes in dress, habitus and comportment was one major part of laying the groundwork for activism in the Green Movement. What we see in this civil rights type protesting is the culmination of several years of resistance.

Although many things have changed over the past 30 years, one cannot help but observe similarities between the public youth protests that fill the streets of Tehran today and what the streets of Tehran looked like 30 years ago. As could also be observed in the 1970s, a number of young people are using their bodies, their style of dress, and even organising venues such as the university, to come together to push for social and political change today. Young people have often been at the forefront of social movements and major historical changes in Iran. Today, when young people take to the streets, they engage in similar strategies as their parents' generation and employ tactics used by youth movements around the world. But their situation is unique and characterised by the particular space and time in which it is occurring.

What started as a sexual revolution and a series of small-scale social movements has become a fairly large-scale civil disobedience movement. What seemed by some to be young people falling prey to the pitfalls of 'sex, drugs, and rock-n-roll', has evolved into a social and political movement that is challenging the Islamic regime and has echoes of the public protests from the 1970s. Perhaps the clothes have changed, and perhaps the slogans are different, but the message remains the same and this group of young people pushing for social and political reform under the collective social movement immediately recognisable by its green hue, has caught the attention of people and press around the world.

Notes

1 Note that while drug use is a significant issue among young people in Iran, many of whom couple most recreational activities with some form of substance use, a thorough discussion of drug use and its implications is beyond the scope of this chapter (see Mahdavi, 2009).
2 To be sure, there are also significant numbers of young people who do not reject Islamist parameters about sociality and habitus. For the purpose of my study, however, I focused on those involved in the sexual revolution, and thus these interlocutors form the basis of my analysis.
3 Found on posters and signs throughout the country.

References

Al-e Ahmad, J (1984) *Occidentosis: A Plague from the West*. Berkeley: Mizan Press.
Allyn, D (2001) *Make Love, Not War: The Sexual Revolution: An Unfettered History*. London: Routledge.
Bayat, A (2007) 'Islamism and the politics of fun'. *Public Culture* 19: 3.
Escoffier, J (2003) *Sexual Revolution*. Philadelphia: Running Press.
Hall, S (1993) *Resistance Through Rituals: Youth Subculture in Postwar Britain*. London: Routledge.
Hebdige, D (1991) *Subculture and the Meaning of Style*. London: Routledge.
Khosravi, S (2009) *Young and Defiant in Tehran*. Philadelphia: University of Pennsylvania Press.
Mahdavi, P (2008) *Passionate Uprisings: Iran's Sexual Revolution*. Stanford: Stanford University Press.
Varzi, R (2006) *Warring Souls: Youth, Media and Martyrdom in Post-Revolution Iran*. Durham: Duke University Press: 147.

CHAPTER 3

TEHRANI CULTURAL BRICOLAGE
Local Traditions and Global Styles of Tehran's Non-Conformist Youth

Mahmoud Arghavan

Would you like me to shred your jeans?
Why? What crime have I committed? Why would you want to do that?

You have violated high school regulations. I can restrain you whilst making a decision about you. We warned you that wearing blue jeans is forbidden.

This was not a recorded conversation between a police officer and a criminal; it took place between one of my high school masters and me in 1997. On that day, my friends and I went to the International Book Fair of Tehran and we decided to go wearing jeans. My friends had worn their jeans under their trousers because of the high school's regulations; I was the only one who had dared to infringe them. At that time, I considered my action to be an overt form of resistance against the unreasonable rules of the high school. Eventually the intervention of one of my teachers saved me from the imminent punishment my schoolmaster was planning, but its memory remains with me after all these years. Ironically, the schoolmaster that was at the ready to shred my jeans went on to found a private high school where students were free to wear whatever they liked, simply because they were paying tuition fees.

When this incident took place in 1997, Iranian society was undergoing a massive social transformation. This transformation was accelerated by generational change (more than 70 per cent of the country's population were younger than 30) and it culminated in the victory of President Khatami in August 1997. Khatami's reformist agenda ignited the passion of young Iranians, who began to hope that they might live in a more tolerant and open society. The most important aspect of Khatami's reformist government was that it tolerated social, demographic and economic change inside Iran. These factors, combined with the impact of globalisation, coalesced to transform Iranian society. The reform movement was ushered out in 2005 when Ahmadinejad assumed office, and in recent years Iranian society has been further repressed under the increasingly conservative policies of the current government. The country is, at present, being forcibly purged of Western influence or subjected to Islamic cleansing.

The government of the Islamic Republic may not be happy with influence from outside the country permeating its staunch geo-political borders, but interaction between different cultures has been happening for centuries and seems to be an inevitable process in a globalised world. In recent decades the speed of these interactions has accelerated change. The increasing availability of communication technologies such as satellite television and the internet has undoubtedly affected sociocultural change, and it is clear that teenagers and young people in closed societies like Iran persistently receive messages from Western culture. Once removed from their original context, these messages have implications that might be completely different from the producers' intended meaning.

In this chapter, which is based on a qualitative study including participant observation and interview, these aspects of youth discourse will be considered to explore the hidden layers of the new generation's lives in Tehran and to explain how local traditions and global styles as two sets of values and beliefs can be reconciled.

Global messages, local meanings: A harmonious coexistence?

Inside Iran's borders, satellite channels broadcast Western music and films and the increasing prevalence of personal computers and mobile phones over the past decade has ensured a cavernous generation gap. Widespread usage of the internet enables Iranian youths to keep up with global events but it often puts them at loggerheads with official discourse. As young Iranians surf the internet, they come face to face with various cultural elements that have very specific effects on their worldviews. Young Iranians are increasingly placed in the midst of both continuity and change.

These transformative factors are much more visible in Tehran, Iran's largest and most cosmopolitan city. For example, Western styles - seen via satellite television in soaps, serials and Hollywood films - appear on the streets of Tehran soon after their broadcast. As well as being Iran's political capital, Tehran is also its cultural heart. Trendsetting Tehranis pioneer new ideas, styles and ways of life, and develops modes of reaction. Tehran's people provide a pattern for other cities and regions to follow. Undoubtedly, these fashions and styles are most popular among youths and teenagers. A longitudinal study of youth culture in Tehran as a pioneering example for Iranian society would reveal seemingly contradictory aspects of their lifestyles, while a short-term look would lead to both misunderstanding and misconceptions about their lifestyles. In this chapter I have chosen to explain these incongruous elements of contemporary youth in Tehran through the concept of cultural bricolage.

Using the terms 'Americanisation' or 'Westernisation' oversimplifies the inherent complexities. Judging Tehran's under 30s on their appearance alone, which are 'fashionable' based on the most recent fashions in Europe and the USA, needs more reflection. For example, a group of boys dressed in clothing typical of the hip hop, rap or heavy metal subcultures does not necessarily understand the implications of their appearance. Their choice of style is not to say that they distrust their cultural (including religious, social, national and Iranian historical) identity and wish to replace it with another. A deeper, more accurate observation reveals that these young people are not ignorant about their cultural identity. In fact, many of them actively engage in Iran's religious and cultural ceremonies and traditional celebrations, albeit in ways that might not be fully consistent with the official dominant discourse.

Considering the new generation's lifestyles and their ways of confrontation with the dominant social order, it appears that large groups of Tehran's youth have constructed their own cultural worlds. In these newly constructed worlds, modern and Western values and the Iranian and Islamic traditions coexist harmoniously. For example, these young people actively take part in reenactments of the Battle of Karbala during Ashura ceremonies but also celebrate Valentine's Day, a Western tradition that has no cultural precedent in Iran, by offering cards and gifts to their girlfriends or boyfriends. While Ashura is recognised, supported and encouraged by the Iranian government, Valentine's Day is contentious. In January 2011, the Iranian state media announced that selling any 'symbols of hearts, half-hearts, red roses, and any activities promoting this day are banned,' and 'authorities will take legal action against those who ignore the ban' (Kaylan, 2011). Thus a number of shops selling paraphernalia for the celebration have been forcibly closed down by the authorities during recent crackdowns. This is just one example of how contemporary Tehrani youth culture can be studied using the concept of bricolage, defined below.

Cultural flows in a postmodern world

The meeting and mixing of different cultures in this age of global communication could be regarded as the main feature of contemporary culture. Using a mountain as a metaphor, the juxtaposition of various elements of different cultures that happened in the age of globalisation saw culture and economy flows from the high mountain ranges to the mountain slopes to the valleys of the world. 'Height' is determined by power in politics, economics and media, and countries (like Iran, Egypt, Greece and others) that had hosted the great civilisations of ancient times, which occupied the highest peaks during their historical heydays, are nowadays wallowing in the valley. From this perspective, the present direction of a majority of cultural flows is from the Western New World to the Old World and Third World. This flow is running within the context of globalisation and, as this chapter will reveal, affects the lives of people in different ways, while changing both their subjectivity and identity.

Pieterse (1995: 62) suggests that 'introverted cultures, which have been prominent over a long stretch of history and which overshadowed translocal culture, are gradually receding into the background, while translocal culture made up of diverse elements is coming to the foreground' (in Barker, 2000: 113). The intercultural communications facilitated by new communication technologies such as the internet and audiovisual media-satellite television channels, have blurred or abolished the traditional boundaries of 'introverted cultures' like Iran and have consequently transformed the cultural identities, tastes and preferences of those nations living in the valleys and mountain slopes.

All things considered, we might argue that geographical and traditional boundaries have dissipated and waves from different sources have penetrated the minds of people across the world. Because of their desire to remain current and attractive, cosmopolitan young people are usually more open to these international cultural emissions. Teenagers and young individuals typically try to detach from their parents' prototypes and examine new ways of life, which are reflected in their clothes, hairstyles, and conversations. Within Stuart Hall's pivotal work *Resistance Through Rituals* subcultures are to be examined from three perspectives: 'resistance/ incorporation; social divisions and fragmentation; and interpretation/

representation' (in Baldwin et al, 1999: 362). Hall's Birmingham School colleague Dick Hebdige argues that subcultures often resist the hegemony of dominant order, both indirectly and symbolically, by adopting certain, possibly contentious, styles. He suggests that youth subcultures use diverse symbols to distance themselves from conventional society in order to challenge its hegemony. Their distinctive aesthetics, which are different from those of the dominant culture, differentiate them from the dominant order or dominant groups (Hebdige, 1979).

Unlike Hebdige, Fred Davis does not perceive clear implications in the selection of clothing, arguing that clothing and fashion are better regarded as aesthetic rather than communicative codes (in Baldwin et al, 1999). Communicative codes convey meaning and ideas that are often difficult to express directly. Davis (1992) believes that, 'the weakening of the formerly tight tie of status and occupation to clothing suggests that the signifier-signified link in contemporary clothing is becoming increasingly loose or under-coded' (in Baldwin et al, 1999: 291). Unlike the 'modernist regime of signification' and modern cultural interpretation of social behaviours, postmodern theorists relying on the variability of styles and the diversity of individual experiences drawing from everyday life, in addition to the effect the media has on identity formation, contest rationalistic views of culture and claim that people's clothing today is not at all socially significant (Baldwin et al, 1999; Barker, 2000).

In the postmodern world, signs and signifiers do not work as accurately as before. Consequently, different elements from various cultural worlds and different times coexist in contemporary cultures. Past and present reconcile to coexist in bricolage and thus everyone acts as a cultural bricoleur, being either consciously or unconsciously selective in his or her lifestyle. Social actors act reflectively or non-reflectively to form a bricolage that takes pleasure from all aspects of life, both materially and spiritually. The rearrangement and juxtaposition of previously unrelated signs and symbols in the form of bricolage produce new codes of meaning in fresh contexts. According to Barker, 'bricolage as a cultural style is a core element of postmodern culture' and is its highlighted feature (2000: 154). This bricolage does not necessitate being homogenous in terms of any former signifying system and thus somebody could have both a very fashionable appearance and a very old-fashioned attitude at the same time.

Currently, to pass judgement on someone's worldview based simply on appearance is increasingly difficult because it involves a process of resignification of cultural signs and objects in relation to other artefacts under new circumstances. Someone who constructs a bricolage by stylising him- or herself through clothing and artefacts of popular culture is called a bricoleur. A bricoleur constructs multiple identities by reselecting elements of material commodities and meaningful signs and rearranging them into a bricolage, which in itself is an important part of their identity formation (Barker, 2004: 17). The next section of this chapter will demonstrate how Tehran's youth actively reselects commodities and codes in order to create multiple identities as cultural bricoleurs.

Tehrani non-conformist youths as cultural bricoleurs

In many parts of Tehran, traditional, modern, local and global cultural signs express themselves next to each other. The somewhat discordant harmony of Tehran's urban space is striking, and is something most foreign observers comment upon when confronted by it for the first time. In fact Tehran is a big bricolage in itself. Sreberny-Mohammadi and Mohammadi (1990) suggest that Iran constitutes one of the most extreme examples of Third World post-modern cultural bricolage (in Shahabi, 2006: 111). Although they based their argument on research conducted in the early 1990s, it serves further to prove that this bricolage has been flourishing over the past two decades. As mentioned before, due to its sociocultural, economic and political position, Tehran and its inhabitants have witnessed tremendous changes during recent years. A general transformation of traditional ways of life has occurred and everyday life, familial and social relationships, clothing style, food habits and leisure patterns have all been affected by the demographic changes of Tehran's population in addition to other influential factors such as globalisation and development in communication technologies and media impacts. The capital city's municipality has played a vital role in reshaping Tehran from an old city to a new modern metropolis. For example, the Milad Tower was built as a symbol of modern Tehran or, phrased better, a new Tehran. This modernisation of the city, obvious even in the renewal of public transportation means, has certainly had its influence upon people's lives and their culture.

Given that today more than 70 per cent of Iran's population is under 30, the issue of Iranian and particularly Tehrani youth is a subject deserving of investigation. This youthful population is living in a communicative world, in which millions of cultural messages are exchanged, and this young generation sees the world very differently from their parents. For this generation, dating, attending private mixed-gender parties, being a fan of certain types of Western music bands, wearing certain clothing, shaking hands with friends of the opposite gender in public and any other transgressions of the traditional or official culture are very common. And even to those youths who do not engage in such behaviour themselves, these ways of life do not appear particularly strange.

These sociocultural changes are taking place in spite of the fact that the government's Islamic laws have been designed to rule over both public spheres and private spaces. These changes may include the popularisation of an individualist pattern of life. This might include a desire for privacy; the ownership of mobile phones by young people (which can facilitate relationships with the opposite sex); the normalisation of having a girlfriend or boyfriend; the secularisation of religious ceremonies; the existence of non-profit schools of different levels with their tolerant and open spaces rather than government-run schools; the presence of a lot of Western brands and their selling agencies in Tehran and some other big cities; and the proliferation of fast-food restaurants and coffeehouses, among many others. It is through these changes in the social, cultural and economic environment, as well as attitudes towards these changes, that young individuals have learnt how to avoid the control of the traditional order in order to fulfil their personal identity in a cultural bricolage.

The official Islamic discourse is present through indicators such as women's dress code, widespread gender segregation, the banning of non-Islamic entertainment, and the propagation of Islamic culture and the humiliation of other cultures through the state-owned national media. Although Iran's more reform-minded religious leaders have supported some of these changes, the red lines of Islamic traditional culture should nevertheless not be transgressed. However, the approval of some new spaces for entertainment such as billiard clubs and coffee shops (which are central places for dating between girls and boys), and the granting of permission for women to enter sports stadiums are just some examples of the demands of society being accepted by the government.

Mahmood Shahabi in his research identifies three ideal types among Iranian young people: first, the locally oriented conventional youth; second, the cosmopolitan, or subcultural youth; and third, the politically radical or activist youth (*Basijis*) (Shahabi, 2006).

According to him, conventional youth conform to the behavioural demands posed by the national media, representatives of Islamic authority, their parents, and schoolteachers. Radical activists are those whose interests are tied very closely to the government and who are basic supporters of the Islamic Republic and its religious leaders.

The 'ideal type' that is the object of discussion here constitutes those young individuals who are neither conventional nor radical activists. Shahabi named them cosmopolitans. Shahabi argues that cosmopolitan youth, coming mainly from the upper and middle classes, are uninterested in ideology and politics (without any definite and homogenous worldviews), tend to be materialistic, hedonistic consumers of mass popular culture despite the government's pedagogic efforts, and have their own definition of normality. Another feature of this type, according to Shahabi, is familiarity with Western culture and the outside world through foreign travels, books, magazines, video, satellite TV channels, and the internet. In a sense global media sources are used by cosmopolitans or subcultural youth as guidelines toward a standard for behaviour, hairstyles and clothing trends that are defused via popular music stars and other entertainment heroes (Shahabi, 2006).

In order to develop Shahabi's study one step further, I explore those contemporary youths in Tehran who are neither conventional nor radical activists as non-conformists. I intend to scrutinise the non-conformist youth from any social strata based on their lifestyles and appearance and not only by their social class.

My examination of the different strata of youth culture highlights how a great amalgamation has happened in Tehrani youth attitudes and lifestyles, which is more complicated than the elucidation that a simple class-based explanation could bring to it. Since a homogenous Western culture is not prominent among non-conformist Tehrani youth, the postmodern conception of bricolage as a process of cultural selection of old and new, global and local components, could offer a convincing explanation. The new generation in Tehran, either consciously or unconsciously, are selective with local customs and various types of imported cultural values. They are also creative in mixing traditional and modern elements in order to construct meaning or make things meaningless. This constitutes an innovative lifestyle, based on a bricolage of elements from different cultural worlds – combining 'parts of several world views into a meaningful entity' (Riis, 1993: 376).

It is worth emphasising that this study does not aim at any kind of generalisation of the whole young population of either Iran or Tehran. Rather, it attempts to explain the social behaviours of the growing group of what I denote as 'non-conformist' youth.

Research method

In going about conducting the research for this study I used both participant observation techniques and open-format interviews to gather data on the social behaviours of Tehran's young people within various regions and different socioeconomic backgrounds. I used two-step sampling to choose the sample of research. Firstly, I divided Tehran into four regions in terms of the general socioeconomic situation of residents in each particular area. Then within each of these four segments, interviewees were chosen at random from a definite age range and were sampled from certain places such as shopping centres, the entrances of cinemas, public parks, popular coffeehouses and restaurants. The interviewees were selected from those with non-conformist appearance. It does not mean that all the non-conformist young residents of those areas will necessarily fit into one of the categories that I have made; rather it means that one type has been more remarkable in one area than another one.

It is worth noting that due to the many Islamic agents who are in charge of controlling people's appearance, many of the young cases of this study either refused to be interviewed or were reluctant to tell their stories. Therefore some limitations were imposed to the sampling for this study. Girls and women were also less interested and daring to stop and answer questions because of the many social constrictions they operate within.

I continued to interview until a pattern of repeated responses began to emerge. This survey allowed me to delineate five types of non-conformist youth, two of which are female and the remaining three male. I have called these five types: distinctive boys, distinctive girls, pretentious boys, hedonistic boys and ordinary girls.

Distinctive boys and distinctive girls

'Distinctive' boys and girls form a small fraction of the upper classes. Their life-world is distinct from the dominant culture and other non-conformist youths in many ways. They grow up in society's wealthiest families and their socioeconomic background allows them to freely choose every aspect of their lives. Having access to several communicative channels that they can afford to use in addition to having many relatives outside the country and the capability of travelling to Western countries themselves, provides them with many links to the outside world and to Western culture. Consequently, these individuals grow up with intimate knowledge of Western, but mostly American, culture. Because traditional values are no longer valid for them, their distinctive way of life and their internalisation of typically American norms like individualism, living independently from family, and having their own car in their early twenties is not surprising.

The way they style themselves (in terms of hair, clothing and makeup) make the differences between them and other types of youth obvious. 'Distinctive' youths often wear original clothes from original brands (as opposed to counterfeit clothing, which is prevalent in Iran) and there is competition among them to have the most individualised and fashionable appearance. They usually spend their time in shopping centres, restaurants and coffee shops where other people could not afford to go. Even though it is illegal since the summer of 2011, they have pets and they bring them out on walks in the afternoons illegal since the summer of 2011.

Their version of religion is largely 'secular' insofar as they believe in God, goodness and living peacefully with others. Their participation in religious ceremonies is limited to some ceremonies such as *Sham-e Ghariban* (Ashura night), which has paradoxically turned to a secular carnival for leisure despite attempts by Islamic radical groups and state agents to avoid this outcome.

'Distinctive' boys and girls typically choose their partners from the 'distinctive' type either because that is what they find the most appealing or in order to prevent cultural problems posed by those with different world views. They do not consider official marriage necessary to cohabitate. Going on vacation with their partners and hosting mixed-gender parties are popular pastimes for them. These young people have their own communities and they work and live within this cultural world. Because they try to minimise the chance of confrontation with the dominant Islamic and traditional order, it is very hard to regard them as being overtly resistant against the dominant culture.

Pretentious boys

The boys whom I have characterised as 'pretentious' represent a majority of young males and come from the middle and lower classes. They are typical bricoleurs and that is why any judgment about their subjectivity based on their appearance would result in misconception. These boys are typically raised in traditional families, with the behavioural measures of a conventional family, in the eastern and southern districts of Tehran. Despite their non-conformist appearance, they are religious people. However, their religiosity is very different from dominant understandings of religious devotion. They do not pray every day and they might not fast during the month of Ramadan, but they do very explicitly believe in the Islamic God, and in some Islamic rites such as *Nazr* (the offering of spiritual vows) and the pilgrimage of Shiite imams.

They are bricoleurs both in terms of their interpretation of religiosity and their selective way of life. These youths like to enjoy material life without abandoning religion. It is plausible to argue that they believe in a semi-secular version of Islam, because they do not see any contradiction between participating in a mixed party that serves alcoholic drinks on one Thursday and in attending a religious ceremony such as *Komeil* prayer on another. In response to a question about his seemingly incongruous way of life, one of my interviewees, Mehrdad, stated, 'Everything is good in its appropriate place and time. I am here in such a way as you are seeing but I will change my clothes and hairstyle accordingly for participation in weekly religious ceremonies.' His garish necklace was the logo of Metal Blade, but he knew little about the band and its social background or attitudes.

A majority of these boys have girlfriends in the Western sense of the term, and most of their relationships are sexual despite it being evidently forbidden in Islam. Paradoxically, they would never tolerate their own sister engaging in such a relationship. It seems that these boys are non-reflective about their way of life and do not care about ensuring any particular sense of homogeneity in it. On one hand they appear religious and on the other irreligious. They celebrate Valentine's Day by presenting gifts to their girlfriends, yet they may also flagellate themselves during Moharram, the month of mourning, which is a critical occasion according to official discourse. Being fashionable is very important to them, and while they cannot afford the original brands, buying forged brands for lower prices is a good option.

These young men are actually imbibing the images and thought patterns of Western and American ways of life from a second-hand source, those so-called 'distinctive boys' from the upper classes. They do their hair and trim their beards in quirky ways and then, wearing tight jeans and t-shirts bearing English words or weird symbols, they spend the rest of the day parading themselves to others by walking in shopping malls and parks in their neighbourhoods with their peers. This is a cheap form of leisure, but the police do impose restrictions upon this kind of time-wasting through what the Western media have dubbed 'Iran's fashion police' (Fathi, 2007)

Hedonistic boys

Hedonistic boys inhabit the western parts of Tehran such as *Shahrak-e Gharb* (West Town) or Geisha Bridge neighbourhoods where the residents are largely middle and upper-middle class. They are fashionable and if they can afford to wear original brands, they try to do so. Living in the present is principal and these boys do not seem to care about the future or the past. They could fairly be categorised as non-reflective people whose main criterion for action is life enjoyment. They rarely think about religion and its restrictions and their participation in religious ceremonies is mostly for entertainment. They spend their free time getting together and watching music clips and films through satellite channels rather than reading books, newspapers or journals. Even though they claim that they are selective, it seems that the juxtaposition of the different parts of their lives is unconsciously based on their demand for enjoyment from life. It does not really matter whether this lifestyle is Western or is derived from Iranian traditions, these young men seek out pleasure and this lifestyle meets their demands appropriately. They celebrate Valentine's Day as seriously as *Chaharshanbeh Soori* (the last Wednesday of the year just before spring solstice), an ancient rite from Zoroastrian religion, the celebration of which generally involves fireworks and fire jumping. Although their parents are very tolerant about their children's differences, some of them live independently from their families and in an unmarried state. Almost all of these boys have girlfriends and they regularly attend mixed-gender parties. Despite being less religious, if religion provides them with an entertaining situation they try to be a part of it.

Ordinary girls

The majority of Tehran's contemporary non-conformist young women can be categorised by the term 'ordinary girls'. These girls do their best not to appear in public places, for example universities or workplaces, without wearing makeup, although the extent to which they wear makeup may vary. Their attitudes are usually very close to traditional and conventional world views. They are interested in the traditional form of marriage with its accompanying rites such as *khastegari* (wooing), *mehriye* (a prenuptial agreement promising the woman a payout of a specified amount if the husband chooses to divorce her) and *jahizie* (dowry). They believe in Islam, even in its orthodox sense (which includes praying every day and fasting during the month of Ramadan), and they believe in the hereafter, predestination, oblation and in going on pilgrimages to the holy shrines of imams or their offspring.

However, these girls do not perceive any serious contradictions between uncovering their hair in mixed-gender parties in the presence of their boyfriends and their rather orthodox religious beliefs. They try to suggest a secular and modern interpretation of Islam, in which the relationship with God is the most important component. Their interpretation of Islam does not conflict with their worldly desires, and thus they practise according to that.

It is hard to find a precise and meaningful relationship between their appearance and their social class. Their socioeconomic backgrounds vary, they are mainly engaged in tertiary education or are employed and have aspirations towards self-improvement that makes them fashionable in public places. They like to be attractive and do not perceive themselves to be imitating a Western pattern. They are rarely resistant against the dominant and official culture and whenever the police enforce new restrictions or dress codes they try their utmost to adapt to the new limitations rather than cause controversy. Nevertheless, police and official discourse consider them to be more or less deviant and non-religious. These young women are largely non-reflective and constitute a special type of cultural bricoleur in Tehran.

Conclusion

In the case of Tehran's society, young people acting as cultural bricoleurs are detaching themselves from the old world and selectively constructing their own cultural worlds based on their own tastes and demands. They are doing this because living solely according to the traditional lifestyle they are taught by official discourse and by generational example does not meet their needs. In their cultural worlds, religiosity does not conflict with the material enjoyment of life. They believe in the core of religion and participate in religious ceremonies yet they also enjoy entertainment forms that have been banned or restricted by the Iranian (and ostensibly Islamic) government.

Nonetheless, the young male or female inhabitants of Tehran from all five above-mentioned types have the common characteristic of being non-conformist in the eyes of official Islamic and traditional culture. The misunderstanding of how youth construct their identities, which borrow simultaneously from Western culture and local tradition, has caused some societal challenges. The dominant culture attempts to simplify a very complicated social and cultural phenomenon by considering such lifestyles as Westernised and their participators as non-religious and blind victims of Western media products, and as an inherent challenge to the authority of the state. As this chapter has revealed, the situation is far more complex than that and has been ongoing for the past two decades.

The dominant order attempts to 'other' these non-conformist youths in order to reinforce the official Iranian Islamic culture as the mainstream culture. State cultural policies try to represent these patterns of clothing and hairstyle as deviant. These non-conformist youths are, on the whole, represented on state television as drug addicts or traffickers, consumers of drugs in their mixed-gender parties, and people who are unfaithful to familial and moral principles. Consequently, these youths are represented as unhappy and mainly marginalised in the real world. This depiction could not be further from the truth.

This 'othering' happens because of the gap between the official system of symbols and the way contemporary youth actually appear. The authorities and conventional people look at non-conformist youth as deviants because their life paths are different from the officially sanctioned patterns of life. The authorities often try to suggest restrictive plans for social and cultural purification and they believe that those who do not observe the rules and dress codes are endangering the social and moral security of society and thus deserve to be punished. These Islamic activists do not like to admit that there is a new signifying system that has been adopted and in many senses shaped by Tehran's youth. The latter are not in the least non-religious and immoral; these young people just want to be fashionable. As this chapter has revealed, many of them do pray to God, attend religious ceremonies, go to mixed-gender parties, celebrate *Chaharshanbeh Soori*, *Sham-e Ghariban* and Valentine's Day without perceiving any sense of contradiction. They observe their own interpretation of Islam and do so in their own constructed world in which religiosity is more private and confined to the person's own relationship with God than a relationship that is enforced by the state.

References

Baldwin, E et al. (1999) *Introducing Cultural Studies*. London & New York: Prentice Hall Europe.

Barker, C (2000) *Cultural Studies, Theory and Practice*. London: SAGE.

Barker, C (2004) *The Sage Dictionary of Cultural Studies*. London, Thousand Oaks, CA: SAGE.

Davis, F (1992) *Fashion, Culture, and Identity*. Chicago: University of Chicago Press.

Fathi, N (2007) 'In Iran, tactics of fashion police raise concerns'. *New York Times*, 4 May. www.nytimes.com/2007/05/04/world/middleeast/04tehran.html.

Hall, S and Jefferson, T (1976) *Resistance through Rituals: Youth Subcultures in Post-war Britain*. London: Hutchinson.

Hebdige, D (1979) *Subculture: The Meaning of Style*. London: Methuen.

Kaylan, M (2011) 'Iran bans Valentine's day, The regime's posture turns the smallest gestures into thrilling acts of subversion'. *The Wall Street Journal Online*, 12 February http://online.wsj.com/article/SB10001424052748703 78680457613829253418676.html.

Pieterse, J (1995) 'Globalization as hybridisation.' *Global Modernities.* M. Featherstone, S. Lash and R. Robertson (eds). London and Newbury Park, CA: SAGE. 45–68.

Riis, O (1993) 'The study of religion in modern society.' *Acta Sociologica* 36: 371–83.

Shahabi, M (2006) 'Youth subcultures in post-revolution Iran: An alternative reading.' *Global Youth? Hybrid Identities, Plural Worlds.* P. Nilan and C. Feixa (eds). New York: Routledge.

Sreberny-Mohammadi, A and A Mohammadi (1990) 'Hegemony and resistance: Media politics in the Islamic Republic of Iran.' *Quarterly Review of Film and Video* 12.4: 33–59.

CHAPTER 4

SOCIAL AND CULTURAL CHANGE AND THE WOMEN'S RIGHTS MOVEMENT IN IRAN

Azadeh Kian

The massive and active participation of several generations of Iranian women in big cities, especially youth, in the protest movement that started following the June 2009 presidential elections (heralding Neda Agha Soltan as their icon), has revealed the crucial role they play in their society. The implementation of Islamic laws founded on traditional jurisprudential interpretations in post-revolutionary Iran institutionalised gender inequality and aimed to reinforce patriarchal order. However, despite the Islamic state's attachment to patriarchal order, revolutionary changes have combined with the implementation of modernisation policies, especially in rural areas and small towns, and have had crucial consequences for women from traditional religious middle and lower class families.

Lower fertility rates, higher literacy rates and better education, an increase both in the age of women at their first marriage and in the number of marriages embarked on by free choice, and the active participation of women in social, cultural and economic realms are some indicators of this change. The average number of children has decreased to two, compared with 7.2 before the revolution, and more than 76 per cent of Iranian women now use contraceptive devices. According to the 2006 national census of population and housing, 85 per cent of Iranian women aged six years and older and 70 per cent of rural women are now literate (compared with 47.5 per cent and 17 per cent in 1976). The number of female university students rose from 57,000 in 1976 (or 30 per cent of the total) to over 1,500,000 in 2008 (about 60 per cent of the total).

Urbanisation has also increased sharply; over 70 per cent of Iranian families now reside in urban areas. The number of towns with more than 100,000 inhabitants rose from 23 in 1976 to 80 in 2006, even though the annual population growth rate has decreased to 1.2 per cent, which is down from 3.9 per cent in 1988. The gap between rural and urban areas has narrowed as the overwhelming majority of Iran's population now has access to education and healthcare facilities, electricity, clean drinking water, roads, etc. This in turn has led to a change in lifestyles and a rise in people's expectations and demands. An acute economic crisis and high inflation rate (27 per cent according to official statistics) have resulted in the decline of the purchasing power of Iranian families and forced an increasing number of lower and middle class women to partake in revenue-earning activities, especially in the underground economy which, according to the Ministry of Economy and Finance, employs over half of the urban workforce (see Kian-Thiébaut, 2005).

To the detriment of peripheral regions and ethnic and religious minorities (especially Sunnis) important regional disparities still persist, but better education and the increasing participation of women in the job market (especially in the informal economy) combined with economic crises have contributed to the increase in the average age of marriage for women. While the legal minimum age of marriage for girls in the Islamic Republic is 13, the average woman is now 23 when she gets married (compared with 19.75 in 1976). Likewise, results of our quantitative survey of 7,600 married women throughout Iran, and including ethnic minorities and rural areas, revealed that marriage based on free choice is increasing among young couples. Fifty-five per cent of married women aged 20–4 had been free to choose their own partner. Our survey also revealed a correlation between the level of a woman's education and the number of children she gave birth to, regardless of her ethnicity or religion. Literate mothers give birth to an average of 2.5 children, while illiterate mothers had, on average, 6.4 children. Moreover, we discovered that literate women often control the wellbeing of their family and play a more assertive role in family decision-making (in Kian-Thiébaut, 2008).

The results of our 2002 opinion poll (Kian-Thiébaut, 2008) suggest that the profound changes that have occurred in the lives of Iranian women as a consequence of a modernising society combined with an increase in women's awareness have weakened traditional perceptions concerning men's authority in the family institution: 90 per cent of sampled women support free choice in marriage, only 30.5 per cent think that housework is the exclusive responsibility of women, 15 per cent believe that childcare should be the exclusive responsibility of women, 86.5 per cent of our respondents believe that men and women should have equal access to education, 77 per cent are agree that men and women should have equal access to work, 53 per cent agree that women and men should equally partake in political activities, 52 per cent think women and men should have equal access to decision-making positions in government, and 69 per cent are in favour of equality in decision-making positions at the local/regional level.

Women's rights movement: From revolutionary era to radical populist period

The paradoxical modernisation of women's attitudes, despite religious precepts and the predominant Islamist ideology that denies women individuality, autonomy and independence, has in turn led to their mounting resistance and opposition against gendered social relations. The existence of a women's movement at the turn of the twentieth century, statutory changes under the Pahlavis (1925–79),[1] and women's participation in the 1979 revolution have largely contributed to the mobilisation of women against gender inequality.

Four periods of time can be distinguished with regard to the Islamic state's policies on women and women's mobilisation: the revolutionary period (which lasted until the end of the Iran–Iraq war in 1988), the period of reconstruction following the war (1989–97), the period of political development during Khatami's two terms as Iranian president (1997–2005), and the radical populist period from 2005 until the present day.

During the revolutionary period, traditional jurisprudence (*feqh-e sonnati*) was predominant. The patriarchal state, with its positivist approach to nature, perceived Islamic laws and institutionalised gender inequality as natural facts originating from the divine will. State authorities attempted to confine women to domesticity and by marginalising women and excluding them from the public sphere they imposed a private patriarchy (see Walby, 1994), denying women autonomy and independence. Indeed, women were perceived exclusively as family members whose rights and obligations should be defined in relation to their male relatives, who the state construed as being leaders and protectors of women.

The imposition of private patriarchy also meant overwhelming privileges were granted to men by law. This provoked the general discontent of many women and forced the Islamist women parliamentarians, who occupied four seats (1.7 per cent of the total) in each of the first three parliaments, to prepare motions to defend more adequately women's needs and rights in the family. Despite their allegiance to the Islamic regime, they believed that the teachings of Islam were not being respected (Dabbagh, 1996). The beginning of the Iraq–Iran war (1980–8) mobilised the country's resources, and was a major impediment to the flourishing of debates on gender inequalities. Although Islamist women contributed to war efforts, and some were recruited by the Pasdaran (Revolutionary Guards) and the Basij (volunteers), their social role was not recognised by the power elite, who considered women primarily and exclusively to be biological reproducers and houseworkers.

For a number of religious authority figures, including Ayatollah Khomeini, when a Muslim country is invaded by non-Muslims, 'defensive Jihad' becomes mandatory for all Muslims regardless of their gender, age or status. Women and men alike should mobilise to defend the honour of Islam. For this very reason Khomeini endorsed women's military training and their enrolment in the army and the Pasdaran. During the Iran–Iraq war women volunteers demanded authorisation to go to the front lines. Khomeini argued that at the time of the Prophet, women went to the front, but only to take care of the wounded. Committed Iranian women thus participated in 'defensive Jihad' through a multitude of activities ranging from taking care of the wounded or the family members of martyrs, to baking bread or sewing uniforms for the soldiers of Islam. Marzieh Hadidchi Dabbagh, a confidante of Khomeini, one of his bodyguards and a member of the second, third and fifth Islamic parliaments was appointed Commander of the Pasdaran in western Iran, but women were never asked to sacrifice their lives for the country (see Kian-Thiebaut, 2004). The sphere of martyrdom as a 'sacred' realm belonged only to men; women entered this sphere solely as family members, the mothers, wives, daughters or sisters of martyrs (see Moallem, 2005). The assassination of Neda Agha Soltan by members of the Basij during the June 2009 post-election protests made her a female martyr who entered this sacred realm as a woman/individual. As such, she became the icon of the whole protest movement, not only of women.

Women were expected to show their commitment to Islam and to the Islamic Republic by accepting these highly gendered roles. Presumed to be main guardians of traditions, they were required to reinforce Islamic family ties, thereby maintaining social cohesion. In addition to traditional instruments of propaganda such as mosques and Friday prayers, the state's ideology for women was perpetuated by school books and modern communication networks, especially by television and cinema. The plight of gender-sensitive women was also overshadowed by the predominant values of self-abnegation, devotion and sacrifice that were rooted in the Shi'a culture and internalised by the young volunteers (*basijis*), hundreds of thousands of whom served in the front. Moreover, the clerical and the political elite, who attributed all shortcomings and problems to the force of circumstances, used the war as a pretext to dismiss women's social problems.

Because women were the first to bear the burden of the rule of political Islam, they were also the first to challenge its legitimacy. Paradoxically, the implementation of Sharia law created a common ground of protest for women, regardless of their social status and political stands. Women activists, both secular women and the disillusioned educated Islamists, challenged the dominant ideological discourse that considered the private sphere of the home the best and the most suitable place for women. They rejected their confinement at home and managed to occupy the public sphere through economic and social activities.

Women not only challenge institutionalised gender inequalities by ensuring their active participation in those economic, social, and political realms not forbidden to them by the religious and political elite's reading of Sharia law, they also assert their authority in the religious and judicial realms where women have traditionally been denied power.

After the end of the war the period of reconstruction started under the presidency of Ali-Akbar Hashemi-Rafsanjani. The power elite, who were forced to concede to women's professional skills due to the shortage of specialists, played a double role and maintained a double ideological discourse. On the one hand, they continued to perceive women primarily as biological reproducers and house workers; simultaneously, however, they responded to the demands of the female population in general, and the pressures of active, professional women in particular. The policies of women's occupation adopted in 1992 by the High Council of Cultural Revolution chaired by the former president Hashemi-Rafsanjani reflected the contradictions of such double standards and discourses. The Office of Women's Affairs (an offshoot of the presidential bureau) was created in 1992 with the aim of finding solutions to women's problems and concerns. With the readopting by the government of family planning and birth control in 1989, the birth rate has diminished sharply. The results of the first national census of the population under the Islamic Republic (in 1986) revealed a total increase of 15 million in the population since 1976, the last national census of the population under the shah. The annual population growth rate at that time averaged 3.9 per cent, one of the highest in the world. The economic crisis, the lack of resources available to respond to the needs of the oversized young generation (in terms of education, health, employment, etc), forced the government to adopt projects to diminish this birth rate, despite clerical opposition and the pro-birth traditions in Islam.

Women also became very active in the realm of journalism. Some women's magazines published in the 1990s by Islamic advocates of women's rights – especially *Zanan* [Women], *Farzaneh* and *Zan* [Woman] – served as a forum for discussion between women activists who criticised gendered citizenship as reflected in the constitutional law, the civil and penal codes, and work legislation. Women's press also played a crucial role in establishing a dialogue between Islamic and secular advocates of women's rights. Despite their political and ideological differences, a gender and class-based solidarity emerged among these women, who overwhelmingly belonged to the urban middle classes. Theses activists can be qualified as 'liberal', because they have attempted to obtain gender equality through reforms in institutions and laws. Their strategy is to question relations of power within both state and society in the context of concrete constraints, a version of what Deniz Kandiyoti (1988) has called 'bargaining with patriarchy.'

Women's magazines also played a crucial role in creating contexts for political interaction between women and the ruling elite (Kian, 2011). They provided women with the opportunity for more active involvement in the public sphere. Women thus could transform their grievances from private issues into public/political stakes, and they started to challenge institutions that they had once perceived as powerful. For example, in 1992, a few months after its inaugural issue, *Zanan* printed a series of articles that examined the obstacles toward women's authority in religious and judiciary institutions and maintained that none of the main Islamic texts justify such prohibitions (Yadigar Azadi, 1992: 24). Azam Taleghani, daughter of the radical cleric Ayatollah Mahmoud Taleghani, is the editor of the magazine *Payam-e Hajjar* [Hajjar's Message]. Her plea for the cause of the disinherited brought her into contact with the plight of women, especially the poor. *Payam-e Hajjar* was the first women's magazine to advocate the reinterpretation of Qur'anic verses, especially *al-Nisa* ('Women', the fourth chapter of the Qur'an) and to refute the legalisation of polygamy (Kian, 2011). These women rejected the divine justifications for gender inequality through a new reading of Islam, which accommodated the equality of rights between men and women. The extent and multitude of queries by the female population led the Qom religious seminary to publish a woman's magazine called *Payam-e Zan* [Woman's Message] to address these issues from 1993 onward.

The aim of women's press, which primarily attempted to reach both educated women and the political and religious elite, was to promote women's status through emphasising legal, social and economic shortcomings, and to propose changes in civil and penal laws and in the constitution. Secular women's contributions to the ongoing debates are manifold. Through articles they publish in women's magazines or interviews, female lawyers and jurists, sociologists and historians, political scientists, artists and writers, sportswomen, film directors, and others, who are often considered to be role models for the younger generation, question the predominant ideological discourse on women. Several lawyers and jurists, including Shirin Ebadi (winner of the Nobel Peace Prize, 2003) and Mehrangiz Kar (a prominent lawyer who was imprisoned and was later forced in to exile), were particularly vocal.

In their publications, they criticised Islamic laws from the perspective of the Universal Declaration of Human Rights and other international conventions that the Islamic Republic has signed. Because they lived and acted in a Muslim society, they were more sensitive to Islamic discourse, using Islam and the Qur'an to argue against gender inequalities. Thus, in their discourse, they too argued that Islam is for the equality of rights between men and women, Muslims and non-Muslims.[2] Based on this interpretation, they were demanding the reform of the Civil Code and Iran's penal laws. In the 1990s, the scope of debates on the condition of women expanded, and conferences started to be organised on various aspects of women's and family issues.

Some Islamist women agreed with the view of Zahra Zabetian, founder of the Hazrat-e Khadijeh Association, that 'the ideals of the revolution cannot be attained unless women are present in the public sphere' (1992: 25), and they created independent associations in order financially and morally to assist deprived women to boost their activity in the public sphere (see Kian-Thiébaut, 2000: 23). These Islamic women's associations, women's religious seminaries, and informal secular women's groups and gatherings reinforced gender solidarity and increased a collective consciousness. Common grievances have led to the emergence of unprecedented gender solidarity between secular and modernist–Islamist women.

The editors of some women's magazines, especially those of *Zanan*, *Farzaneh* and *Hoghough-e Zanan* [*The Rights of Women*], demanded the contribution of secular women specialists. This call for co-operation has provided both a challenge and an opportunity for secular social activists. Some secular lawyers, jurists, economists, sociologists, artists, historians, novelists and film directors, took up the challenge and seized the opportunity to present their opinions and works through writings and interviews with these magazines. Indeed, these secular intellectuals, who had been forced into isolation for several years, adopted a new strategy, asserting their social identity through critical writings. Thanks to the pressures of women activists, women judges were rehabilitated in the judiciary and started to serve in the courts. However, they still do not have the right to append their signature to judgments and despite women's plights and struggles, only a few legal changes occurred during the period of reconstruction – for example the amendment to the divorce law (called *Ojrat-ol Mesl*) that tended to prevent unjustified divorce through financial pressures, by forcing men to make a lump sum payment in lieu of the unpaid housework that had been carried out by the woman during the marriage. In order words, the ruling elite continued to perceive women as minors who needed assistance.

The third period started with the election of Mohammad Khatami, which women played a large role in. Among women voters, some demanded a radical and wholesale change of the Islamic laws (especially the family law and the penal code), while others argued that the reform of laws would not be sufficient as long as social customs and cultural perceptions remained unaltered. Therefore, it was with a strong hope for a radical political, juridical, and cultural change and the improvement of their status and condition that the majority of women, from diverse social and family backgrounds, participated in the election, using their right to vote as a potent agent to implement change. Through their involvement in politics, women attempted to present a different reading of Islam and Islamic laws in order to promote gender equality.

Nonetheless, gender inequality was largely absent from debates between reformers and conservatives. Some reformers even argued that the question of women and their legal and citizenship rights was not intertwined with the building of democracy and therefore did not constitute an urgent issue for democracy ideologies (see Abdi, 2002). Likewise, the law continued to consider women to be minors, placing them under the guardianship of their fathers or husbands for life.[3] Although the 13 female members of the sixth parliament were gender conscious and quite active in proposing motions to ameliorate women's status (for example, to modify the civil code, facilitate women's access to divorce, send female students abroad, increase the minimum age of marriage for girls from 9 to 18, or adopt the Convention of the Elimination of All Forms of Discrimination Against Women (CEDAW)), only a few legal changes were actually implemented. The Guardian Council systematically disapproved of these motions, arguing that they were incompatible with Islam. Finally the minimum age of marriage and penal responsibility for girls was increased from 9 to 13 and for boys from 15 to 17. President Khatami discounted the request for government intervention to help promote the status of women, arguing that it was superfluous, as the development of a civil society, his broader goal, would inevitably contribute to satisfying women's demands and would provide women with the means to transform their demands into laws (Khatami, 1997: 3). Nonetheless, in 1998 secular feminists finally obtained the authorisation to publish a magazine called *Jens-e Dovvom* [The Second Sex], which was edited by Noushin Ahmadi-Khorasani. Despite the crucial role played by women in his election in 1997 and re-election in 2001, Khatami conceded to conservative pressures by refusing to nominate women ministers in his second cabinet. The policies of the Islamic state remain ambiguous with regard to women. As Zahra Shojaei, President Khatami's advisor in women's affairs argued:[4]

> More than two decades after the revolution, we still ignore the Islamic Republic's doctrine with regard to women. Should the number of employed women be increased or not? We are devoid of a comprehensive program concerning women. It is not the four principles of the constitution, Ayatollah Khomeini's sermons or the history of women at the advent of Islam that can lead us to conceive such a program!

This doctrinal ambiguity does not only concern women. Its roots can be located in the very foundations of the Islamic regime, which claims with reference to different clauses in the Constitution to be both republican and Islamic. Its republican component praises gender equality while its Islamic component advocates gender inequality. For this very reason, women's fate is intertwined with the fate of the Republic.

The persistence of gender inequality during Khatami's presidency and the reformer-dominated sixth parliament has disillusioned the women activists who had supported them, and has widened the gap between the female population and the state. Jamileh Kadivar, a member of the sixth parliament from Tehran, criticised Khatami arguing, 'We know that nominating one or two women ministers will not resolve women's problems, yet we are convinced that such nominations could have had positive social and cultural consequences' (Kadivar, 2001). Likewise, Isfahani MP Akram Mansurimaneh declared, 'President Khatami's refusal to nominate women who are more competent than male ministers humiliates the entire female population' (*Zanan*, 2001: 12). Faced with these severe criticisms President Khatami said he was sorry (Kadivar, 2001). Women's disillusionment with the reformers has further radicalised the women's movement, which now relies exclusively on their own members and activities to promote the status of women and the equality of rights.

The political demobilisation of middle class women, several of whom refused to run as candidates and many others of whom did not vote, led first to the election of a neo-conservative seventh parliament (2004–8), and then to the election of a radical populist president, who was supported by fundamentalist clerics and gender segregationists, in 2005. Contrary to women members of the sixth parliament who had attempted to reform laws, anti-feminist women members of the seventh parliament supported polygamy, advocated more repressive measures against 'badly veiled women', and rejected the approval of the CEDAW. These regressions led to the rupture in relations between women activists and the state.

In post-revolutionary Iran, especially from the 1990s onward, the number of women writers, novelists, journalists, publishers, film directors, etc grew sharply. Women directors are using their cameras to unveil the mechanisms of patriarchal control and to demonstrate their collective struggle against gender disparities. They highlight women's legal and social problems and portray women as active and courageous beings with a strong personality. The important success of their films shows that the urban population is interested in modern interpretations of gender questions. Rakhshan Bani-Etemad, Tahmineh Milani, Pouran Derakhshandeh, Manijeh Hekmat, Marziyeh Meshkini, Samira Makhmalbaf and Nikki Karimi are among the most well-known of these film directors. But the active presence of women is undoubtedly the strongest in the realm of literature. Among them, Simin Daneshvar, Goli Taraqi and Shahrnoush Parsipour started publishing prior to the revolution. Qazaleh Alizadeh (d. 1996), Monirou Ravanipour, Fariba Vafi, Zoya Pirzad, Sepideh Shamlou and Mahsa Moheb-Ali are some among many women novelists who started writing from the 1990s onward. These novelists aim to occupy public space through written expression and to give a better visibility to women, their problems and their struggles. In literary works, women also deal with the issues of sexuality and the body that are usually considered to be taboo subjects and are prohibited in films.

Women's increasing access to education and revenue-earning activities, their increasing social participation and their disaffection with official Islam, combined with their inferior positions within social and economic hierarchy, have all had an important impact on the structuring of their political behaviour.

The emerging Iranian civil society is also marked by the vitality of debates on the social, civil and political dimensions of women's citizenship. The arrest of many women's rights activists, the closure of several women's magazines (including *Zanan* in January 2008) and women NGOs (the number of which has increased from 54 in 1995 to over 600 today), and many other attempts by Ahmadinejad's government to intimidate women's rights activists attest to the increasing importance of women's issues as a political stake. Although state authorities qualify feminism as a sign of Western cultural invasion, it has become commonplace in the discourse of women's rights activists, and self-identification with feminism is no longer taboo.

Among women's rights activists, some present a new and dynamic reading of Islam to demand citizenship rights for women, while others refer exclusively to universal human rights and other international charters. The limitations set by the current government on freedom of expression and action and the closure of women's press has led women's rights advocates to express their views, overwhelmingly on internet sites, in weblogs, books, novels, paintings, theatre, cinema and through ongoing campaigns (including the One Million Signature Campaign, to change discriminatory laws, the Campaign Against Stoning and all Forms of Violence against Women and the White Scarves Campaign against Sex Segregation in Stadiums).

The conservatism and sexism of President Ahmadinejad and the segregational policies implemented by his government on the one hand, and the protest activities of Muslim and secular women on the other, have caused some traditional and anti-feminist women (including some members of the parliament) to criticise the low number of women in decision-making positions and Ahmadinejad's refusal to appoint women cabinet ministers. On the occasion of the legislative elections of the eighth parliament (April–May 2008), Maryam Behrouzi, former member of parliament, member of the conservative Islamic Coalition Party and president of the conservative Zeynab Association, declared, 'Women should actively participate in decision making. There is no legal impediment preventing women from obtaining a significant number of seats in parliament. It is the predominant patriarchal system that wants to thrust women aside from the public sphere.' (Behrouzi, 2008)

Before the June 2009 presidential elections, the speaker of the Guardian Council declared that women could indeed run in these elections.[5] However, the Guardian Council, which vets all of the presidential candidates, did not permit any of the 42 women applicants to progress through to the candidacy stage of the presidential elections. A large coalition of secular and Muslim women published a declaration demanding that the future president take measures to ratify the CEDAW, which was promulgated by the reformist majority sixth parliament (2000–4) but rejected by the Council of Guardians and the seventh and eighth conservative majority parliaments. They also called for a change in discriminatory articles of the constitutional law and the civil code.

Faced with a new set of regressions, some advocates of women's rights opted for gender solidarity and overlooked their political divisions, joined hands and worked together to oppose the Family Protection bill that the government of Ahmadinejad had presented to the Parliament in 2007. In September 2008, over 50 secular and Muslim women who had decided to prevent its ratification went to the parliament and demanded to meet with those members concerned. They argued that, in its current form, the bill would inevitably be detrimental to the interests and rights of women, and they presented proposals to change the controversial provisions of the proposed bill. Following in-depth discussions with the members of the judiciary commission and other MPs, they succeeded in convincing the parliament to retract the two articles.

The contested results of the June 2009 presidential elections,[6] the post-electoral protests and the repression of millions of opponents have overshadowed women's demands and activities. Women's rights activists, several of whom have been arrested and imprisoned, can no longer think of interacting with the current parliament and government, which they consider to be both illegitimate and repressive. Contrary to the reformist era, during which these women interacted with the power elite to implement change, it is now through social activity and the mobilisation of civil society that women activists are attempting to implement change from below.

Conclusion

The social, demographic and cultural changes occurring in post-revolutionary Iran among the female population have started to shake the traditional harmony that has been founded on male domination and the patriarchal power that state ideology and legislation tend to enforce.

The instrumentalisation of Islam, the masculinised construct of the Islamic state, essentialist discourses and gendered concepts of citizenship have been challenged by both Islamic and secular women activists. Through their social struggles they have attempted to introduce structural, institutional, or cultural change and have been involved in public debates and interacted with political processes and political institutions. Faced with those who use a conservative interpretation of Islam to justify sex discrimination and perpetuate patriarchal logic, many Iranian women activists are now presenting their own interpretations and readings of Islam in order to oppose gendered social relations.

The women's rights movement, however, still remains largely confined to the educated urban Persian middle classes living in big cities. These activists need to strengthen their ties with rural, lower class and ethnic women in mid-sized and small towns where the majority of the population live. Many of these 'ordinary women', some of whom are working to ameliorate women's conditions in their villages or towns, are unaware of women's rights campaigns. These campaigns, including the One Million Signature Campaign, several of whose activists have been arrested and imprisoned for defending women's rights, are almost exclusively active in Tehran and large cities and are better known outside Iran than inside the country.

If women's rights activists do not consider adopting popular mobilisations that are more relevant to traditional modes of social organisations in order to reach out to non-elite women, they will isolate themselves from the majority of Iranian women (and men). It is risky for them to construe themselves as being saviours of subaltern women, and to speak on their behalf instead of clearing space to allow them to speak. They risk endorsing a linear vision, seeing the experiences of ordinary women as a variation of their own meta-narrative, thereby implying their cultural, social and political superiority. (Spival, 1999; Chaterjee, 1993)

The results of my research suggest that the agency of change is located in an alliance between various categories of women, which will bring about the conditions for all women to step out from subalternity.

Notes

1 The legal status of women underwent change following the Shah's grant of political rights to women in 1963. In 1967, the Family Protection Law was adopted. It gave women the right to divorce, with custody of their children upon the court's approval, and the increase of the minimum age of marriage for girls to 15 and later to 18. Laws were approved to facilitate women's access to jobs, including the judiciary and the army.
2 See, for example, articles published by Shirin Ebadi and Mehrangiz Kar in Zanan and Jami'eh-ye sâlim (following a court order, the latter monthly was closed down in early 1999).
3 For example, in order to travel, Iranian women must receive written permission from their father, or their husband if they are married.
4 I am grateful to Mahboubeh Abbasgholizadeh who provided me with the text of her interview with Zahra Shojaei in Tehran, in the Spring of 2001.
5 www.radiofarda.com/content/o2_women_iran_election/1606943.html.
6 For an analysis of the results see, Ansari et al, 2009.

References

Abdi, A (2002) 'Rawshanfikri-yi dini va masa'il-i fawritar az masa'il-i zanan ['Religious intellectualism and more urgent questions than the women's questions']. *Zanan* 58: 38.

Ansari, A, Berman, D and Rintoul, T (2009) *Preliminary Analysis of the Voting Figures in Iran's 2009 Presidential Election*. London: Chatham House and the Institute of Iranian Studies, University of St Andrews, 21 June.

Behrouzi, M, interview with Deutsche Welle, 19 February 2008 (www.dw-world.de/dw/article/0,2144,3137038,00.html.)

Chatterjee, P (1993) *The Nation and its Fragments: Colonial and Post-Colonial Histories*. Princeton: University Press.

Dabbagh, M (1996) 'Zanan va naqsh-e anan dar majlis' ['Women and their role in the Majlis']. *Neda* 17–8: 9.

Kadivar, J (2001) interview with *Siyasat-e Ruz* 115, 4 September.

Kandiyoti, D (1988) 'Bargaining with patriarch'. *Gender and Society* 2, 3: 274–90.

Kian, A (2011) 'Gendering Shi'ism in post-revolutionary Iran' in Bahramitash, R and Hooglund, E (eds) *Gender in Contemporary Iran: Pushing the Boundaries*. London: Routledge: 24–35.

Kian-Thiébaut, A (2005) 'L'Iran: Etat islamique entre structures monopolistiques et modèle de l'Etat social'. *Revue des mondes musulmans et de la Méditerranée* 105–6: 175–98.

——— (2000) 'Women's religious seminaries in Iran'. *International Institute for the Study of Islam in the Modern World Newsletter* 6: 23.

——— (2004) 'Women, gender and Jihad: Iran and Afghanistan' in Joseph, S (ed) *Encyclopedia of Women and Islamic Cultures*, Leiden: Brill: vol. 2: 325–6.

——— (2008) 'From motherhood to equal rights advocates: The weakening of patriarchal order' in Katouzian, H and Shahidi, H (eds) *Iran in the 21st Century. Politics, Economics and Conflict*. London: Routledge: 86–106.

Khatami, M (1997) interview in *Zanan*, 34, April–May 1997: 2–5.

Mansurimaneh, A (2012) interview in *Zanan* 79, September 2012: 12.

Moallem, M (2005) *Between Warrior Brother and Veiled Sister: Islamic Fundamentalism and the Politics of Patriarchy in Iran*. Berkeley, Los Angeles: University of California Press.

Spivak, GS (1999) *A Critique of Postcolonial Reason. Toward a History of the Vanishing Present*, Cambridge: Mass. Harvard University Press.

Walby, S (1994) 'Is citizenship gendered?'. *Sociology* 28(2): 379–95.

Yadigar Azadi, M (1992) 'Qezavat-e Zan' ['Women's judgment']. *Zanan* vol.1, No. 5, Khordad-Tir 1371 [May–July]: 21; and 'Ijtehad va marja'iyyat-e zanan' ['Women's religious authority']. *Zanan* No. 8, Aban-Azar 1371 [October–December]: 24.

Zabetian, Zahra, interview in *Payam-e Zan* 9, first year, Azar 1371 (November–December 1992): 25.

CHAPTER 5

EMERGING FORMS OF MASCULINITY IN THE ISLAMIC REPUBLIC OF IRAN

Mehri Honarbin-Holliday

This chapter aims to illuminate and reflect on the emerging forms and expressions of Iran's variegated masculine identities through the ownership, sensation, presentation and management of the body.[1] This is occurring both in the private and intimate as well as the public and social spheres. My research findings demonstrate that among the generation of males born after the Iran–Iraq war (1980–8) the idea and the role of the masculine body is neither monolithic nor influenced by the state's messages of 'Islamic' corporeal restraint and modesty. My observations indicate that young men are increasingly taking ownership of their bodies, each adopting it as a tool to relate individual perceptions and lived experience. I define this as the sovereign body, the resource to make meaning and mark differentiation. I will argue that whilst such manifestations are personal and cultural in form, they encompass a chain of ideas that are political in nature. They demonstrate the young men's critique of their sociopolitical location, their resistance and objection to a lack of freedom of expression and persistent forms of censorship, and their demand for autonomy. I argue that seeking differentiation through body presentation is to alter expected male identities in order to reconstruct and project more layered, complex and individual identities. The chapter ultimately posits the question of how changes in masculine identities might indicate a demand for change in the patriarchal and constricting societal structures. I reference the interplay of the elements of a rich masculine discourse of the body, which is evident in classical literature, the rituals of Shi'i Islam, and the performing arts on the one hand, and the development of urban space related to the dynamics of the Iranian higher education system, which I define as Iranian cosmopolitanism, on the other.

Why masculinities?

The terms 'masculinities' and 'masculinity studies' are increasingly used in interdisciplinary scholarship in cultural studies, humanities and the social sciences to discuss a vast range of ideas and concepts relating to and documenting power differentiation in male gender sexuality. While studies are often devoted to addressing the historical imbalance of the male as an absolute or 'implicit subject,' they tend to place men and masculinity at the centre of analysis, thus positioning them as 'explicit subjects' (Adams and Savran, 2004). I use the term 'masculinities' to mean the range of inherited, constructed and adopted sociocultural ideas and patterns in behaviours that male participants in Iran have projected. The biological qualities of the participants are not of concern. Rather, I subscribe to the notion that masculinity is a set of fluid social and cultural performances, which are not necessarily a product of men's hormonal states (Whitehead and Barrett, 2001). There has been much focus and discussion by scholars in Iran and in the diaspora about women, their lives and shared histories, and their often neglected legal status in the past hundred years. In comparison, studies of men and forms of masculinity have been lacking so the subject area and the nature of my enquiry consolidate a highly relevant and new area of knowledge construction.

Educational revolution and Iranian cosmopolitanism

The initial site for my fieldwork was the metropolis of Tehran and my interviews were conducted in April 2009, before the controversial presidential elections of 2009. Most of the young men I interviewed had migrated to Tehran so to contextualise the site of research I highlight some of its significant characteristics.

The capital city has increasingly become a demographic melting pot and as one of the largest cities in the Middle East, Tehran offers demographic complexities and a wealth of potential research participants from diverse cultural backgrounds and regions. Economically, these include the wealthy and powerful who are able to access a wide range of material goods, the financially challenged, and the considerable majority who fall in between the two categories. The 17 young men I interviewed for this study are from financially challenged backgrounds, even though some of their families have improved their economic circumstances by deploying more members of the family, including mothers, to become wage earners to various degrees. For example, the mother of one of the young men in this study who is from a farming background has managed to take advantage of her weaving skills in recent years to make and sell rugs on occasion.

Since the 1930s Tehran has undergone processes of urbanisation in waves that have brought educational, economic and civic development. This was intensified by the oil boom in the 1970s and the catastrophic and devastating eight-year war with Iraq escalated the process, as the war-weary and war-damaged were driven to the capital city in search of both shelter and economic survival (Bayat, 1997; Keddie, 2003). Furthermore, the government's efforts in urban reconstruction during the post-war decade and a discourse of globalisation attracted substantial numbers to urban centres from the country's regions. People came looking for opportunities whether empty handed and in search of any form of employment with the hope of improving their lives, or with the intention to invest their capital and take advantage of growth opportunities. Further, and with the state's encouragement in the aftermath of the war and the tragic scale of the loss of lives, Iran witnessed a baby boom resulting in an unprecedented rise in the population. As a consequence a steep population rise during the post-war period worked in parallel with urban growth and resulted in Iran becoming young, urban, and increasingly cosmopolitan (Nooshin, 2005).

Urban reconstruction in the post-war era has also meant the expansion of educational opportunities. 'Educational Jihad', the Islamic Republic's goal to narrow the gap between those who had a familial tradition or the financial ability to go to university and those who previously had no such ambitions, has facilitated the means for significant numbers from rural areas to join the urban mainstream in pursuing higher education. Since the republic's 'cultural revolution' in 1983 and the reopening of higher education institutions after a three-year period of closure and academic and administrative 'cleansing' the Islamic regime has responded to the demand for an increase in the number of universities across the country. This, alongside the cross-disciplinary cross-regional nature of the new higher education system, has created unprecedented fertile ground for the development of Iranian cosmopolitanism with specific qualities.

Iranian cosmopolitanism has developed organically and is plural, indigenous, widespread and intellectually fluid in nature; this is contrary to the state's isolationist stance. It is the result of significant and intersecting elements implicated in the increased access to higher education, intra-national mass migration, and a discourse of political reform. It reflects the people's creative and layered identities, and greater understandings of their sociopolitical location and place in society. As such, Iranian cosmopolitanism possesses the potential to overcome imposed social, cultural and religious barriers, accommodating ethnic, religious and class diversity to unprecedented levels. It is unlike the enlightened but highly exclusive social groups that developed in the 1940s interconnected with the politics of the left and left-over aristocrats, and the few among those branded, rightly or wrongly, as 'Westernised' in the subsequent decades.

The national university entrance examination, the *concour*, and the standardised student selection and placement procedures, have forced thousands of first-year university students from Tehran to take up their studies in cities as diverse as Qom, Shiraz, Isfahan, Mashad, Tabriz, Karaj, Kerman, Zahedan or Yazd. In turn it has become possible for large numbers of students from the country's regions to end up on the capital's numerous campuses, and many stay behind after completing their studies. Thus, Persians, Azeris, Lors, Kurds, Baluchis, Armenians and Arabic speakers from the four corners of the country, possessing varied ethnic identities and belonging to diverse religious and cultural practices, come together and occupy and share urban space. The scale is highly significant because by the time they complete their studies, several million young people will have shared spaces of public transport, restaurants and coffee shops, parks and cultural centres as well as the university campuses, which also provide high speed access to the internet. While the internet has been available in Iran since the late 1990s, many students will have first encountered its possibilities upon arrival in higher education. Thus, considerable numbers will have heard one another articulate aspirations and ideas, engaged in political debate, participated in social acts, and more often than not explored physical intimacies and sexuality for the first time in this urban space. Whilst class differences persist in universities, ideas and demands from the grassroots can unlock and spread in such an environment more than ever before due to its diversity. Youth consciousness, political awareness, the understanding and exchange of new ideas (both real and imagined) and, most significantly, the recognition of the rights of the individual and the need for a more developed democracy and civil society, are among the specific goals and qualities of this Iranian cosmopolitanism.

Considering the desire and struggle for reform from the mid-1990s, including the work of political activists, journalists, and women's press demanding change in the legal system, which led to the 1997 election of Mohammad Khatami as president (1997–2005), and juxtaposing this with the worsening civil rights and economic situation and the hardline politics of fear imposed during Mahmoud Ahmadinejad's presidency since 2005, this cosmopolitanism is political at its very heart. It is concerned with freedom of speech and expression, human rights, democracy, transparent governance and the sanctity of the rights of all citizens. Its potential power is yet to be realised. Two-thirds of the population is under the age of 30, over three and half million aspiring youth are in higher education,[2] and the national literacy rate is projected to be 92.1 per cent by 2015 (Salehi-Isfahani, 2008). These demographic and educational figures, when coupled to the power of the internet and contemporary digital technologies, suggest the extent of Iranian cosmopolitanism and posit major implications for the country's political and cultural trajectories (Sreberny and Khiabany, 2010).

A heritage of the discourse of the masculine body

Many aspects of Iranian cultural heritage implicitly or explicitly engage with a discourse of the masculine body. The disposition and construction of male identities, as indeed any process of identity construction, are dependent on histories and social influences past and present. While the paradigm of maleness in Iran is as complex and layered as it would be anywhere in the world, it is nevertheless clear from the interviewees' reflections on the male body that it is grounded in their heritage. This is contrary to the views of the authorities in Iran who consider the young generation's expressions of individuality alien and irrelevant, and borrowed from and planted by foreigners. Indeed, the young men's conceptualisations draw on Iranian mythology with contemporary referents including frequently cited poetry, literary fiction, religious ritual and visual and performative art forms.

In the grand narrative of the *Shahnameh*, Hakim Abolghasem Ferdowsi Toosi's *Epic of the Kings* (1009 CE), we read of the legendary Rostam, the *pahlavan* of noble birth and the eponymous symbol of absolute masculine might.[3] We become aware of and familiar with the force of Rostam's body and his endurance during the course of his seven trials and exploits. His might, we are told, is comparable to that of lions and elephants, and his grip is leopard-like (Shah Nameh Ferdowsi, nd, 93–7). He is given to us as the ultimate hero, the chivalrous and noble warrior, the defender of the territory of *Iranzamin* the land of the Aryans. The performative arts of *naghali* and *pardeh khani*- narrating and enacting stories from a painted canvas for an audience- have kept the narratives of Rostam's exploits alive in the minds and hearts of Iranians. This is despite the Islamic regime's desire to eradicate teaching and referencing of the *Shah Nameh* in the education system.[4] Nevertheless despite this opposition, Iran has its first officially licensed female *naghaal* (storyteller), Gord Afarid under the tutelage of Morshed Torabi.

Further, the third Caliph of Islam, Ali Ebn Abi Taleb (600–1 CE), and his son, Hossein Ebn Ali (626–80 CE), who was killed in the Battle of Karbala (680 CE), embody the concept of selfless sacrifice and martyrdom in Shi'i Islam. To the Shi'i believers, the two imams are symbols of purity, spirituality, chivalry and brotherhood, or *javanmardi* and *fotovat*. (*Nahjolbalagheh*, 1980; Aslan, 2006). The youth are called upon by the state to emulate such qualities and protect Shi'i identity, especially during Ashura, the anniversary of Imam Hossein's martyrdom, when *ta'ziyeh* (passion plays) are performed in remembrance (Beyzaei, 2000; Chelkowski, 1998). However, spirituality and male aesthetics are taken to a different realm in Persian classical mystic poetry. Some of the most renowned was written in the thirteenth century by Mowlana Jalal-al-Din Mohammad Balkhi (1207–73), also known as Rumi. In his love odes Mowlana reflects on his passionate love of the divine through the physical presence of his beloved Shams (d. 1248) (Holliday, forthcoming; Andrews and Kalpakli, 2005; Shamissa, 2002). We are frequently reminded of Shams's cypress-like body and tulip-like face, his touch, his sweet breath, his agate and ruby lips, the subtle and seductive movement of his eyelashes, and the locks of hair upon his forehead that the lover longs to behold. Shams embodies cosmic love, and who knows maybe earthly love too, for Mowlana (Kadkani, 1370/1997; Chittick, 2005). Both homo-eroticism and desiring the male friend have been intertwined with Sufi love poetry and practice since the mid-ninth century, with particular attention placed on the figure and face of the young adolescent man (Javadi, 2008).

Young men in Tehran

I conducted biographical interviews in Tehran and my interviewees introduced me to other young men with whom I could speak, and as we talked we focused on their life histories and their lived experiences. The majority were students, some of whom were also relatively recent arrivals in Tehran. The data presented here comes from the young men's accounts of their lives and lived experiences, and is not as a result of my direct questioning about their bodies.

Educated under the government's 'Islamic' ethical codes and theories, any regard for bodily 'self' should be inhibited if not totally prohibited by law. Haadi, a student in mechanical engineering at Sharif University, illustrates this point.

> Look, there is some kind of a confusion and cover up about male bodies, about all bodies... As far as the government is concerned we should not know anything about bodies at all, they only connect it to the sexual act. The scientific teaching of anatomy for the sake of understanding it at the very

least is totally lacking in our education system unless you are specialising in medicine at university. Our Islamic Ethics tutors are clerics, and their teachings in upper secondary and university education allude to a confused picture of the male physique oscillating between sin and sacrifice. The message is to ignore the *nafsani* or bodily desires and functions in order to maintain Islamic modesty and purity. Certainly in my books at school the whole physical appearance of the male body and organs were either censored or distorted, whilst from the age of four I understood something about bodies which I now relate to gender difference, warmth, beauty, and humanity.

Confusion and differentiation among governmental organisations exists. While the complete anatomical illustration of the body is deemed unsuitable in textbooks, discussing it in the context of injury in war and martyrdom are highly desirable if only to prompt the youth to emulate attitudes of sacrifice and selflessness. When I consulted a respected war veteran in high office, a member of the Basij Revolutionary Guard volunteers who went to war at the age of 14, about pained, maimed, and chemically affected bodies of veteran soldiers, he announced unexpectedly that his body belonged to his wife and was not up for discussion! He momentarily confused my academic interest in the topic with illusions of implied intimacy. The very mention of the word 'body' made him nervous. Yet in the later stages of the interview he managed to speak at length about the mental torment related to the physical injuries he both witnessed and sustained, which are central to his own fiction and non-fiction writing and film-making. He explained that when he was injured and lost in battle away from his battalion he found the charred crouching body of an Iraqi soldier, which he was not able to ignore and leave behind. He said that although he was alone, injured and frightened, he was compelled to think about the burnt body as an emblematic representation of a life, belonging to someone and deserving of attention and buried the charred remains out of respect for another human being.

One student explains that he has given up his studies because of lack of finances. He has borrowed and raised a small amount of capital to keep a stall in a busy shopping precinct, where he sells jeans and t-shirts for young men. He is aggrieved that his stall has been shut by the morals police and that his work licence taken away. His crime? His upper arm was exposed. His shirt sleeves were rolled up according to contemporary fashion trends. While he knows that he can pay a fine and renew his licence, he is angered and devastated by such harassment, the prospects of a lack of income for several weeks, and the infringement on his sovereignty and civil rights. He is not alone, the morals police regularly harass shop owners for displaying items of clothing such as a short skirt or sleeveless top in their shop window because in their view they are suggestive of sexual misconduct and therefore morally corrupt.

Resistance however is widespread. The youngest men I interviewed were 19-year-old Hooshyar and 20-year-old Ashraf, who study in one of the universities in the south-east of Iran (see figure 5.1) The two spoke at length about how disillusioned they are with the country's politics, the lack of relevant cultural activity and programmes for youth, the prevalence of media censorship and the pressures put on young people's freedom by the morals police in the street, on campuses and in coffee shops. They said they feel 'mentally squeezed' because they are constantly under surveillance. They said there is no political accountability and the regime has no plans for the future of youth and employment. Ashraf added that at times he reverts to self-harm, cutting his own skin in deep frustration. They spoke for each other using 'we' and analysed their thoughts and actions as follows:

> For us, our bodies represent our minds, the way we think is reflected in the way we dress and style ourselves. We use our bodies as the point of identification [*ta'een-e hoviyat*] and differentiation [*tafavot sazi*]. We want to show our sensitivity through the details of our appearance, our sense and choice of colour and our attention to the textures, designs, and materials of our clothes. For example, when Ashraf shaves his eyebrows off, or when he wears black nail varnish, or when we design and paint our own t-shirts, we

Figure 5.1 Hooshyar and Ashraf.

mean to say something specific and particular about us, we present ourselves in this fashion to say something about our very personhood.

We share an attention to detail. I look at something and I look at Hooshyar and he gets it, and we say yes, that's it... Then we create together. The ideas we had already seen in our minds become realities on our bodies. It's a personal system, it is a system of control, it gives us the possibility of being at least in peace with ourselves. This is how we can best be who we are against all the difficulty for young people here.

As well as the political pressures, as soon as we turned 14, even our sisters and mothers started treating us differently; they suddenly didn't play around with us as they did before and they watched their language, being careful not to mention anything to do with sexuality. They closed themselves to us all of a sudden just because our bodies were changing ... Hooshyar and I have created a kind of trust, deep trust, to experiment with ideas to do with our bodies, even our sexuality. We feel we are exploring what our body means, we want to know how it functions. We are not homosexual, but we discuss and explore our sexuality openly with each other, and if there are girls who want to join in the discussion, well that is also great.

These accounts show how Hooshyar and Ashraf make meaning through body management and presentation. Their use of words such as 'identification' and 'differentiation' demonstrate intent and resistance. These young men are determined to construct personal identities that relate to their own perceptions and lived experiences rather than adopting the deferred sense of identity promoted by the regime. Their initiation of a free and private space for being, labelled with terms such as 'a personal system' (*yek system-e shakhsi*) and 'deep trust' (*e'temad-e amiqh*) reflect their anxiety about their environment and their need for expressions of sovereignty. Ashraf and Hooshyar are representative of considerable numbers of young men – and women – who face harassment and are denied freedom of speech and expression, and political voice. For them the body becomes the central and sovereign tool needed to escape alienation, perceiving and creating a meaningful and personal lifeworld.

Attention to grooming, stylised eyebrows and hair, facial and body piercings and cosmetic surgery are becoming widespread among young men in Iran. While many progressive parents in Iran view and tolerate these forms of grooming in relation to freedom of expression and economic ability, others tolerate them simply because these young men are bringing home salaries. The following account given by a thoughtful and sensitive 21-year-old conscript illustrates the point. Sporting a delicately bandaged nose because of a recent cosmetic operation he spoke of his impatience to complete his military duties in order to look like himself again and to go back to work earning proper money.

I have had to tell my sergeant major that the nose operation was because it had broken when I was a child and was preventing me from breathing properly. But in fact I wanted to change the shape of my nose to fit my face better. He will not understand these things though. He thinks this is the military and we should only be thinking of defending Iran from the foreign forces. He reprimanded me for shaving one side of my hair in criss-cross patterns. My hair was very short anyway but I wanted to see one side with a pattern because that's how I am. I have paid for my nose operation myself, I saved up for it when I worked in the catering industry before military service. I am counting the days of the seven remaining months when I will finish my service and can be myself again, wear my own clothes, have my hair style and have a new girlfriend.

Abbas, who refers to himself as 'Joljota' to mark his intellectual transformation, is an art student about to graduate in painting. He explains that his adopted name means a journey of resurrection. He often speaks in verse, reciting poems by himself as well as Ferdowsi, Mowlana, and Shamloo. He does this to either make a point about what he believes in or to suggest parallels between his own philosophical contemplations and those of the great poets. Born and brought up in a small and at times financially struggling farming community, military service has been fruitful for Joljota as it has facilitated the possibility to train and become a primary school teacher for the villages near his hometown. This training has enabled him to benefit from governmental regulations and skip the national university entrance examination and enter university for a degree in art. He explains to me that he felt he could no longer breathe in his birthplace Zarin Shahr and had to leave in search of new experiences and ideas. He speaks of the landscapes and soundscapes of his childhood and of his grandfather who was the village *chaavush* (harbinger and orator), with a good voice, sound knowledge of epic poetry, and excellent ability for religious recitations.

Performing is rooted in Joljota's family history and is part of his cultural capital. It has shape-shifted significantly and been influenced by his new environment at university and his art training.

Aware of his own transformation he has persuaded his parents to allow his younger sister to learn the violin. Joljota himself routinely participates in classical dance sessions, which are held sporadically in private homes in Tehran because of the political climate. He regards his body as his primary tool of communication when facing an audience; it has been his key to enter new and imagined worlds (see figure 5.2). While he is struggling with the economic challenges and demands of the capital city he thrives on the shared intellectual and artistic trajectories of his peers. In the following extract, he reflects on his childhood near Isfahan and speaks of his body as an archaic tool.

> I have a special mental and physical relationship with movement and space, it is part of my childhood in farmlands in a village near a small town near Isfahan; open spaces are free spaces and you can claim them. I have left all that behind now. I live with the sensation and emotion those wide open spaces provoked in me. I want to be a performance artist, I am a performance artist. I have stepped out of the cocoon, I have resurrected in

Figure 5.2 Joljota bound in metal cable in performance.

my body... First I did figurative painting, then sculpture, and then I brought my real body into real space. You see, my body is all I possess, it is my archaic mythic tool for creating new myths. It has become my pen, with it I write a story in space, I tell that story with movement, I draw in space with my body leaving traces of ideas, hanging there in the mind of the audience. It is then that I feel I can breathe again! If anything I imagine and wish I could return to the landscapes of our origins and perform in the nude using my body as an archaic element. Well, isn't that what it is... I use metal cables to show struggle and entrapment and small bells to create rhythmic soft sounds born out of movement, a faint echo of the sounds of my childhood.

A similar case for using the sculptural qualities of the body as a tool to express intellectual and political location comes from an interview with Mahmoud. He is from Sabzeh Vaar where Ashura processions (*dasteh*) are taken to heart and performed by representatives of every trade. As tradition demands, groups of men, led by physically stronger men who carry large heavy metal standards decorated with peacock feathers, march down the city's main streets in an organised and precise fashion towards the mosque. Stopping and starting, they chant the names of the sacred imams to the sound of drums and beat their chests or whip their shoulders and backs with chains in sympathy and rhythm. Mahmoud explains how, influenced by such traditions, he and his friends have employed the sculptural qualities of their bodies to make a political point about their own experiences, rejecting the constant surveillance of the morals police and a change in the ownership of the public space. Mahmoud's design of a group performance on campus suggests the profound and synergistic relationship he draws between the sovereign body and the ownership of public space. He explains,

I organised a group performance involving 40–50 students... Here, right here, in front of all of them. We wanted to stand out, so we got ourselves kitted out in black, highly tailored suits, black ties, the whitest shirts you could find, and dark glasses. Walking in clusters we paused for short intervals, sometimes closing in towards each other and sometimes on the verge of dispersing. We marched through the campus, we stunned them all, they did not know what was happening for a while. Who were these men in black suits and what were they doing? Eventually they realised, or were told that we were sculpture students considering versions of ourselves in space.

Evidently religious ritual carries deep significance for many young men and they are alert to the potential wider meanings such acts could project. Energised and motivated by intellect and a fertile imagination they give themselves permission to transform such acts and to juxtapose their own experiences and struggles with those of the imams. They thus register new personal and collective identities and claim the public space even if momentarily.

Hojat is from a pious farming family in Lorestan. His knowledge of Persian mystic poetry is impressive and, as a devotee of Imam Ali, he frequently references him in verse and describes him as the just and magnanimous prince of the Shi'is. Hojat's father, uncle and other relatives are participants in the yearly ta'ziyeh passion plays enacting the Battle of Karbala. He stresses the belief that Imam Hossein symbolises peace and a love of humanity and that he was forced into battle for the sake of freedom.

Hojat jokingly commented that when he was an art student he told some of his relatives and the bus drivers shuttling him back and forth between

Figure 5.3 Winged Man.

Tehran and his hometown that he had become a plasterer in Tehran because they were too traditional to understand what it means to be an artist. Hojat's photographic works draw on *pardeh khani* performance and co-constructs, but he resists the expected norms by replacing the sacred and the noble with the ordinary. He carries his canvas of painted wings to public spaces and invites members of the public to collaborate, imagining themselves as if angels and about to take flight (see figure 5.3). The idea of flight and the concept of the winged deity are deeply rooted in Iran's history and iconography; they symbolise Ahura Mazda, the deity in Zoroastrianism, the religion of ancient Iran. Hojat's work suggests the conquest of self rather than its subduing:

> When I return to Lorestan I take myself to the massive rocks with carvings and reliefs from thousands of years ago. I lie there touching the rock, feeling the rock energising my body, imagining that my body is part of the solid rock sensing eternity itself. (figure 5.4) My photographic works with angel wings create a moment for self-identification where imagination and desire meet; I hope to capture the integrity of the self. So the wings say something about possibilities, resisting limitations and the mundane. I wish to restore to the body the possibility to signify both the inner longing and desire and the outer physical presence.

The few commercial billboards in uptown Tehran often adopt the masculine figure to promote forms of consumerism. Regardless of the

Figure 5.4   Hojat and the Lorestan rock.

Figure 5.5 Billboard in Tehran.

merchandise, it is the image of the well-attired man, often in a pose comparable to those of late Renaissance painting and sculpture, which dominate (see figure 5.5). The goods appear to be a secondary concern. Recently some of these images have been removed by the government because of their 'immodest' messages of desirability. Noteworthy is the erasure of Leonardo da Vinci's *Vitruvian Man*, also known as the *Cannon of Proportions* symbolising divine proportional values shared between geometry and the male figure, which was placed in the corner of several large billboards promoting men's clothing.

Consumerism's link to the male body also springs to mind when considering the recognisable and iconic image of Imam Hossein, which I found placed in the window of a framer's shop (see figure 5.6). The large, mass-produced framed poster introduces the imam as 'the standard-bearer of Karbala' in an inscription in the upper right-hand corner. Unusually he is shown wearing a delicate open-fronted shirt rather than a heavy cloak concealing anatomical detail. He suffers a small and neatly painted wound on the forehead instead of the slashed throat often depicted. Most significantly however the imam is shown to possess a well-proportioned, toned, and muscular upper body.

We might question who executed this image and for whom, who does this image aim to represent, and why is this poster allowed to be published and displayed in the shop window when our young man's clothes stall was shut down and he was fined because of exposing a muscular arm? As Haadi put it earlier, the state is 'confused'. Does the imam represent youth, and is the poster evidence of youth resisting the absolutist moral stance of the

Figure 5.6 Contemporary poster of Imam Hussein.

state about the body, engaging in reidentification and redefinition of identities through it? We see in the poster that the past runs into the future, and that the imagination and self-perception of youth allow the image of the Imam to reflect creative expression and freedom relevant to the narratives related above and disallowed by the regime.

Conclusion

Being masculine and 'becoming a man' in contemporary Iran is neither monolithic nor controlled entirely by the discourses of the state. Further, the state has not been successful in implementing its Islamic model of maleness based on a discourse of martyrdom and suppressed bodies under the banner of religion. Rather than suppressing masculinity this particular discourse has intensified the promotion and projection of sovereign bodies by many young men in order to make meaning and relate a rich cultural heritage of masculinity. Narratives of resistance and reidentification thus emerge where young men adopt bodies as tools of differentiation and expression, with specific perceptions of themselves and who they wish to be as individual citizens. The young men I interviewed demonstrated the ways in which their 'sovereign body' facilitates the means for communicating ideas relating their inner and outer worlds, both social and psychological, as well as complex and fluid identities.

The post-election events of summer of 2009 in Iran brought millions of citizens together in public space, on campuses and streets, disputing the election results collectively and enquiring about the plight of their votes. Though treated brutally by the regime, the contingency of young reformists demonstrated to the world that they resist and reject the regime's ideological stance and modes of governance. This study has demonstrated that a demand for change in both culture and politics runs through the grassroots in young people's daily social acts, beyond the narrow interpretations of the state. Further, Iranian cosmopolitanism and the educational revolution are increasingly bringing the young generation together to jointly participate in a battle of ideas. Young women especially have been at the forefront of civil society debates in mind and body in recent decades, insisting to be visible in all aspects of life. Equipped with self-knowledge, education, and the desire to be seen and heard they have sought reform in the legal system and equality based on human rights (Honarbin-Holliday, 2009). It is increasingly the case that young men are joining forces with the women in new ways, emulating their self-knowledge and desire for self-definition. Together they reinforce a civic demand for the recognition of the rights of the individual whilst also consolidating the nation's demand for justice and rule of the people in a democratic system of governance. Together, they will no doubt return to the streets afresh when the time is right, demanding their individual rights to freedom of speech and expression and a more developed civil society.

Acknowledgements

I thank the young men in this study for accepting my presence among them and am grateful for their generosity and openness.

Notes

1 The material and discussion presented here grows out of the first leg of my research in Tehran and Isfahan in April 2009 for a volume entitled Masculinities in Urban Iran; Men in Contemporary Iranian Society to be published by I.B.Tauris.
2 Author's calculations based on the figures released by the Office of Iran's National Statistics in Tehran in 2005. Over 15 million Iranians are in education, and the sum of the male and female participants in tertiary education comes to 3 million. However, in her plenary address at 'Thirty years on: The social and cultural impacts of the Iranian revolution' 5–6 June 2009, The Centre for Media and Film Studies, School of Oriental and African Studies, University of London, Professor Shahshahani of Tehran University suggested a figure of over 3.5 million.
3 Shah Nameh Ferdowsi, with an introduction by Mohammad Ali Foroughi Zaka-ol Molk (1877–1942) published by Sazman-e Entesharat-e Javidan, Tehran. This volume is not dated and carries over 60 plates, and has been in my family for decades which I have inherited.
4 These were among the views expressed by Naghal Khoshhal Pour of Esfahan in an extended interview with the author in April 2009. Mr Khoshhal Pour comes from a long line of Naghals or narrator-interpreters of Shah Nameh and has dedicated his life to continuing with the tradition and training two young assistants.

References

Adams, R and Savran, A (2004) 'Introduction' in Adams, R and Savran, D (eds) *The Masculinity Studies Reader*. Oxford: Blackwell Publishing: 1–8.
Andrews, W and Kalpakli, M (2005) *The Age of the Beloveds*. Durham and London: Duke University Press.
Aslan, R (2006) *No God but God; The Origins, Evolution and Future of Islam*. London: Arrow Books.
Bayat, A (1997) *Street Politics*. New York: Columbia University Press: 19.
Beyzaei, B (2000) *Namayesh dar Iran [Performance in Iran]*. Tehran: Roshangaran.
Chelkowski, P (1998) 'Popular arts: patronage and piety' in Diba, LS and Ekhtiar, M (eds) *Royal Persian Paintings: The Qajar Epoch 1785–1925*. London: I.B.Tauris: 90–7.
Chittick, W (2005) *The Sufi Doctrine of Rumi*. Bloomington, Indiana: World Wisdom Books.
Honarbin-Holliday, M (2008) *Becoming Visible in Iran; Women in Contemporary Iranian Society*. London: I.B.Tauris.
——— (2009). *Becoming Visible in Iran: Women in Contemporary Iranian Society*. London: I.B.Tauris.

―――― (nyp) *Masculinities in Urban Iran; Men in Contemporary Iranian Society.* I.B.Tauris.

Javadi, H (2008) *Obeyd-e Zakani: Ethics of the Aristocrats and Other Satirical Works.* Washington: Mage Publishers.

Keddie, NR (2003) *Modern Iran; Roots and Results of Revolution.* New Haven and London: Yale University Press: 89, 153, 164.

Nahjolbalagheh translated by Mohsen Farsi into Persian (1980), Tehran: Amir Kabir. Publications.

Najmabadi, A (2005) *Women with Mustaches and Men without Beards.* Berkeley: University of California Press.

Nooshin, L (2005) 'Underground, overground: Rock music and youth discourses in Iran'. *Iranian Studies* 38, 3: 463–94, 470.

Salehi-Isfahani, H (2008) 'Human resources: potentials and challenges' in Katouzian, H and Shahidi, H (eds) *Iran in The Twenty-first Century: Politics, Economics and Conflict.* Oxford: Routledge: 243–72.

Shafi-e Kadkani, MR (1997) *Gozideh-ye Ghazaliyat-e Shams [Selected Ghazals by Jalal-al-Din Mohammad of Balkh (Rumi)].* Introduced by Dr Mohammad Reza Shfi'i Kadkani. Tehran: Sherkat-e Sahami-ye Ketabha-ye Jibi 132 and 165.

Shah Nameh Ferdowsi (This volume is undated, it has an introduction by Mohammad Ali Foroughi Zaka-ol Molk (1877–1942). Tehran: Sazman-e Entesharat-e Javidan.

Sirous Shamissa (2002) *Shahed Bazi dar Adabiyat e Iran*, Tehran.

Sreberny, A and Khiabany, G (2010) *Blogistan.* London: I.B.Tauris.

Whitehead, SM and Barrett, FJ (2001) 'The sociology of masculinity' in Whitehead, Barrett (eds) *The Masculinities Reader.* Cambridge: Polity Press: 16.

PART II

PERFORMING ARTS AND CINEMA

CHAPTER 6

CONTEMPORARY IRANIAN THEATRE

The Emergence of an Autonomous Space

Liliane Anjo

In the aftermath of the 1979 revolution, the Islamic state attempted to impose its authority over any kind of public representation, especially artistic practices. Since its establishment, the Islamic Republic has strived to shape Iranian society in its own image, in accordance with its ideology (Khosrokhavar, 2006). Given the Islamic state's desire to attain conformity between the public sphere and official dogma, artistic practices represent decisive stakes. For the Islamic leaders, it is a matter of controlling any form of public representation. For Iranian civil society, the arts embody a unique form of expression and a possible space of autonomy. Artistic practices are a fertile ground for dissent and social criticism. Thus, theatre becomes a privileged research topic, as it is a discursive and performative space made significant by the audience's presence and interaction with the actors and the events occurring on the stage.

The recent revitalisation of Iranian theatre has made possible the emergence of a both a both physical and imaginary space that can elude the state's influence and official credo. This space appears to contribute to the elaboration of a shared consciousness of resistance to the regime's authoritarianism nowadays. How can theatre embody a public space for disobedience in spite of censorship? My research attempts to outline how the renewal of the repertoire and the development of an original scenic language have enabled the emergence of a public space that disregards the official doctrine. In other words, the objective of my chapter is to examine how contemporary Iranian theatre aspires to create an autonomous space from within the Islamic state.[1]

The revival of Iranian theatre

Following the establishment of the Islamic Republic, theatre became 'socially, religiously and, above all, politically suspect' (Floor, 2005). A strict censorship was imposed on theatre, hence Iranian artists had to learn how to compose and perform within a set of specific new rules and tacit norms. First and foremost, a respect for the elementary principles of public life was imposed on stage. Theatre directors were expected to show their allegiance to the fundamental principles governing public life on stage, including in interior settings. Thus, in post-revolutionary Iran, theatre artists must align their works with the compulsory wearing of the *hijab* (veil) and the prohibition of any tactile contact between female and male actors. Women are no longer allowed to dance or sing solo on stage. In addition to these principles, which also govern everyone's behaviour in the public sphere, actors are officially banned from generating empathy towards negative or morally elusive characters from the audience. Nor may they expose situations regarded as immoral, blaspheme on stage, or spread ideologies contrary to the core values of the Islamic regime. Before being staged, any performance has to be submitted to a commission depending from the Ministry of Culture and Islamic Guidance verifying whether it complies with the specific rules and tacit norms imposed on public representation. If approved by the commission, the director of the performance obtains an authorisation of public staging. This authorisation may however be conditioned by some rectifications or censured scenes.

The conditions imposed on theatre have placed a considerable strain on artists accustomed to working under the former regime. While it has been difficult for them to adapt, the younger generation of artists – those who were born after or raised during the Islamic Republic – are adept at working under these same conditions. Even though it is difficult to distinguish between explicit regulation and unspoken rules, Iran's theatre artists all seem to master what is required of them. The massive contribution of young authors, directors and actors to the annual Fajr International Theatre Festival illustrates the important role youth have played in the revitalisation of Iranian theatre after the 1979 revolution and the Iran–Iraq war. The Fajr Festival, whose programme showcases the main successes of the past theatrical season and outlines the scenic prospects of the coming year, represents a yearly opportunity to appraise the state of theatrical activities in Iran. Considering the important proportion of young directors who took part in the recent editions – not only in the categories specifically planned for the participation of young artists, but in all sections of the festival[2] – the role of this new generation in the dynamics of theatrical life is obvious.[3] As Hossein Parsai, the former director of the Dramatic Arts Centre (2005–9) says, Iranian theatre is not merely 'youth-oriented' but literally lead by the young generation of artists (Parsai, 2010).

Educated under the Islamic Republic, these young artists have learned to accommodate its imperatives and requirements on stage. They have perfectly assimilated the rules and conventions of performing arts. Furthermore, they confront the ordeal of public representation at an early stage in their careers, through Iran's many regional and national festivals (Yeganeh, 2007). Several of these festivals are devoted to young theatre companies like, for example, the Festival of University Theatre annually held in Tehran. These festivals offer Iran's young theatre artists an opportunity to experiment with audience expectations and acquaint themselves with the constraints imposed upon theatrical art in Iran. Despite their young age, they have been able to gather experience of the stage before they collaborate with their elders in more demanding programmes and theatrical events. This young generation of theatre artists is not only growing and gaining in stature. As the Iranian director and researcher Farhad Mohandespour points out, they are 'turning their back on the values of Iranian ideological theatre' by creating performances experiencing inventive techniques and exploring new themes (Mohandespour, 2008).

Contributing actively to the emergence of an original theatre, this young generation of artists has grasped the exigencies and particularities of the profession. However, the crucial involvement of the youth in revitalising Iranian drama is not limited to the dynamism of young playwrights, directors, actors or scenographers. Khosrokhavar and Roy (1999) suggest that given the lack of leisure activities, places to socialise and opportunities to go out, young Iranians have turned their interest towards art and culture. They have undeniably taken possession of the theatrical space, a meeting and interaction place not only between artists and audience, but also between the spectators themselves. It is through their massive attendance at theatre performances that young Iranians have participated in the revival of Iranian drama. Also interesting to note is the fact that Mohammad Khatami, a former Minister of Culture and Islamic Guidance famed for his open-minded views on arts and widely appreciated among young Iranians for his liberal cultural policy (Balaghi, 2009), was elected President of the Islamic Republic of Iran in 1997 – at the very moment the younger generation was taking possession of the cultural scene.

Indeed, the late 1990s witnessed the emergence of a new generation. This younger generation, which did not take part in the revolutionary rupture, cannot identify with official ideology – especially as a majority of the older generation has grown away from revolutionary idealism (Khosrokhavar, 2001). Campaigning for reform, Khatami's candidature for presidency was widely supported by this new generation who have been striving for a comprehensive change towards cultural autonomy and social openness.

A renewed dramatic repertoire

The peoples of Iranian theatre have learned to master the restrictions imposed on their art to such an extent that their ingenuity has finally led to the emergence of an original theatre scene. The revitalisation of Iranian theatre is partly due to playwrights who have been devoting themselves to renewing the dramatic repertoire. Their work strives to create original genres that could be characteristic of contemporary Iranian drama. The exploration of theatrical language extends from literary naturalism to poetic symbolism, but the development of new writing styles is inseparable from the development of new themes in Iranian drama. According to my observations on the field, Iran's contemporary dramatic repertoire, excluding indigenous traditional drama and religious theatre, seems nowadays to revolve mainly around four themes. Although none of these categories are hermetic, this categorization will help us to discern key motifs.

Plays referring to the literary and cultural heritage of Persia

These plays draw their inspiration from pre-Islamic heritage and literature, such as the *Shahnameh* written by the Persian poet Ferdowsi, the work of the mystic Attar or more generally the Persian Sufi tradition. These plays sound out the memory of Persian civilisation and reassert the value of an important chapter of history that the Islamic Republic has initially attempted to conceal.

Pari Saberi (born in 1932) is renowned for directing works constantly referring to the literary and cultural heritage of Persia. Her latest *mise-en-scéne*, *Rostam and Esfandiar*, performed at the end of 2010 in Tehran, follows numerous other productions directly inspired from ancient Persian literature, among others: *Rend-e khalvatneshin* ['The Isolated Libertine' based on the poetry of Hafez, 2001] 'Mourning for Siavash' (based on the *Shahnameh*, 2003), 'Flying Shams' (based on Shams Tabrizi and Rumi's works, 2007) and 'Rostam's Seven Labours' (based on the *Shahnameh*, 2009).

It is here interesting to note that whereas she used to work with a Western repertoire before the revolution, she dedicates herself nowadays exclusively to performances dealing with Persian identity and culture. Considering the upheaval following the 1979 revolution, Saberi believes that Iranian society needs to delve into its ancient traditions in order to rediscover its own cultural identity[4] – as if, after the establishment of the Islamic ideology as the state credo, it has become necessary to explore the pre-Islamic components of Iranian culture.

Directors belonging to the generation raised during the Islamic Republic have also shown their interest in the ancient Persian heritage. Zahra Sabri (born in 1967) wrote and directed several creations inspired by the Persian Sufi tradition. Her latest performances, *Tooti Par* [Parrot's Feather, 2006] and *The Earth and the Universe* (2009), both based on the mystic tales of Rumi, create a dreamlike atmosphere of infinite beauty conveying a message of humanity transcending any religious or geographical boundary. Her work does not only pay tribute to the cultural heritage of Persia, but it also places emphasis on the spirit of universality carried by Rumi's thought – thus rejecting the pre-eminence of Islamic ideology. Ali Asghar Dashti (born in 1976) has acquired his notoriety by directing several plays blending techniques of indigenous performing traditions – especially *ta'ziyeh*[5] – with contemporary Western stories. He has nevertheless also been attracted by ancient Persian literature, which he directly drew inspiration from in his performance 'Tale of a Woman's Play Reading' (2001) based on a female character found in Attar's writings. Whereas Ali Asghar Dashti's work is regarded as one of the most experimental theatres in today's Iran and considered as one of the directors marking a 'turning point in modern Iranian theatre' (Mohandespour, 2010), his plays are nourished by ancient performance rituals and traditions. Furthermore, despite the fact that his theatre places emphasis on the physical elements of performance, he also refers to literary texts borrowed from ancient Persian heritage.

Plays discussing the revolution or the war against Iraq

The second theme comprises those plays based on or set during more recent historical events, such as the Iranian revolution and the war against Iraq (1980–8). The production of these performances is strongly encouraged by the theatrical authorities. The Fajr festivals of theatre, film and music were established to celebrate the anniversary of the revolution, and some recent editions of the Fajr Theatre Festival have included a special section in tribute to the Islamic revolution (in 2000, 2008 and 2009). In addition, there is an annual festival commemorating the Iran–Iraq war, known as the 'Holy Defence' (*defa'-e moghadas*) Theatre Festival – which has its corresponding version in other artistic fields (cinema, poetry, etc).

This type of repertoire is usually ambivalent. While some performances tend to exalt martial or revolutionary bravery, others are obviously a criticism of the state ideology that glorifies the sacrifice of the martyrs. Indeed, this chapter of Iran's history is used symbolically by many theatre artists to depict a disoriented society that is trying to rebuild itself after a long period of conflict. It is also interesting to note that even the plays explicitly praising the glory of those who dedicated themselves to the defence of the nation ('the Holy Defence') do not ignore the cruelty of war and its impact on the Iranian population.

'Symphony of Awareness', written and directed by Hossein Farrokhi (born in 1959) at the occasion of the 2008 edition of the Fajr Festival, was staged at Vahdat Hall – one of the most prestigious venues in Iran. The play narrates a dichotomous historical confrontation between the forces of Good and Evil, starting from the Creation until the victory of the 1979 revolution depicted as the triumph of the divine will on Earth. Designed as an homage to Islamic revolution glorified as a sacred achievement, the performance however ends with images from the Iran–Iraq war – thus reminding the audience how brutal and terrifying the war had been for Iranian society despite it being considered holy by the official rhetoric.

During the 27th Fajr Festival, the street theatre section dedicated to the 1979 revolution was exclusively attended by young directors (all born between 1978 and 1984[6]). Among these performances, several plays focused on the Iran–Iraq war following the revolutionary period by portraying how young people went through the conflict. Rather than submissively praising the revolutionary uprising that the festival's section (and actually the Fajr itself) is supposed to pay homage to, most of the young directors preferred to examine its controversial consequences. Interesting to mention here is 'A Sigh of Peace' (*Ahi-ye sefid*), written and directed by Rasoul Haghshenas, whose research on theatre therapy has led him to perform a play delving into children's emotions and reactions towards war.

Plays examining the contemporary social condition

These plays present a critical outlook on the current sociopolitical situation and compose a sort of mirror of Iranian society. In an attempt to shed light on a dramatic repertoire embodying social criticism leading to the possible emergence of a space of alternative expression, I would like to mention here three plays that are, in my opinion, significant examples of this type of repertoire.

'Unwritten Whispers' (*Najvaha-ye naneveshteh*) is a play written by Afrooz Foroozand and directed by Narges Hashempoor (born in 1967) that stages four women who have decided to commit suicide. One evening they meet up in an apartment where they intend to carry out the act. But before they do so, they begin discussing the reasons behind their resolution: one argues continuously with her daughter, another feels neglected by her husband whom she believes is unfaithful. In a society dominated by men and within which the expression of femininity is stifled, the four women are convinced that they are condemned to lead a superficial existence. They reach the conclusion that their life is gloomy and senseless. However, they cannot bring themselves to perform the irreversible act. While gambling and drinking alcohol, they are transported by a sudden burst of enthusiasm. *Unwritten Whispers* portrays ordinary women confronted with the absurdity of their existence and at odds with themselves. The reason for their distress lies less in the individual difficulties each one has to cope with than in the impossibility of escaping their role as mother or wife, and asserting themselves in their femininity. Although this play is noticeably critical towards the established order in Iran – considering that the female characters plan their suicide, drink alcohol and attack the regime's patriarchal values on stage – it nevertheless received authorisation from the Ministry of Culture and Islamic Guidance, and was performed in the Tehran City Theatre. The official approval of the play is probably related to the appearance of a priest supposed to hear the women's confession, whose very presence indicates that the protagonists on stage are not Muslims.

'Kiss You and Tears' (*Miboosamet va ashk*) is a text written by Mohammad Charmshir and adapted for the stage by Mohammad Aghebati (born in 1975). The play depicts a political prisoner sentenced to death who is anguishing in his cell while waiting for his execution to be carried out. Throughout the play, a succession of imaginary visitors appear in his cell, each one attempting to convince him to embrace a particular point of view and follow a certain path. The dialogues he has with the imaginary visitors raise issues as thorny as political dissent, the death penalty, devotion to a cause greater than oneself, despair at having dedicated one's life to defending convictions and being misunderstood by all – all motifs that strike a chord with Iranian society.

'Where Were You on January 8th?' was written and directed by Amir Reza Koohestani (born in 1978) shortly after the massive street protests following the disputed presidential elections in June 2009. Rather than dealing right away with the question 'Where is my vote?' – which became the catchphrase of the movement – Koohestani imagined a story about a missing gun triggering a chain of reactions reflecting Iranian society's situation at that time. Apparently constructed as a detective story – as the title suggests – the play actually raises issues echoing the questions Iranians where confronted with after the violent crushing of the protest movement: What is justice? How shall we act in response to physical or verbal violence? How do fear and lies interact? Moreover, the key role assumed by Iranian women in the events following the disputed elections resonates in Koohestani's female characters who are radically fighting for their rights.

These three plays – and also many others – boldly despise the rhetoric advocated by the authorities. They focus instead on the troubles tormenting Iranian society today, such as the status of women, inter-gender relations, the generation gap, the issue of confinement, the question of power and the absence of future prospects as perceived by youth. Here, the work of these dramatists dissects the system they live under. The plays, devoid of political activism and without any devotion to a sacred cause, merely denounce the deadlocks and the absurdity of certain norms of the Islamic Regime.

Though maybe less topical than 'Where Were You on January 8th?', I have chosen to mention 'Unwritten Whispers' and 'Kiss You and Tears' for two reasons. Not only are they significant examples of contemporary Iranian plays that critically examine sociopolitical life in Iran, but they are both based on Western texts. 'Unwritten Whispers' is a remote adaptation of Neil Simon's *The Odd Couple*, and 'Kiss You and Tears' is – as the subheading of the play announces – a 'rereading of Vaclav Havel's *Letters to Olga*'. This adds a further dimension to contemporary Iranian repertoire: it is capable of borrowing stories from abroad and recreating them as if they were its own. Furthermore, these two examples also show the Iranian artists' openness to the world repertoire and their deep knowledge of Western arts.

Foreign plays

This leads us straight into foreign plays, which is the fourth theme in the theatrical repertoire of Iran today. Considering that the works of most foreign playwrights were banned from the Iranian stage as the result of the cultural revolution declared in 1980 in order to counteract Western influence, the now frequent performance of foreign plays can be regarded as a true revival. Among the foreign works most staged in Iran today we find the plays of Bertolt Brecht, Federico García Lorca, Henrik Ibsen, Anton Chekhov, William Shakespeare, Samuel Beckett, Jean Genet and Eugène Ionesco. The comedies of playwrights such as Molière and Carlo Goldoni are also popular. Without going into detail concerning Iranian directors' interpretations of these authors, I would nevertheless like to point out that most of these works focus on issues surrounding social and political oppression or, more generally, the question of power. In other words, there is always a social or political ingredient blended into the foreign plays that Iranian artists choose to perform on stage.

As Willem Floor notices in his *History of Theatre in Iran* (2005), 'contrary to expectations the Islamic government did not ban theatre', to a certain extent because 'it realised the importance of theatre as a political propaganda tool'. Hence, tragic, religious and ideological dramas praising the triumph of the revolution were the only theatrical activities to be authorised by the Ministry of Culture throughout the 1980s. This type of drama still belongs to the repertoire performed in Iran. However, after the end of the war with Iraq (1988) and during the course of the 1990s, the determination of Iran's playwrights led to the emergence of new genres, which now dominate theatrical programming in Iran. The contemporary dramatic repertoire has thus moved away from the official credo. Far from adhering to the moralistic pretence of the official rhetoric, this new Iranian theatre shows a culture in motion and depicts a changing society. Many plays now draw their inspiration from everyday Iranian life and are critical, albeit in a subtle manner, of the restrictive laws repressing society.

An original scenic language

The revitalisation of Iranian drama has also been nourished by the talent of directors, as they have had to learn how to express themselves within the restrictions imposed by the Islamic Republic. Critical reflections on the Islamic Republic, the established system and romantic relationships have had to be expressed in different ways. For example, since any tactile contact between female and male actors is forbidden, the stage director will dress an actress in thick leather gloves; this artifice allows her to touch her male stage partner. The fact that female performers are required to hide their hair on stage generates incoherence in interior settings, where women are usually unveiled. In an attempt to circumvent the Islamic requirement that women cover their head, directors frequently ask their actresses to wear wigs or woollen hats rather than a scarf. But the ingenuity of Iranian directors goes further than their ability to skirt restrictions. Beyond their craftiness, they have created imaginative and expressive codes. Through an exploration of the possibilities of non-verbal expression and non-descriptive modes of representation, Iranian directors have managed to create an original scenic language. They use a language of colours and gestures that is particular to their theatre and understood in the context of the Islamic Republic of Iran.

Many directors base their *mise-en-scéne* around a chromatic idiom, a device that is freely inspired by the chromatic symbols and techniques of indigenous drama forms like *ta'ziyeh*. For example, they design a monochromatic scenography and introduce subtle touches of colour into the scenic space, so that the colour of a costume or a stage accessory enables them to point out a particular significance without putting it into words. In Ali Rafii's latest stagings, like Federico García Lorca's *Blood Wedding* or his recent 'Fox Hunting' (*Shekar-e roubah*), co-written with Mohammad Charmshir, the stage design is entirely composed of white elements, while some touches of colour are daintily brought into the scenic space: a black accessory or a red piece of clothing contrasts with the pale backdrop, making the narration of innocence oscillate between passion and impulsion on the one hand, adversity and grief on the other. Colours operate here as a language in the first sense of the term, ie a medium of expression and communication.

Contemporary Iranian theatre also resorts to an original spatial language and many directors use codes of *mise-en-scene* to suggest the distant displacement of the characters. For example, the actors may complete a rotation around the stage in order to represent the crossing of extensive land or the journey from one locality to another and if they walk around a bowl of water it means that they are crossing a river. And here again, it is interesting to note that most of these codes are drawn from indigenous performance traditions.

Besides chromatic and spatial codes, Iranian directors have also been exploring various practices of physical expression, thus creating a sort of lexicon of gestural phrasing. For instance, while bodily contact between actors of the opposite sex is prohibited, many directors employ a slow-moving exchange of a veil or a cloth between an actress and her male acting partner in order to express their love feelings, or even to allude to sexual relations. Thus, the Iranian directors have learned to elude interdiction by inventing non-discursive and non-figurative expression codes. They have developed a visual language that is capable of evoking ideas without making use of verbal articulation. The use of chromatic, spatial and physical codes of expression today composes a genuine scenic language, some elements of which are shared by several Iranian directors.

Conclusion

Alongside contemporary playwrights, who have strived to revitalise the Iranian dramatic repertoire, directors have succeeded, through their imagination and perseverance, in creating a space of expression. After the 1979 revolution and the harsh period cultural activities went through during the Iran–Iraq war, theatre has regained its dynamism. Willem Floor writes that the change occurred 'when the country could focus once again on living rather than dying' (Floor, 2005). Given the government's gradual acceptance of theatre and in a context of enthusiastic demand, theatrical activities have flourished. But its current vitality would not have been possible if the theatre artists had not absorbed the demands and particularities of their profession in a remarkable way. Their ability to work within new restrictions led to the emergence of an original theatre, nourished by a creative vital force that takes root in a deep desire for expression. The past decade has demonstrated that the Islamic state's attempt to impose a rigidly defined ideology upon arts has engendered lively creation rather than submissive conformity.

While the reform and revitalisation of the theatre industry accelerated during Khatami's tenure as president, under the cultural policy of President Mahmoud Ahmadinejad's administration, the theatrical scene has been suffering the consequences of harshly reinforced restrictions. The procedure for obtaining an authorisation has become more complex. Directors suspected to be opponents to the regime have always somehow been kept away from the boards. However, it is nowadays less frequent that certain plays are merely not permitted to be staged. Instead of openly banning a performance, the authorities prefer to impose cuts and rectifications – it is then up to the artists to accept performing a modified play or eventually abandoning the whole creation. And if the artists decide they still want to perform in spite of the possible changes imposed to their work, the authorities keep a Sword of Damocles dangling over their head. Some recent plays, for example Ibsen's *Hedda Gabler* directed by Vahid Rahbani (born in 1979) and *Born in 1983* (*motevaled-e 1361*) written by Naghmeh Samini (born in 1973) and directed by Payam Dehkordi (born in 1978), were thus banned after having previously been approved by the Ministry of Culture and Islamic Guidance. The decision to ban the plays was not taken by the Dramatic Arts Centre, nor by the Ministry of Culture itself, but by some enigmatic judiciary authorities – which also reveals the divergences existing between decision-making powers in Iran. We must here keep in mind that theatre is a live performance: that embodies its strength and its Achilles' heel all at the same. Performed in the interaction with its audience, theatre can only find its deep meaning on stage – well after it has been inspected by the commission of censorship. But because it is alive and subject to the necessity of being de facto *performed* again and again as long as it is meant to exist, the authorisation delivered by the ministry is not definitive.

However, the government is in general supportive of the global expansion of Iranian theatre, funding an increasing number of performances and supporting the organisation of theatre festivals. While some theatre professionals bolster the regime's official ideology by producing compliant plays, many theatre artists continue their efforts to navigate around the state's censorship and create works reflecting Iranian society. Theatrical spaces do not abound in Iran, even in Tehran. Though the capital's theatres are much better equipped than in the provinces, the general lack of professionally equipped facilities remains a real problem for theatre practitioners (Habibian and Aghahosseini, 2011). Also, the number of Iranians who have access to the theatre is by definition limited in comparison with artistic practices like cinema or music that are recordable and reproducible. Nevertheless, the symbolic impact of the possibilities offered by theatrical art is undoubtedly far-reaching. An increasing demand has thus lead to the construction of new theatrical spaces. During autumn 2009, a brand new theatre was inaugurated in Tehran's city centre: *Tamashakhane-ye Iranshahr*. It has rapidly become one of the favourite stages in the Iranian capital, not only in the eyes of the artists who appreciate its two professionally equipped venues, but also from the perspective of the audience who attends the programming in great numbers. In addition, other theatrical scenes are currently being built in Iran that will most likely share the same successful destiny as the capital's main theatres, embodying a possible space of expression in spite of the tight surveillance imposed by the authorities.

Notes

1   This chapter is mainly based on my personal field research and observations during several long stays in Iran between October 2007 and July 2011, as well as discussions and interviews with theatre directors, playwrights, actors, spectators and administrators of Iran's Centre for Dramatic Arts.
2   The Fajr International Theatre Festival is subdivided into a dozen sections; several categories are explicitly dedicated to student's theatre or new experiences. However, the young generation of artists is also attending the most prestigious sections of the festival. For example in recent years, the number of young directors participating in the official competition, probably the most appreciated section of the festival because of its international dimension, is significant. During the 2008 edition, five out of ten Iranian directors selected in this section were aged between 28 and 34 years. During the 2009 edition, seven out of ten

Iranian directors were under 40 years and in the following edition in 2010, seven out of eight.
3   Official Catalogue of the International Fajr Theatre Festival, 2008, 2009 and 2010.
4   Interview with the author, Tehran, 25 September 2007.
5   Ta'ziyeh is a ritual passion play performed in Shi'ite countries which narrates the tragic martyrdom of Hussein and his companions in the plain of Karbala (680 of the Christian Era/61 of the Muslim Calendar). Some scholars suggest that ta'ziyeh originates in pre-Islamic mourning rites, though it reached its full development during the nineteenth century in Iran (Chelkowski, 1979).
6   Official Catalogue of the 27th International Fajr Theatre Festival, 2009.

References

Balaghi, S (2009) 'Cultural policy in the Islamic Republic of Iran'. *Middle East Report* 39, 250: 15.

Chelkowski, P (ed) (1979) *Ta'ziyeh, Ritual and Drama in Iran*. New York: New York University Press and Soroush Press.

Floor, W (2005) *The History of Theater in Iran*. Washington DC: Mage Publishers.

Habibian, N and Aghahosseini, M (2011) *Theatres of Tehran – From 1868 to 2011 [Tamashakhaneha-ye Tehran az 1247 ta 1389]*. Tehran: Afraz Publications.

Khosrokhavar, F (2001) 'L'Iran, la démocratie et la nouvelle citoyenneté'. *Cahiers internationaux de sociologie* 111, February: 291–317.

—— (2006) 'The public sphere' in Göle, N and Ammann, L (eds) *Islam in Public. Turkey, Iran and Europe*. Istanbul: Bilgi University Press.

Khosrokhavar, F and Roy, O (1999) *Iran: Comment Sortir d'Une Révolution Religieuse*. Paris: Editions du Seuil.

Mohandespour, F (2008) 'Iran' in Majumdar, R and Hoque, M (eds) *The World of Theatre. An Account of the World's Theatre Season 2005–2006 and 2006–2007*. Dhaka: Bangladesh Centre of the International Theatre Institute.

—— (2010) 'On Iranian theater' in Atebbai, M (ed) *Theater in Iran*. Tehran: Namayesh Publications.

Parsai, H (2010) 'Iranian theater' in Atebbai, M (ed) *Theater in Iran*. Tehran: Namayesh Publications.

Yeganeh, F (2007) 'Iranian theatre festivalised' in Hauptfleisch, T, Lev-Alagdem, S, Martin, J, Sauter, W and Schoenmakers, H (eds) *Festivalising! Theatrical Events, Politics and Culture*. Amsterdam/New York: Editions Rodopi BV.

Other sources

Official Catalogue of the 26th International Fajr Theatre Festival (2008). Tehran: Dramatic Arts Center Publications.

Official Catalogue of the 27th International Fajr Theatre Festival (2009). Tehran: Dramatic Arts Center Publications.

Official Catalogue of the 28th International Fajr Theatre Festival (2010). Tehran: Dramatic Arts Center Publications.

CHAPTER 7

DANCE AND THE BORDERS OF PUBLIC AND PRIVATE LIFE IN POST-REVOLUTION IRAN

Parmis Mozafari

Introduction

State interference in the public and at times private lives of the Iranian people has been one of the major causes of confusion and suffering throughout the history of Iran. In the pre-modern era (c. 1600–1900), factors such as the fear of social exclusion or religious persecution resulted in the formation of a marked difference between the public space as a locus of respectability, reputation and honour, and the house as a private space in which one could mostly do what one liked so long as it did not disturb neighbours. During the twentieth century, this divide found a new momentum.

The nation-building projects of Reza Shah, the first Pahlavi king (1925–41), required a total transformation of the public space, which not only changed the outwards appearance of people but also transformed the balance of power and normality inside private spaces. Reza Shah took some drastic measures to implement his vision of modernisation in Iran. For example, during the late 1920s he made Western clothing compulsory in governmental organisations. This was disliked by many, but it did not generate much protest. Conversely, in 1935 when he banned women from appearing in public spaces wearing the *hijab*, the country was outraged. This interventionist decision was intended to help the less religious sections of society overcome the social and cultural pressures that were preventing them from showing a more open attitude towards women's presence in the public space. As with many other plans of enforced 'modernisation', however, it created negative reactions rather than positive results (Chehabi, 1993).

Ironically, this radical move was annulled less than half a century later, in the early 1980s, by the dictates of another form of nation-building, which introduced the Islamic dress code as an anti-colonial measure and made women's *hijab* obligatory. In the context of Iran's rapid developments during the twentieth century and the expansion of access to the global media, this swinging from one extreme to another has created a sense of confusion and intense reactions in people, and has resulted in the intensification of the divide between the public and private spaces.

The confusion became particularly apparent following the restrictions imposed on public life after the Iranian revolution (1979). Due to the restrictions on many public activities and art forms people who were confused by the rapid changes in their lives had to find new ways to negotiate their public and private personas. Since these restrictions also coincided with the sober atmosphere that overwhelmed the lives of Iranians during the years of the Iran–Iraq war (1980–8), the new government were particularly severe when restricting activities that involved public expressions of happiness such as singing and dancing. Music-related activities, therefore, were among the major targets of the new government.

This religious and revolutionary ethos was also intensified, at least in its earliest stages, by the tendency among some people to associate sobriety with maturity and wisdom and merriment with vulgarity, which became more intense immediately after the revolution and provided an excuse for the government to suppress entertainment in music, arts, and even life. Despite all the legally-imposed restrictions, however, the people's desire for artistic activities and entertainment created a space for a tacit process of negotiation between the people and the artists, on the one side, and the authorities, on the other. The process that began immediately after the imposition of the bans gradually expanded the public space for those activities that the Islamist revolutionaries had originally described as useless or frivolous. It has also continued to transform the cultural landscape of Iran during the last three decades despite facing severe obstacles.

The opening up of the public space for entertainment has partly become possible because some of the restrictions have been matters of controversy between different religious scholars and because those responsible for imposing them have in some cases recognised the futility of their attempts. Thus the relative relaxation of the bans on some cultural activities can be attributed to people's resistance against unwanted regulations and the influence of the religious or political figures who have been ready to change the rules to increase public satisfaction.

The existence of these areas of controversy among the various factions of the political and religious establishments creates a situation in which, while some factions of the government are arguing for increased limits to be placed on artistic activities, some others respond positively to the peoples' and artists' attempts to challenge the bans and push the boundaries. This contested legal space resulted in the revitalisation of classical Iranian music between 1988 and 1998, and popular music between 1997 and 2005. However, dance has faced more difficulties in challenging the bans.

In this chapter I document the presence of dance among the urban middle and upper middle classes in post-revolution Iran. To begin, I give a brief historical overview of dance in Iranian life and then focus on its position in post-revolution Iran. I argue that Iran's social conditions, a number of contradictory readings of the Islamic tradition, and the attempts of certain factions of the Iranian government to suppress dance have all led to a process of tacit negotiation between the people/artists and officials, which has gradually reshaped dance and brought it back to the public life of contemporary Iran.

Historical background

The historical references to dance in pre-Islamic Iran demonstrate that it mainly functioned as a means of entertainment during non-religious ceremonies. Both literary and historical texts suggest that a great number of dancers and entertainers lived in the courts of the pre-Islamic Iranian dynasties. This may suggest that Iran's ancient dancers were prosperous and enjoyed a good quality of life. However, a close reading of the texts reflects that the social conditions of dancers and entertainers was rather precarious. As Shahbazi and Friend (1993) put it:

> The third group of harem women were concubines, beautiful girls (Plutarch, *Artoxerxes*, 27; Diodorus, 17.77.6; *Esther* 2.3) bought in slave markets (Herodotus 8.105; Plutarch, *Themistocles*, 26.4), or received as a gift (Xenophon, *Cyropaedia*, 4.6, 11; 5.1, 1; 5, 2, 9, 39) and tribute (Herodotus 3. 97), or collected from different parts of the empire (*Esther* 2.2–3;), and even captured from rebellious subjects (Herodotus 4.19, 32; Cf. Grayson, 1975, p 114). While still virgins, they were kept and groomed in the harem's 'first house of women' (*Esther* 2.9), and trained as musicians, dancers and singers in order that they might entertain their king or the magnate lord at banquets or throughout the night (Aelian, *Varia Historia*, 12.1). Any child born to such concubine was regarded as inferior to the 'rightful' offspring...

The situation remained similar during the Islamic era. The paintings depicting dancers and musicians performing in front of the king and the descriptions of the court performances written by European travellers indicate that dance was popular and central to all courtly celebrations. The travelogues of European travellers recount that during the reign of Shah Abbas (1587–1629) court dancers sometimes performed in the streets of Isfahan to welcome foreign merchants to the city (Mashhun, 1994: 295). Sasan Fatemi (2005: 400) states that during the Safavids (1501–1722) and the Zands (1722–50) 'dancer/prostitutes were held in high regard' and that some 'European travelogues' mention dancer-prostitutes 'who were quite wealthy'. Nevertheless, it is doubtful that these entertainers were held in 'high regard' (see figure 7.1). The support these entertainers received from the king may have helped them prosper financially, but it never helped them to be accepted or treated as normal citizens.

Therefore, one can argue that despite its popularity in private spaces, dance has never had a positive reputation as a public form of art. During Mohammad Reza Shah's reign (1941–79), attempts were made to improve

Figure 7.1 A mural depicting Safavid entertainers displayed in Chehel Sotoon Palace, Isfahan, Iran.

the stature of dance as an art form and enhance its public reputation as a profession by founding dance institutes and supporting promising dancers. Thus, at the time of the revolution, dance was performed in public spaces by ordinary people as an amateur entertainment activity and by expert dancers as an art form. Nevertheless, dance in urban contexts was appreciated most by secular sections of society, and when it came to professional training even the educated, liberal and Westernised layers of Iranian society had their reservations about sending their sons or daughters to dance schools.

Dance after the 1979 revolution

After the revolution, dance's existence as a performing art form encountered serious setbacks. Dance institutes were closed and its performance was made illegal. It was also denied any official public presence for nearly two decades after the revolution. During this time dance continued to be practised indoors and in various spaces as a leisure activity or for family entertainment. It was not until the late 1990s that dance began to reappear as an art form in public space.

To clarify the forms through which dance continued to exist in post-revolution Iran and later reappeared in the public space, I will discuss them in the order they occurred after the Iranian revolution.

(1) Dance as an illegal leisure activity performed in
  (a) Public-in-private spaces
  (b) Public spaces outside the country
  (c) Private-in-public spaces inside the country.
(2) Dance as an art form
     Dance as part of cinematic theatrical performances
  (a) Dance as a performing art by itself (not as part of cinematic theatrical performances).

(1) Dance as an illegal leisure activity

The total ban on some public practices after the revolution gave back to the house its pre-modern multi-functional role. This private space was transformed into a space for holding private tutorials (on such activities as music, dance, sports, sewing), small family parties, wedding ceremonies, etc. Dance has had a special place both in tutorials and in parties. Since the majority of religious people associated it with promiscuity and frivolous attitudes towards life, dance became the most demonised art form after the revolution and the secrecy surrounding it became so intense that for a while nobody even dared to utter the word *raqs* ('dance') in public spaces. However, while the dominant political discourse attempted to annihilate this aspect of people's identity by force, it continued to evolve by any means possible. Therefore, despite all prohibitions, dance remained popular as a house-bound activity in spaces that were away from the direct gaze of officials.

(a) *Public-in-private spaces*: In spite of the occasional raids of people's mixed parties (mainly during the first and second decades of the revolution) by the Revolutionary Guards (a militia force dedicated to upholding Islamic morals in society), dance remained a central part of all indoor parties, mixed or segregated. Dance in such parties was influenced by video tapes of Bollywood films, Western popular music videos, music videos of Los Angeles based Iranian pop singers and the dance tutorial videos of Mohammad Khordadian (b. 1957), which were all available on the black market in Iran. In his videos, Khordadian introduced and taught some popularised versions of the main forms of Iranian *melli* (national) and *mahalli* (regional) dances. For a time his work was so popular that those who had seen and learned from his videos were distinguishable from others because of the similarity of their movements. The considerable influence of Western popular music videos, particularly those of Michael Jackson and of films such as *Breakin'* (1984), was also apparent.[1] As a more recent example I can refer to my observations during several house parties in Iran in 2009, where moves from Anne Fletcher's *Step Up* (2006) seemed to be very popular among younger people and some of the featured routines were being practised and performed.

(b) *Public spaces outside the country*: Since the early 1990s some people have visited neighbouring countries – specifically Dubai and Turkey – to participate in the concerts of Los Angeles based Iranian pop stars. As dancing at pop concerts inside Iran is forbidden, these concerts provide those who are able to travel outside Iran with an opportunity to dance to Iranian music in a public space. The Iranian government has tried to stop people from going to these concerts or celebrations on several occasions, but they are still well attended.[2]

(c) *Private-in-public spaces inside the country*: After the political reforms of the late 1990s, when some forms of popular music were legalised and there was an increased sense of social freedom, some people, especially the younger generation, occasionally danced in the public space when they had the opportunity. For instance, when Iranian youth go hiking or go to picnics in the woods they may dance if they find a place that is free from the direct gaze of the authorities. Or on group outings, they may draw down the bus blinds and start dancing. When Iran's national football team qualified for the World Cup in 1998 and in 2006, widespread public celebrations created a challenge for the police. On both occasions people came out of their houses to celebrate their team's success by dancing, singing and cheering; but the police, who had been taken by surprise, though widely present did not get involved to stop the crowds.

Similar situations also develop during the annual *Chaharshanbeh Soori* celebrations (the last Wednesday before the Iranian New Year), during which time the ritual of jumping over fire is at times accompanied with dancing in alleys or even on roundabouts. The same tends to happen on *Sizdah be Dar* (the 13th day of the Iranian New Year), where the tradition of spending a day in nature is often made more interesting by playing music, dancing together and singing if the occasion allows. There are also instances that young men dance in parks. In general one can relate this to the tendency of Iranian people at stretching the rules on public holidays.[3]

Occasionally during concerts of pop music, some members of the audience dance in their seats, even though they know that the security guards, who are often the members of the Islamic Vice Squad (*Entezamat*), may see and ask them to leave the hall. The legal procedure for issuing permits for concerts involves the Ministry of Culture and Islamic Guidance checking the music to make sure that its rhythm and tempo does not encourage dancing. However, in reality performers may play faster renditions of their songs in their concerts to satisfy their audiences. In any case, young people seem to share an intense desire to express their feelings through movement.

If one ignores these furtive, private, occasional or overseas transgressions, dance, as a form of entertainment, is absent from the public space in Iran. However, dance as an art form has had a different destiny. Although it nearly vanished entirely during the first two decades of the Islamic Republic, dance as art began to carve out a little space for itself in public after the reforms of the late 1990s.

(2) Dance as an art form

Although dance is an often present part of most house parties in Iran, for many it is still considered to be a worthless hobby that can be enjoyed and cherished, but never turned into an artistic profession. As Anthony Shay states in his *Choreophobia*, in Iran 'dance is encouraged for an individual at specific times, but denied to the same individual at other times' (1999: 8) Thus, adults may encourage children, both boys and girls, to dance with each other on special occasions, praising them for the beauty of their movements, but when they grow up they are gradually indoctrinated to limit their dancing to avoid giving out wrong signals, particularly to members of the opposite sex. The controversial status of dance in Iranian society and culture, which is deeply rooted in religion and patriarchy, accounts for why dance has been slow to evolve as a modern art form in Iran.

(a) *Dance as part of cinematic or theatrical performances:* Dance was reintegrated with the public life of Iranian cinema through short scenes depicting men or children dancing regional or folk styles in historical films and television series such as Mohammad Ali Najafi's *Sarbedaran* (1984) or Davoud Mir-Bagheri's *Imam Ali* (1990). It was also included in its popular forms in scenes depicting weddings or house parties. However, in these cases the director was careful to show it as a trivial practice and not as an art form.

Dance movements were also included in theatrical pieces performed with puppets fairly early on after the revolution. This way of suggesting dance movements was, for a time at least, the only way to represent dance in a public performance. The fact that dance movements could be performed by puppets but not by actors emphasises the importance of the human body, and particularly the female body, in registering dance as a transgression. In later developments of dance as a part of theatrical activities, women have been directed to perform dance moves in ways that suggest the movements of a puppet, an animal, the wind or even a tree, to detract from their sexuality.

The reform movement in the second half of the 1990s gradually allowed dance more space to breathe. Some renowned pre-revolution dance practitioners began to hold private tutorials and to apply for permission from the Ministry of Culture and Islamic Guidance to perform dance in public. These developments allowed professional dancers to transform themselves from victims into survivors and argue for dance to be recognised as an art form. Yet whereas male dancers were gradually allowed to have occasional performances in front of mixed audiences, female dancers were and still are more limited in the variety of moves that they can do on the stage.

One reason that made the evolution of dance possible was the reintroduction of it under a new name – 'Rhythmic Movement'

(*Harakat-e Mozoon*). This name, officially recognised by the authorities, made it possible to re-establish a society for dance in Iran. The establishment of the Rhythmic Movement Society in 1999 was itself of great importance, as nobody could have dreamed of it two decades earlier. Artists and audiences alike accepted the new name because it made it possible to talk about dance in public in an objective way.[4] The Office for Rhythmic Movements is a subdivision of the Office of Theatre (*Edareh-ye Taatr*), and its members are officially known as actors (*bazigaran*) rather than dancers (*raqsandegan*). Therefore, as in the case of other art forms, dance has gone through a process of transformation, and dancers have been forced to adjust themselves to the new regulations by inventing new ways of practising their profession, among which the use of 'rhythmic movements' in narrative/dramatic contexts has been the most frequent one.

Choreographers and theatre directors use a variety of techniques to incorporate dance movements into their narratives. I have observed two types of scenes in which dance moves are often used. The first are scenes that require actors to express intense emotions such as mourning, separation, delight and pain. For instance, Farzaneh Kaboli (b. 1951) used 'rhythmic movements' to convey a rape scene in Hadi Marzban's (b. 1944) staging of Akbar Radi's (1939–2007) *The Night on the Wet Cobblestone* in 1999. The second types of scenes are those in which animals or supernatural beings appear on the stage. These scenes are particularly prevalent in Pari Saberi's (b. 1932) works. In *Haft Khan-e Rostam* [*The Seven Labours of Rostam*], which was staged in Tehran's Rudaki Hall in the summer months of 2009, the main sequences of rhythmic movements were performed by female dancers who were cast as Rakhsh (Rostam's celebrated horse), a goat and a witch. A male 'actor' also made heavy use of 'rhythmic movement' in his characterisation of the *simorgh* (the mythical bird of wisdom).[5] The witch in *Haft Khan-e Rostam* first appeared as an attractive woman but danced later dressed as a robotic doll. It seems that it is unacceptable for a performer to dance as a beautiful woman, while dancing as an animal or a mythical object creates fewer problems. However, the boundaries are not as obvious as one might suppose. In the same performance, I was surprised to see that the dancer performing the role of the goat did the splits, as I had assumed that officials would not permit this type of movement. If the performer had not been dressed as a goat, this type of movement would certainly not have been allowed.

(b) *Dance as a performing art by itself (not as part of cinematic or theatrical performances):* These kinds of performances have faced more obstacles than the above-mentioned, and they first occurred in women-only semi-public spaces. One early example of this was a series of performances held in the Italian embassy.[6] Held as part of a charity event, these performances continued for three years from 1997 to 1999. Such performances cannot be fully described as public, because they were performed by women for women, were not publicly advertised and the audience was a select group of luminaries and famous charitable individuals who had been offered the tickets. Thus such performances may be called 'border performances', where diplomatic immunity (in both a metaphoric and literal sense) creates a space for a selected number of people. A similar case occurred during the opening ceremony of the Muslim Women's Olympics, held in Tehran in 2005; the event was choreographed by Farzaneh Kaboli and performed in a sealed stadium in front of a women-only audience.

Some dance practitioners have also attempted to organise actual public performances of dance as an art form by itself rather than as a part of a theatrical performance, but have had to endure so much during the permission-seeking process that they have refrained from any further attempts. To get a permit a practitioner must perform the programme for the heads of several different offices who will then decide whether to authorise or reject the performance. This is a devastating process because it causes a great deal of stress and encourages self-censorship. But this task must be undertaken in order to perform in public, and professionals who want to perform must undergo this arduous process to gain approval from a number of officials who may not know anything about the artistic aspects of their profession.

On one occasion, while seeking permission for an event that involved the performance of regional dances, the officials stated that while finger-snapping was permitted for men, the women should refrain from it. The choreographer decided that to maintain the aesthetic balance, it would be better to change it to clapping for both men and women, even though snapping is the dance's original feature,

While in other countries, a particular show may run for several months or years, a dance performance is like the coming of Halley's Comet in Iran – one may need a second life to see a performance again. The performers undergo a lot of stress to get official permits which, due to pressures from radical and ultraconservative groups, do not guarantee a performance will take place. In fact, there have been musical concerts and dance performances that have had their permits revoked just hours before the performance; or even during the show's brief season. There have also been cases where dance performances have been given permits for semi-public and gender-segregated performances. However, some performances have received permission on the condition that even in front of female-only audiences, the dancers observe the Islamic dress code.

Due to these restrictions, most dancers who were active in pre-revolution Iran either left the country or changed career. For those who remained in Iran however, one career option has been to choreograph for other dancers who perform abroad.

Teaching/Learning dance

In his *Choreophobia*, Anthony Shay explains that 'Iranian dancers... overwhelmingly learn their skills in informal settings...' (1999: 36). These informal settings are mostly limited to family parties and unofficial tutorials delivered by family members. Besides these basic forms of learning, the music videos of Los Angeles-based singers and Khordadian's instructional videos have also been very influential in post-revolution Iran. With the gradual expansion of Iran's post-revolution musical culture since the 1990s, it has also become possible to take part in tutorials that teach different forms of dance, from Iranian regional dances to ballet and salsa.

When music institutes were closed after the revolution most musicians and singers who had remained in Iran switched to private tutoring. But the case of dance was not as straightforward. During the 1970s, dance was still in the early stages of being institutionalised as a public art form and it was mainly treated as a form of entertainment or as a private leisure activity. Consequently, serious dance tutorials did not translate as easily into a home environment as did music. In addition, within the borders of dominant cultural discourse and the unwritten rules of the post-revolution government, attending indoor music lessons was less problematic than joining dance tutorials. Thus it was only later that formal dance tutorials gradually found a space in the houses of former dancers.

During the 1980s joining female-only sport clubs was a leisure activity that many middle-class women engaged with. Since exercise to music (ie roller-skating or choreographed exercise routines) is not considered to be dance, these aerobic clubs were among the few semi-public places where one could hear Western popular music, albeit with the omission of the singer's voice.[7] Some dance tutorials have emerged from inside these aerobic clubs. Some women's clubs – and recently men's – have become spaces for teaching and practising a variety of dance forms. The government is aware of these activities, but does not usually interfere with their activities unless there is clear evidence of mixed-gender training or performance.

As it is forbidden to include dance as part of the curriculum in any official institution, the main method of advertising the opening of a dance class has been through personal connections and word of mouth. Recently some classes have also used methods such as fliers or even small billboards, which have often led to problems. One report from a newspaper states that 'tutorials for teaching *raqasi* [a pejorative term for dancing] working under the name of "rhythmic movements" have grown fast in Tehran' (*Jomhuri-e Islami*, 2009). The report aims to criticise the existence of dance classes in an Islamic country, but the result is often contradictory. Even these kinds of reports may intrigue readers and encourage them to seek out these classes, particularly as the report also details the different styles of dance taught illegally in one of these classes: 'Arabic, Iranian, Spanish, Turkish, Techno, Hip Hop, Indian, and Ballet' (*Jomhuri-e Islami*, 2010).

In these private and semi-public spaces the difference between dance as an art form and dance as entertainment is not clear. Because there are no regulatory bodies, there are also no systems in place for the evaluation of dance teachers. This is a major problem as it is very likely that through the misguided approaches of unqualified teachers, those who have the potential to become leading Iranian dance practitioners may lose or never discover their talent.

Conclusion

While dance as entertainment maintained its place in post-revolution Iran through house parties and celebrations, its presence as a performing art faced enormous difficulties and disappeared entirely from the public lives of Iranians. However, since the early days of the revolution and the initial banning of dance and other cultural art forms, artists and audiences have tried to push the political boundaries on cultural activities. Thus, a tacit process of negotiation began immediately after the imposition of the bans. Following this it became possible for dance to emerge as a theatrical technique, which subsequently opened the space for a few performances of dance as a performing art form during the last ten years.

The implicit process of negotiation between artists and officials still continues. Thus while at the moment the pressures from a more radical government seem to have reduced the frequency of dance-related activities, there are still instances of dance performance which manage to pass through the permitting process by adjusting themselves to new regulations. For instance, in the 15th International Festival of Ritual and Traditional Theatres of Iran (*Jashnvareh Beinolmelali-e Namayesh-ha-ye Aeeni va Sonati-e Iran*) in 2011, the director Qotbedin Sadeghi used Kurdish regional dances, which though appreciated by the audience was heavily criticised by some radical newspapers.[8] What is significant in the history of this ongoing negotiation, therefore, is the constant transformation of forms and attitudes, which has made the official approach to art more flexible than seemed possible in the early 1980s.

Notes

1 For a sample video from a lower class wedding ceremony, please see 'Tehran 1991 Javad dance' at www.youtube.com/watch?v=1g-g7nBzg30 (accessed 5 June 2011). 'Javad' is a common name and a Persian slang describing the qualities of a pretentious young male from a lower or lower middle class background.
2 During the early 2000s for instance, flights to the Anatolian shores, which have become a favourite destination for the Iranian people, were cancelled by the authorities on several occasions.
3 For some visual examples, see 'Break dancing in Park Melat in Tehran – Iran' and 'mp4.Haft Howz حوض هفت' at www.youtube.com/watch?v=c5m5rAqHLXI& feature=related, www.youtube.com/watch?v=4WLsXj_1GEg&NR=1.
4 In 2008 the name 'rhythmic movements' generated some debate among the more radical sections of the conservative government and the society was renamed 'The Society for the Actors of Silent Movements' (*Anjoman-e Bāzigarān-e Harakāt-e Bi Kalām*). It seems that under the new ultraconservative government, 'rhythm' and 'movement' are deemed to be too provocative for public use.
5 Rostam is the main hero in the epic section of Ferdowsi's (940–1020) *Shāhnāmeh* (c. 1000).
6 Such performances have been possible because embassies do not need to adhere to the rule of the Islamic Republic as strictly as other public spaces within Iran.
7 Some forms of Western popular music are acceptable to the Iranian authorities as long as the words are removed.
8 See 'Raqs va Paikoobi-e mokhtalet be bahane-ye namayesh-e aeeni va sonati' [Mixed dance under the pretext of ritual and traditional theatres], in *Mobasheroon* at www.mobasherun.ir/index.php?option=com_content&view=article&id=655: 1390-05-11-23-15-14&catid=1:news1&Itemid=59.

References

'Amoozesh-e Anva'-e Raqs dar Gheflat-e Masoolan-e Farhangi' ['Teaching different dance styles and the negligence of the officials']. *Jomhuri-e Islami* 11 May 2010 (www.jomhourieslami.com/1389/1389_0221_03_jomhori_islami_akhbar_dakheli_0025.html) (last accessed 21 June 2010).

Binesh, MT (1376/2003) *Tarikh-e Mokhtasar-e Musiqi-e Iran* [*A Brief History of the Music of Iran*]. Tehran: Chakad.

Chehabi, Houshang E (1993) 'Staging the emperor's new clothes: Dress codes and nation-building under Reza Shah'. *Iranian Studies*, vol. 26, no. 3/4: 209–29.

Fatemi, S (2005) 'Music, festivity, and gender in Iran from the Qajar to the early Pahlavi period'. *Iranian Studies* 38, 3: 399–416.

Joneidi, F (1372/1993) *Zamineh-ye Shenakht-e Musiqi-e Iran* [*An Introduction to the Study of Iranian Music*]. Tehran: Part.

Mashhun, H (1373/1994) *Tarikh-e Musiqi-e Iran* [*The History of Music in Iran*]. Tehran: Simorq.

'Raqs va Paikoobi-e mokhtalet be bahane-ye namayesh-e aeeni va sonati' ['Mixed dance under the pretext of ritual and traditional theatres'] in *Mobasheroon* (www.mobasherun.ir/index.php?option=com_content&view=article&id=655:1390-05-11-23-15-14&catid=1:news1&Itemid=59 (last accessed 5 August 2011)).

Shahbazi, S and Friend, RC (1993) 'Dance' at *Iranica* (www.iranica.com/newsite/; http://www.iranica.com/articles/dance-raqs).

Shay, A (1999) *Choreophobia*. California: Mazda Publication.

Youssefzadeh, Ameneh (2000) 'The situation of music in Iran since the revolution: The role of official organization'. *British Journal of Ethnomusicology* 9, 2: 35–61.

CHAPTER 8

BEYOND GENDER

Women Filmmakers and Sociopolitical Critique

Saeed Zeydabadi-Nejad

Iranian cinema and Hollywood have very few things in common. One of the commonalities is the small number of female directors in comparison with their male colleagues. According to Martha Lauzen in her article 'The celluloid ceiling' (2008), women directed only 6 per cent of the top box office films in the USA in 2006. Contrary to what one would expect, there has also been a downward trend in the number of women directors as of late. As the title of Lauzen's article suggests, a 'celluloid ceiling' seems to hinder women's progress within the film industry not just as directors but also in other professions. The situation is no better in the rest of the Western world (Jacobs, 1998). Given Western pretentions of gender inequality to be a problem for the rest of the world, the situation is rather ironic. In Iran women directors whose films do well at the box office are also very few.

However, box office returns do not reflect the overall trend for Iranian women in the film industry. In post-revolutionary Iran the number of women filmmakers has been increasing, in contrast to what is observed in Hollywood. In addition, an increasing number of them have made significant feature and documentary films that have been met with critical acclaim both inside and outside Iran. Some have won national and international awards.

The emergence of a number of women filmmakers in post-revolution Iran has come as a surprise to many. In the West, this trend is generally considered in terms of individual women filmmakers' brave defiance of the Islamic Republic's gender-based restrictions. While this is partially true, the phenomenon should also be considered in correlation with the women's movement in Iran (Zeydabadi-Nejad, 2010). Thus, rather than considering women filmmakers as the exception, the enlightened elite from the orient, their work should be related to the specific geo-political context in which they are embedded.

Research so far has almost exclusively considered Iranian women directors' contribution to Iranian cinema in relation to the feminist content of their films. The fact that women filmmakers have challenged gender discrimination and patriarchy is undeniable. The films of Tahmineh Milani, Rakhshan Bani-Etemad, Samira Makhmalbaf, Manijeh Hekmat, Nikki Karimi and Mina Akbari and their contemporaries have both explicitly and implicitly challenged Iran's deeply embedded patriarchal gender configurations. However, I believe that by concentrating solely on the feminist content of these films, the filmmakers' significant role as social critics in a wider sense has been neglected. Inadvertently, focus on gender representation ghettoises both the filmmakers and their films, implying that the only notable social commentary from Iranian women directors is gender related. This is not only reductive of their contribution; it can be considered sexist. In addition, such an approach is out of touch with the realities of film reception in Iran where the impact of female directors extends far beyond gender. This chapter is an attempt to get away from ghettoisation of women filmmakers and their work.

Tracing women's presence in film from the front to behind the camera, this chapter begins with brief foray into the cinema of pre-revolution Iran. Much of the early developments in post-revolution cinema, particularly to do with women, were a reaction to the (perceived) sexuality in pre-revolution films. In addition, one has to contextualise the works of women directors within the development of post-revolution cinema in order to understand their emergence. To exemplify the impact of a woman director's sociopolitical critique, as it reaches beyond gender, I will then analyse *Women's Prison* (2002), a film directed by Manijeh Hekmat. I will draw on fieldwork carried out in Iran to discuss the controversy surrounding the film.

Cinema before the revolution

Pre-revolutionary cinema can be broadly divided in two categories: *film-farsi* (mainstream films) and the New Wave art-house variety. Both types of films have their beginnings in the 1960s, when a few significant films led to major transformation of the cinema industry. The immense popularity of *Croesus' Treasure* (1965), a film by Yasemi, heralded a new era for cinema in Iran. The film was a melodramatic feel-good, featuring many song and dance routines that had already been popularised through the screening of Indian films. The immense popularity of *Croesus' Treasure* resulted in a large number of new cinemas being built around the country (Golestan, 1995: 81). Local film production, inspired by the success of this film, also grew exponentially, thus consolidating the film industry (Omid, 1998: 411).

The mainstream cinema of the time, including the cycle of films that followed the musical formula of *Croesus' Treasure* hoping to attain the same level of popularity and success, became termed *film-e farsi* or *film-farsi* (lit. Persian film). At times, film critics who rejected the low production qualities of the commercial cinema used this label pejoratively.[1] The films also used the sexualised image of female film characters to lure the predominantly young male audience to cinemas. The dance sequences provided ample opportunity to package images of the scantily clad female characters for the 'male gaze' (Mulvey, 1999). As discussed later in this chapter, it was precisely the issue of the sexualisation of film that led to the rejection of cinema by the Shi'ite clergy, who would later take a leading role in the revolution and the Islamic republic.

In the early 1960s a number of socially conscious documentary and fiction films were made that were distinct from the mainstream cinema of the time. Many of the films were made in close association with intellectuals including novelists and poets such as Ebrahim Golestan and Gholam-Hossein Sa'edi. One of the earliest examples of this type of cinema was Gaffary's *South of The City* (1958), a film about life in the poor suburbs of Tehran. Gradually many more such films were made including: *Night of the Hunchback* (Ghaffary, 1964), *The Brick and the Mirror* (Golestan, 1965), *Mrs Ahu's Husband* (Mollapur, 1968), and *The Cow* (Mehrju'i, 1969). These films were well received by Iranian film critics. In Iran this film movement was named *sinema-ye motefavet* or Alternative Cinema, and in the West it became known as the Iranian New Wave.

Unlike mainstream cinema, which generally painted a flattering picture of Iran, New Wave films pointed at social issues and were thus inherently political. Many of them highlighted the social and economic problems that the monarchist regime tried to gloss over with a veneer of Westernisation, thus leading to various problems with the authorities, which resulted in many of the films being censored or banned. Censorship was meant to stop any efforts to undermine the flashy image of the nation that the regime wished to project. For example, one of the articles of the 1959 censorship code prohibited films from showing 'ruins, poverty, backwardness and scenes that damage the state's national prestige' (Golmakani, 1992: 20).

Gender depiction in the works of male directors in the New Wave was no better than in *film-farsi* (Lahiji, 2002). Like in *film-farsi*, female characters were denied subjectivity and were thus either submissive background figures (the mothers or sisters of film heroes) or, if they were in the foreground, sexualised objects of desire.

One important figure among the New Wave filmmakers was the female poet Forough Farrokhzad. By the time she made *The House is Black* (1963), her first and, sadly, only film, she was a very well established poet (on her poetry, see Hillman, 1987). Filmed in the confines of a lepers' colony, the documentary depicts the grievous conditions of life within the colony. Farrokhzad's highly creative filmmaking style raised the film above a simple reflection of the lepers' lives a poetic and socially conscious masterpiece. Her film was read in Iran in a variety of ways, including as an allegorical censure of social predicaments of Iran. Importantly this, the first significant film by a woman director, was not specifically addressing the condition of women. Rather, while Farrokhzad's feminine sensitivity and compassion are as undeniable in the film as they are in her poetry, the film represents the leper colony as a whole. Farrokhzad's filmic and poetic career met a tragic and premature end with her death in a car accident in 1967.

The Islamic revolution and its aftermath

The Shi'ite clergy, who saw themselves as the guardians of public morality, were opposed to cinema's depiction of women. To them, the 'immoral' images and messages of films were a cause for concern, as they contended that the films would lead men astray. The puritanical clergy that took power after the revolution were particularly incensed by the sequences in films depicting scantly clad women dancing in café bars in front of the often intoxicated male clientele. The clergy did not differentiate between New Wave films and *film-farsi*, rejecting cinema as a whole. Famously, over the course of the 1978–9 revolution, almost half of Iran's 436 cinema halls were set on fire. In all cases except one, the cinemas were not in use at the time of arson attacks. However on 10 August 1978, about 400 people died in an inferno in the Rex Cinema in the city of Abadan. From then until directly after the establishment of the Islamic Republic in 1979, cinemas remained closed across the country.

Matters of culture were top of the agenda for the newly established Islamic Republic. Interestingly, in Ayatollah Khomeini's first speech upon his return to Iran, and just ten days before the eventual victory of the revolution, he stated that he was against vice and not cinema *per se*. The 'immorality' of cinema obviously concerned the Ayatollah. To him and others, the representation of women was a central concern.

Islamisation of cinema

In his numerous speeches broadcast on TV and radio, Ayatollah Khomeini called repeatedly for the Islamisation of Iranian society and cinema was a key cultural arena where this was to take place.[2] Some of the early indicators of culture change were more about what the ruling clergy did not want the cinema to show than what it was supposed to become. In the early period, 1979–82, *paksazi* or 'purification' was an institutional move to 'purify' cinema of 'contamination' of those practitioners, from actors to producers, who were closely associated with pre-revolution cinema (see Naficy, 2002). Actresses, particularly those who were young and attractive, bore the brunt of this shift. The on-screen depiction of 'un-chaste' behaviour was believed to have affected these actresses' real personalities. Actors had a better chance of redeeming themselves. From Saeed Rad to Jamshid Mashayekhi, most of the male stars of pre-revolution period have continued to act in the post-revolution period.

In 1982, a few of the Ministry of Culture and Islamic Guidance's (MCIG) more open-minded religious intellectuals began to take charge of cinema. The minister in charge, Mohammad Khatami, who became the country's president in 1997, was also in favour of expanding quality filmmaking in Iran. Over the course of a few years, film production grew from just a handful to 40 in 1984 (Talebinejad, 1998: 54–5). To encourage the production of better quality films, MCIG rewarded compliant producers/directors with better funding opportunities for their future projects.

The question of what constitutes an Islamic film was settled by an attempt to eliminate everything considered to be un-Islamic. The ministry came up with a censorship code that was intended to exclude any scripts or completed films that could be considered to be out of line with the state's Islamic ideology. The code prohibited the exhibition of films that would:

- directly or indirectly insult the prophets, imams, the supreme jurisprudent, the leadership council, or the qualified jurisprudents;
- encourage wickedness, corruption, and prostitution;
- encourage or teach abuse of harmful and dangerous drugs or professions that are religiously sanctioned against such as smuggling, etc;
- encourage foreign cultural, economic and political influence contrary to the 'neither West nor East' policy of the Islamic Republic of Iran;
- express or disclose anything that is against the interests and policies of the country that might be exploited by foreigners.

In addition, a sub-clause declared that the *nezarat* (literally 'supervision' but in fact 'censorship') committee should be responsible for determining the regulations regarding the way women can appear in Iranian and foreign films. They may only appear in a way that will not be at variance with the high position of women, bearing in mind the *shari'a* laws. The regulation should apply to makers of Iranian films and the importers of foreign ones (Nuri, 1996: 191–3).[3]

The code was open to interpretation: for example how can one decide with any certainty that a film has encouraged 'wickedness' or that it has undermined 'the high position of women?' In addition, there were always at least a few sympathetic/progressive people in charge of various cinema-related organisations. The combination of these elements meant that film censorship was always negotiable. But this very much depended on the political context of the time. In the crisis-ridden first decade of the Islamic Republic, the regime was too concerned about its own survival to allow any heterogeneity of expression to emerge. The state kept tight control of the media and cinema was no exception.[4]

The end of the Iran–Iraq war in 1988 and the death of Ayatollah Khomeini a year later heralded a new opening for media in general and cinema in particular. Earlier banned films were now released and some films with oblique social critique received permission to be made and were subsequently exhibited. However, the ups and downs in the political atmosphere continued to have a strong bearing on the degree of leniency towards films with critical themes.

The year 1997 was of utmost significance to the history of Iranian cinema and indeed the Islamic Republic. In that year, the election of Mohammad Khatami to the presidency brought much hope for political and social reform. Khatami, who had earlier worked as Minister for Culture and Islamic Guidance, had the support of almost the entire film industry. Some made his campaign videos and others issued supportive statements as well as rallying for him on the streets.

Khatami's win brought together a number of political groups under the banner of reformism. His opponents became known as the conservatives. With the supreme leader, Ayatollah Khamenei, the judiciary and the armed forces belonging to the conservatives, they held much power against the reformists. Khatami's cabinet included Ayatollah Mohajerani as his Minister of Culture and Islamic Guidance. Mohajerani oversaw a major transformation of the media scene in Iran where the number of newspapers and magazines rose dramatically. In cinema, filmmakers who had not been allowed to make films for years (such as Bahman Farmanara) or films whose scripts had been rejected (such as Milani's *Two Women*) finally received the necessary permissions. Social and political criticism became more frequent, and some of the leading filmmakers who turned to such themes were women. In 1999, Mohajerani was unsuccessfully impeached by conservative parliamentarians for matters that included his handling of cinema.

The particular sensitivity of the regime to cinema and the attempt to keep in check any criticism of the regime on film has politicised cinema. The banning of films and, at times, the persecution of filmmakers has contributed to the perception of cinema as a political institution. Women filmmakers have not shied away from venturing into the restricted zone of criticism of the regime and hence have suffered the consequences.

Women directors and the revolutionary transformation

It may seem ironic that an Islamic political context considered oppressive of women would be the place where a number of prominent women film directors have emerged. This is more of a surprise if one considers that before the revolution, apart from the above-mentioned Forough Farrokhzad, only two other women ever directed films. Shahla Riyahi and Korba Saidi each have one love story to their credit, *Marjan* (1956) and *Mariam and Mani* (1979) respectively. The low number of women filmmakers in pre-revolutionary Iran contrasts with the social breakthroughs achieved by women in Pahlavi-era Iran. These included the 1967 Family Protection Law, which diminished the rights of men to divorce and polygamy. At the same time, led by women with close links with the ruling elite, women's organisations progressed on many fronts including women's education.

In contrast, under the Islamic Republic, Pahlavi-era gains in women's rights were initially reversed and the role of women was redefined as nurturing (would-be) mothers. The 1967 Family Protection Law was revoked and family planning services were halted. Women were forced to wear *hijab* in spite of the fact that Ayatollah Khomeini had promised otherwise during the revolution. Women were also prohibited from studying certain university courses in the engineering fields. How, in such a context, women filmmakers grew in number and importance is a dilemma that requires attention to broader changes in Iranian society.

One of the main post-revolution changes was the Islamisation of public life in Iran. The puritan representatives of the state intended workplaces, public spaces and even the private lives of Iranians to be policed in order to ensure that at least on the surface people did not behave contrary to the edicts of the Shi'ite clergy. As an unintended by-product, participation in public life became easier for women with religious backgrounds. While they or their families considered Pahlavi-era public life secular and hence prohibited for women, this was no longer the case under the Islamic Republic (Gerami, 1996; Higgins and Ghaffari, 1994). In addition, for many women whose husbands were involved in the war with Iraq (1980–8), increased participation in public life was a matter of necessity. Thus, religious women joined the workforce and public arena in droves.

Cinema was also no longer the religiously prohibited arena of the Pahlavi period from which women had to stay away. In fact, an Islamic cinema was supposed to develop that would be a bastion of religiosity. On screen characters must comply with rules of *hijab*: cover their hair and bodies, and appear modest. In the early post-revolutionary phase, however, they had to almost completely hide from view. In contrast to the dancing girls of *film-farsi*, women appeared as supportive mothers/wives in the periphery of the screen as background figures. Later, particularly in the post-Khomeini period, women played many key roles and lead characters. Behind the camera, what began with a few women directors casting mildly assertive female leads in their films, turned into self-assured directors producing films that critiqued issues that were not just to do with gender but were of larger political relevance. One of these directors was Manijeh Hekmat.

Manijeh Hekmat

Hekmat began her cinema career as a 'script girl' in the early 1980s and then worked as assistant director from 1988. From the mid 1990s to the present day she has produced a large number of feature films. In 1999 she began her research into female prisons, which culminated in her directing a documentary called *High Walls* (2000) and then the feature film *Women's Prison* (2002). It took her almost a year to gain the necessary permits to have the film screened both in Iran and internationally. Her debut feature was shown in around 120 festivals and won a number of prizes including the 'Best Film' award from Iranian film critics[5] and the 2003 Amnesty International DOEN award from Rotterdam International Film Festival. She has since directed the film *Three Women* (2008).

Women's Prison (2002)

True to the *cinéma vérité* style of Iranian films, *Women's Prison* depicts the lives of female inmates. This is a bold move in the history of Iranian cinema, because no film has ever been made within an Iranian prison, let alone in a women's prison. The natural acting style of the characters, a real prison as the film's set, the makeup and costumes, as well as the dimly lit interiors of the prison, give the film a bleak look which adds to the film's realism. To augment the realist effect, women appear without appropriate head cover in numerous scenes.[6] There is hardly any male presence in the film, and the protagonists and antagonists are all women.

The film spans 17 years of the post-revolution period and is segmented into three episodes. The first is set in 1984 and opens with the arrival of the new warden Ms Tahereh Yousefi (henceforth Tahereh) at the women's prison, where the prisoners have been disobeying rules. Witnessing the unhygienic, cluttered and unruly conditions of the prison, the impassive Tahereh introduces a strict new control regime that involves harsh punishment, including frequent solitary confinement. In a short while she manages to bring a draconian order to the jail.

The characterisation of the prison warden is central to the film: she is a *chador*[7]-clad ultra-religious and very strict person who does not seem to allow anyone including herself to have any material pleasure.[8] In one sequence we see her trying on lipstick that she had confiscated earlier from an inmate. This does not seem to have made an impact on her, as we see her in the next scene without the makeup and adhering to a strict dress code for the rest of the film. She seems to be a metaphoric prisoner of her own strict boundaries, a fact emphasised in the final sequence of the film.

Tahereh is often challenged by Mitra, a former university student in midwifery, whose studies were cut short after she was imprisoned for murdering her abusive step-father. Tahereh sends Mitra to solitary confinement a number of times. Mitra objects to the treatment of prisoners at the hands of Tahereh, and to the society beyond the confines of the prison that seems to target the effects of crime rather than the causes. Mitra tries to protect the most vulnerable among the prisoners, particularly the younger ones.

One of the young prisoners called Pegah (a Persian name meaning Dawn) appears to be there for political reasons. Although this is not stated explicitly in the film, there are many clues as to her status. Pegah is eventually taken away from the prison in a sequence indicating that she is going to be executed.

To emphasise the significance of what happens to Pegah, this sequence is placed at the end of episode one. The sequence begins with Pegah in the prison yard with other prisoners when her name is called to the office over the PA system. Mitra, looking worried, follows Pegah into the prison building. The next shot shows Pegah as she is being led out towards a gate with her eyes covered and in handcuffs. She is led through the prison corridor where two men are depicted painting the corridor white. This is followed by a shot of Mitra's sad face as Pegah is being led away. Mitra looks down at the newspaper covering the floor that is turning white beneath the dripping paint. The colour white is not only a reference to the innocence of Pegah or symbolic of the many of her generation who were executed by the Islamic Republic in the 1980s, it is also the colour of the long white cloth used as a shroud (*kafan*) to wrap a dead body in Islamic burial, hence a reference to the imminent execution.

The inclusion of a political prisoner among the inmates and reference to her execution were bold moves by the filmmaker. Up until then, no film had ever referenced the fate of thousands of young people, generally loosely affiliated with leftist political groups, who spent years in jail and/or were executed in the 1980s. Furthermore, to depict a political prisoner as an innocent-looking and vulnerable person was significant. The reference to political prisoners was not lost on Iranian critics and audiences.[9]

In the second episode, set in 1990, the prison is crowded with prostitutes, some women convicted of adultery, drug-dealers and addicts among others. A young addict called Sahar (another Persian name meaning Dawn) is in jail for a minor drug-related offence. She works hard to save money for her family outside jail. When Sahar is apparently raped by Zivar, a drug-dealer, she commits suicide in her cell. The relationship between Tahereh and Mitra reaches a sort of truce at this point. They both know and despise the drug-dealer/rapist. Intriguingly, the actress playing the part of Sahar is the same as the one that had earlier appeared as Pegah. She later reappears in the third episode as Sepideh (yet another Persian name meaning Dawn). As the director explains below, this is meant to emphasise the predicament of Iranian youth in society.

Set in 2001, the third episode shows the older Tahereh and Mitra on better terms. The prison is now bursting at the seams with a very large number of mainly runaway teenagers as well as prisoners' children. Many of the inmates spend brief periods in jail for not observing the strict dress code or being caught at a mixed sex party. As in episode two, the guards appear to be corrupted. Mitra meets a young inmate who turns out to be Sepideh, a 17-year-old girl whose baby Mitra had helped deliver in the prison in episode one using her knowledge as a midwife.

When Sepideh gets out of jail, she informs Mitra that she is about to go to Dubai. Worried about the prospects of Sepideh being exploited by prostitution gangs in Dubai, Mitra requests that Tahereh help her get furlough so that she can find Sepideh and prevent her from going to Dubai. Tahereh then personally puts up the hefty bail for Mitra.

The film ends with a long and highly metaphoric sequence. As Mitra is exiting the prison, Tahereh stands facing the closing gate. We see the figure of Tahereh from behind, as the black colour of her *chador* blends with the dark colour of the door. Tahereh's figure hence becomes almost indistinguishable from the prison gate. In a film throughout which the prison itself and life within it is presented in documentary style, the final shot stands out as a metaphoric representation of Tahereh's imprisonment by her own personal restrictions. More significantly, the darkness of this closing shot of the film contrasts with the white of the final shot of episode one. The latter is associated with the victim of the Islamic Republic and the former an appointed authority. The contrast between the two could not be any starker.

Hekmat's treatment of the prison as a microcosm encourages an allegorical reading of it as Iranian society at large. Tahereh's tyrannical rule within the prison, which begins close to the time of the revolution, and her strict religiosity reinforces this interpretation. However the allegory does not have a one-to-one correspondence with the political reality of the Islamic Republic. For example, power within the prison is monolithic with Tahereh never being challenged by any of her colleagues. In contrast, in the Iranian regime the powerful conservatives have been seriously challenged a number of times by reformists within the establishment, particularly since 1997. Therefore, while encouraging an allegorical reading, the filmmaker has shown the prison to be a *real* prison and not simply an allegorical element.

Reception of the film in Iran

The Ministry of Culture and Islamic Guidance (MCIG) banned *Women's Prison* shortly before it was due to be shown at the Fajr International Film Festival (Cheshire, 2002). Mohammad Hassan Pezeshk, the deputy minister in charge of cinema at MCIG, was reported to be absolutely against the screening of the film (Anon., 2002: 28). *Etemad*, a reformist newspaper, quoted the conservative authoritarian Mohammad Hejazi in his condemnation of *Women's Prison*, which he argued was implying that the Islamic regime is a prison as large as the country (Mohammadi, 2002). When the film was eventually screened across Iran, a cinema where it was being shown in Isfahan was set on fire. During the same period, it was taken off the screens in a number of cities. Although the film did well at the box office in Tehran for several weeks, it was controversially removed from cinemas (Mohammadi, 2002). Nevertheless, and perhaps surprisingly for an art film with bleak subject matter, it became a box office hit, ranking fourth among the top grossing films of the year even though bootleg copies of the film were in wide circulation at the time (see table 8.1).

The reformist press had shown interest in the film since it was in pre-production and frequently published news about it until it was eventually released (Nikpur and Hadisi, 2002). Significantly, the main focus of analysis in reviews and interviews about the film was not gender. For example, Shoraka (2002: 81), a female critic, wrote, 'Since the film's main and peripheral characters are all female, gender conflict does not develop that would encourage feminist readings [of the film].' In fact, critics and interviewers were interested in allegorical representation of Iran's post-revolution history in the film. Nikpur and Hadisi (2002) asked Hekmat about this in an interview:

> Nikpur: The film is divided into three parts, three time slices corresponding to three periods in the recent history of this country. Each of these periods has its own specificities, which we can see in a way in the film. It is remarkable that you have taken the camera inside the prison. How come [the camera] does not come out of prison?
>
> Hekmat: The work is a whole and I don't focus on a [single] sequence or character... [the camera] looks inside the small society within the prison and need not come out. In my story 'outside' [the prison] does not have a place.... the film reflects the larger society and you don't need to get out of prison.
>
> Nikpur: But the main events of the 1980s [1360s in Iran] do not feature in your film.
>
> Hekmat: The historical trend of these 20 years shows itself in the film. I mean you can see all social, economic and political conditions in it...

Table 8.1. Box office rankings for the top 10 films in Tehran 1381/2002[10]

Raking	Film
1	*Kolah-Ghermezi and Sarvenaz*
2	*Pastry Shop Girl*
3	*I, Taraneh, am 15 Years Old*
4	*Women's Prison*
5	*Bother*
6	*Bread, Love & a 1000cc Motorbike*
7	*Low Heights*
8	*Last Supper*
9	*Blue*
10	*Sam and Narges*

Nikpur: You can take Tahereh as representing [political] 'power' [in the Iranian society]. In the first two episodes her character fits in with how 'power' showed itself in Iran. In the third, however, when she puts up the bail, her character is not [representative].

As the interviewer points out, Tahereh's putting up the bail is a show of compassion, which may seem incongruent with the reality of the powerful and uncompromising conservatives. Hekmat responds:

Hekmat: If we look around ourselves and read the papers, we see the same thing happening ... You can see that Tahereh has lost everything. If she had thought in a more balanced way, certainly she would not find herself in such predicaments.

Unlike the more 'realist' representation that the interviewer would have preferred, Hekmat appears to be addressing and attempting to educate the conservatives within the Iranian power structure to be more compassionate, as Tahereh appears to have become.

Nikpur: How about Mitra? Who does she represent in society?

Hekmat: She could be anyone, anyone who cannot accept force and pressure and looks at issues seriously. In our society [people with any] social status may not give in to certain pressures.... Mitra objects... She was an objector who would not put up with even her [bullying] step-father's impositions.... These characters are shaped in a particular context and then they become milder, eroded.... But I am not at all a political person. I say this everywhere. In any case, we should see the present social predicaments and the past and see how we can help mend them....

Nikpur: Is this [film] a warning for the next twenty years?

Hekmat: Yes. The young generation is our future. If this generation is not motivated by any ideals, does not have an identity and is unmotivated what will happen to this society in twenty years? This is my warning! This is my worry![11]

Hekmat wishes her film to be read as a critique of the political hierarchy in Iran, while at the same time claiming she is 'not a political person', but rather a social filmmaker. As I have shown elsewhere (Zeydabadi-Nejad, 2010), 'social filmmaker' is a label that progressive directors prefer over 'political filmmaker', which is certainly likely to land them in much more trouble with the Islamic regime. Nevertheless by allegorically addressing political issues, female filmmakers such as Hekmat engage in Iranian politics.

In another interview conducted at the time with Iranian film magazine *30nema*, the interviewer suggests the film could have been made about male prisoners (Naghibi, 2002). Hekmat agrees, saying she is not a feminist and made the story about female rather than male prisoners because she had researched the conditions of women prisoners in preparation for the film. As a woman she could not study men's prisons.

Although not the central theme of her film, it does address issues of gender inequality and injustice; Mitra's imprisonment is due to her standing up against the abusive behaviour of her step-father. In a sequence in the third episode it appears that a male prison guard had attempted unsuccessfully to make a sexual advance towards Sahar. However, these are subthemes within the narrative.

Intrigued by the boldness of the film and how Hekmat had managed to make it in spite of the restrictions, I interviewed Manijeh Hekmat in her office in central Tehran in early 2003, when her film had just been taken off the screens across Tehran. In the interview, excerpts of which appear below, I began by asking about the reactions to the film:

> Hekmat: I am not a political person. I am not the leader of a political party. I am a social filmmaker and this is my perspective. I don't have anything against the regime but I am worried about the fate of the people. I have a responsibility towards these people as a filmmaker....
>
> Zeydabadi-Nejad: Why do you have the same actor playing three roles in the three sections of the film?
>
> Hekmat: This is the youth in all three periods in these 20 years; I wanted to show who has replaced who. I will never forget that in the early 1980s there was a well-read, intellectual generation who were worried about the future of this country. They were decent and good. And now the youth have other wishes, which is their right. Some try to get what they want and others have just given up. Who has replaced who? Was it worth it to replace that well read intellectual generation with a generation of drug addicts [like Sahar in the second episode replacing Pegah in the first]? This was a betrayal I believe.... All three have the same innocence and in every period their problems have a different shape.
>
> Zeydabadi-Nejad: Tell me about the problems you had with the making of the film and what you did to overcome them.

Hekmat: Well to start with they would not give me a director's certificate to make this film. So my husband, who is a director, got a permit to make it so that we could start the film. But in fact I directed it. Because of all the problems I had faced before, the day I was going to start the filmmaking I had no energy left, I was drained. I persisted and finished the job but the film was banned for the next two years. I kept going to the MCIG so many times to get a screening permit. I tolerated so many insults and rude behaviour. Nevertheless, I got the permit to show it. They cut ten minutes of the film but I said that did not matter because I wanted the film to be shown and I could see that the totality of the film was still there. I accepted this although I felt pretty bad when I saw the censored version. Then the film was screened and there were some negative reactions including the burning of a cinema. However, I was standing firm. Filmmaking in Iran is difficult. If you are not related to the regime it is harder for you, particularly if you want to focus on sensitive issues like I did in my film. These are related problems and one has to be really tough to enter this arena and stand up against them.

Zeydabadi-Nejad: What about the fact that you are a woman?

Hekmat: This was an extra reason. There was a period that I was depressed and I was close to a nervous breakdown. I passed a very tough period but I stood, in spite of all these and in the end I got the permits (for further details, see Zeydabadi-Nejad, 2010).

It is significant how the filmmaker made the film as a reflection on Iranian society at large and that it was indeed received as such. The rapid social change in post-revolutionary Iran is represented through the changes in the prison environment. At this level, the film becomes an allegory about post-revolution Iran. Such reflection at times of social upheaval has been discussed by Turner, a cultural anthropologist. According to Turner (1984, 1986, 1990) at liminal junctures of major social change, 'cultural performances' such as theatre and film are employed to reflect on the instability that the society is experiencing. Thus cultural performances are 'a metacommentary, implicit or explicit, witting or unwitting, on the major social dramas of social context (wars, revolutions, scandals, institutional changes)' (Turner, 1990: 16).

Obviously in these commentaries the voice of the creator of the work, such as Hekmat in case of *Women's Prison*, predominates. Discussing this creative role, Turner refers to it as 'the supreme honesty of the creative artist who, in his presentation... reserves to himself the privilege of seeing straight what all cultures build crooked' (1984: 40). The critique that Hekmat offers is that of a committed social commentator that emphasises instances where revolutionary Iran appears to have gone wrong. Such criticism was met with force by conservative authorities within Iranian society and manifested in the ban and censorship of the film.

In order to understand the political impact of the film, I discussed the issue with Habibollah Kasesaz, the former head of the censorship section of the MCIG. He was the appointed intermediary between Hekmat and the MCIG when Hekmat pursued the release of her banned film. When I asked Kasesaz about the film he said:

> When the film was completed *Nezarat* [the censorship section of the MCIG] considered it anti-regime. However there were some reformists in the Screening Permit Council who wanted to go against the judiciary and gave the film a permit.[12] The judiciary wanted the film to be banned and had got Pezeshk (the cinema deputy of the MCIG) to act. In order to counteract them, Hekmat had shown the film to reformist parliamentarians, including Mehdi Karoubi [the speaker for parliament at the time] to gain their backing.[13]

However, with Pezeshk blocking the film, Hekmat was forced to compromise and she agreed to have Habibollah Kasesaz, former head of censorship and an independent film producer at the time, to arbitrate. Kasesaz told me that he felt the weight of responsibility as he had to respond to a number of sides including the judiciary, Pezeshk, and *Ansar Hizbullah*, a conservative pressure group that often resorts to violence against what they oppose. After Kasesaz cut about ten minutes of the film, he recommended it for screening. The judiciary and Pezeshk wanted Kasesaz to go further and censor more of it but he would not accept. He told me that *Ansar Hizbullah* still wanted to attack some cinemas in Tehran but he spoke to their leadership and dissuaded them. The same group, however, did attack a cinema in Isfahan as mentioned earlier.

The interview with Kasesaz shows that Hekmat's film had been taken very seriously by some of the highest authorities within the Islamic Republic. Obviously this had much to do with their interpretation of the film as 'anti-regime'. Had it not been for the Hekmat's tireless efforts and mobilisation of support from the reformists the film would have not been screened.

Other women filmmakers and sociopolitical critique

While the direct political connotations embedded in the film's representation of a prison were unique, *Women's Prison* was not the first or the last time that a woman filmmaker made a politically contentious film in Iran. Milani's *Hidden Half* (2000) is about a young woman involved with leftist groups in the early 1980s. Famously, Milani gave an interview to a reformist newspaper in which she referred to those political activists as young victims of repression who genuinely cared about Iran. She added that she wanted to raise the issue for the society to come to terms with it (Mazra'eh, 2001: 230). Milani was subsequently arrested and spent six days in jail.

Bani-Etemad, another major woman filmmaker, has also made films that have been intended to make a political impact. The most important of these was a documentary she made on the eve of the disputed presidential elections in 2009. Filming a range of women's rights activists posing questions about topical contemporary issues, Bani-Etemad asked the four presidential candidates to respond to the questions on camera. Three candidates took part, while Mahmoud Ahmadinejad, the ultimate winner of the elections, declined to participate. Many of the activists seen in the film were later arrested in the post-election protests.

Hana Makhmalbaf, the younger daughter of Mohsen Makhmalbaf, made a film called *Green Days* (2009) about youth whose lives get entangled in political activism during the 2009 elections and its aftermath. Not only does the film stand no chance of ever being screened in Iran under the current regime, in June 2011 it was banned in Lebanon where the Iranian-backed Hezbollah holds much power.[14]

The political activism of women directors does not end with filmmaking. As I have demonstrated elsewhere (Zeydabadi-Nejad, 2010), women filmmakers can be considered as active participants in the women's movement, a highly political movement, particularly since the 2009 elections. In addition, Bani-Etemad, Hekmat and some other women filmmakers have actively taken part in the Green Movement, which protested against and contested the legitimacy of the post-2009 Iranian regime. This is a fact that has not been lost on conservatives commenting on these activities in their blogs.[15] Bani-Etemad has not been allowed to make films since the disputed elections.

Conclusion

Since the 1979 revolution, a small but growing number of women filmmakers have been making films in Iran. Overcoming difficulties and prejudice, they have carved a place for themselves and other emergent women directors. These women's contribution to Iranian cinema has so far been generally acknowledged exclusively in relation to their input to the gender discourses. Reading women director's films solely through the lens of gender would not only be reductive of their multifaceted films, but also out of touch with the reality of film reception in Iran. In this chapter, tracing women's participation in pre- and post-revolution Iranian cinema and focusing on Manijeh Hekmat's *Women's Prison*, I demonstrated the significance of films by women filmmakers in the Iranian context. Beyond being directors, these women have a strong presence on the Iranian political scene.

During the 1978–9 revolution Iranian women who took part in the struggle against the Pahlavi regime subjugated their gender-related demands to the larger political aims of the revolution. At the time none of the women revolutionaries had a public profile comparable to men's and without such a profile their distinct voices were drowned in the post-revolution mayhem. The prominence of Women filmmakers and other women activists at the present political juncture can help to ensure that their voices remain in the fore if and when positive political change occurs in Iran. Women's demands will then have to be listened to, whether they are gender related or otherwise.

Notes

1 The instigation of the pejorative use of this term is attributed to Hushang Kavusi, an influential Iranian film critic at the time.
2 I am referring to the Ayatollah's insistence on *eslami kardan* (making Islamic) or *eslami shodan* (becoming Islamic) of all affairs in Iran.
3 The above does not include all the clauses in the code. For the full list see Nuri (1996).
4 For a thorough discussion of the censorship and the political context in Iran see Zeydabadi-Nejad (2010).
5 The award was part of the House of Cinema's event honouring the best contributions to Iranian cinema every year. The organisation houses cinema guilds and is relatively independent of the state.
6 As mentioned earlier female characters are expected appear in full *hijab* in film even when they are in their own house with their family members. When in real life they would not cover in front of relatives, on film male audience's gaze is acknowledged. Hekmat managed to get a permit for her finished film by arguing that the women's hair in the film look unkempt and dirty, hence making the women look unattractive. The inclusion of many such scenes was a major risk for the filmmaker, because if the censors had insisted on censoring them, the film as a whole would probably have become incomprehensible.
7 A head-to-toe loose-fitting cloak covering the whole of the body apart from the face of the wearer.

8   A conservative website associated with Qom seminary recently criticised the film as having shown a negative representation of a highly religious person, i.e. Tahereh, as tyrannical (Naghizadeh, 2010)
9   See for example Asadi's (2002) review of the film for BBC Persian published outside Iran. That Pegah was a political prisoner who was executed was not mentioned in reviews of the film in Iran. Given the fact that Tahmineh Milani was arrested in 2001 after discussing with a newspaper the fate of political prisoners in the 1980s, it is not surprising that the Iranian press would avoid the topic.
10 Figures obtained by author from MCIG. According to MCIG ranking of films in Tehran generally reflects the nationwide ticket sales for a film. Among these films only *Women's Prison* is directed by a woman.
11 These are sections of a much longer interview published in the newspaper. Translated from Persian by the author.
12 Persian: *Shora-ye parvaneh-ye namayesh*. According to Kasesaz, members of the council consist of representatives of the censorship section of the MCIG, the minister in charge of the MCIG, the cinema deputy of the MCIG and the parliament.
13 Karoubi is one of two figureheads of the Green Movement that began in 2009.
14 See www.france24.com/en/20110621-lebanon-bans-screening-iran-film-green-days (last accessed 21 June 2011).
15 See for example: http://warnarm.parsiblog.com/ and http://warnarm.parsiblog.com/ (last accessed 30 May 2011).

References

Anon. (2002) 'Qazi-ye monsef'. *Mahnameh-ye sinema'i-ye film* 291: 28.

Anon. (2002b) 'Ancheh gozasht'. *Iran* 2416 (www.iran-newspaper.com/1381/811228/html/art.htm (last accessed 5 May 2010)).

Anon (n.d.) 'Baz ham in arusake dust dashtani' (http://30-nema.persianblog.ir (last accessed 10 May 2011)).

Asadi, S (2002) 'Zendani va zendanban har do ghorbani' (www.bbc.co.uk/persian/arts/020823_la-cy-cinema.shtml (last accessed 1 May 2011)).

Cheshire, G (2002) 'So Fajr away' (www.villagevoice.com/2002-02-19/film/so-fajr-away/ (last accessed 10 May 2011)).

Farrokhzad, F (1963) *The House is Black*. Iran.

Gaffary, F (1958) *South of The City/Jonub-e Shahr*. Iran.

——— (1964) *Night of the Hunchback*. Iran.

Gerami, S (1996) *Women and Fundamentalism: Islam and Christianity*. New York: Garland Publishing.

Golestan, E (1965) *The Brick and the Mirror*. Iran.

Golestan, S (1995) *Fanus-e khiyal: sargozasht-e sinema-ye Iran az aghaz ta piruzi-e enqelab-e Islami*. Tehran: Entesharat-e kavir.

Golmakani, H (1992) 'New times, same problems'. *Index on Censorship* 21, 3: 19–22.

Hekmet, M (2000) *High Walls*. Iran.

—— (2002) *Women's Prison*. Iran.

—— (2008) *Three Women*. Iran.

Higgins, P and Ghaffari, P (1994) 'Women's education in the Islamic Republic of Iran' in Afkhami, M and Friedl, E (eds) *In the Eye of the Storm: Women in Post-Revolutionary Iran*. Syracuse: Syracuse University Press: 5–18.

Hillmann, M (1987) *A Lonely Woman: Forough Farrokhzad and her Poetry*. Washington DC: Three Continents Press.

Jacobs, K (1998) 'The status of contemporary women filmmakers' (www.libidot.org/v2/articles/womenfilm-print.html (last accessed 2 July 2010)).

Lahiji, S (2002) 'Chaste dolls succeed unchaste dolls: Women in Iranian cinema since 1979' in Tapper, R (ed.) *The New Iranian Cinema: Politics, Representation and Identity*. London: I.B.Tauris.

Lauzen, M (2008) 'The celluloid ceiling' (http://womenintvfilm.sdsu.edu/files/Celluloid%20Ceiling%202007%20Full%20Report.pdf (last accessed 25 May 2011)).

Makhmalbaf, H (2009) *Green Days*. Iran.

Mazra'eh, H (2001) *Fereshtehaye Sukhteh: Naqd Va Barrasi-i Sinemaye Tahmineh Milani*. Tehran: Nashre Varjavan.

Mehrju'i (1969) *The Cow*. Iran.

Milani, T (1998) *Two Women*. Iran.

Milani, T (2000) *Hidden Half*. Iran.

Mohammadi, Y (2002) 'bazkhaniye kalbod shekafi-ye majaraye ghate ekrane zendan zanan baraye sabt dar tarikhe sinema' (www.bamsin.com/?p=482 (last accessed 9 May 2011)).

Mollapur, D (1968) *Mrs Ahu's Husband*. Iran.

Mulvey, L (1999) 'Visual pleasure and narrative cinema' in Braudy, L and Cohen, M (eds) *Film Theory and Criticism: Introductory Readings*. New York: Oxford University Press: 833–44.

Naficy, H (2002) 'Islamizing film culture in Iran: A post-Khatami update' in Tapper, R (ed.) *The New Iranian Cinema: Politics, Representation and Identity*. London: I.B.Tauris.

Naghibi, K (2002) 'Goftegu ba manijeh hekmat: man bakhtam shayad yek dowre az omram ra!' *30nema* (http://mag.30nema.com/mag8106/810613-c.asp (last accessed 10 November 2002)).

Naghizadeh, H (2010) 'Sinema va hejab (1)' (www.hawzah.net/Hawzah/ Magazines/MagArt.aspx?LanguageID=1&id=76964&SearchText=% 22%D8%B2%D9%86%D8%AF%D8%A7%D9%86%20%D8%B2% D9%86%D8%A7%D9%86%22 (last accessed 10 May 2011)).

Nikpur, A and Hadisi, H (2002) 'Se dorehye tarikhe in joghrafia: episode chaharom ra man hanuz nadideham'. *Hayat-e No*, 6 September 2002: 8.

Nuri, A (ed.) (1996) Majmu'e-ye qavanin va moqarrarat-e vezarate farhang va ershad-e eslami va sazemanha-ye vabasteh. Tehran: *daftar-e hoquqi-ye vezarate farhang va ershad-e eslami*.

Omid, J (1998) *Tarikh-e sinema-ye Iran 1900–1978*. Tehran: Entesharat-e rowzaneh.

Riyahi, S (1956) *Marjan*. Iran.

Saidi, K (1979) *Mariam and Mani*. Iran.

Shoraka, A. (2002) 'Hameye zendanhaye zanan' in *Mahnameh-ye sinema'i-ye film*, 291:81.

Talebinejad, A. (1998) Dar hozur-e sinema: tarikh-e tahlili-ye sinema-ye ba'd az enqelab, Tehran: Farabi Cinema Foundation Publications.

Turner, V (1984) 'Liminality and the performance genre' in MacAloon, J (ed) *Rite, Drama, Festival, Spectacle*. Philadelphia: Institute of Study of Human Issues.

───── (1986) *The Anthropology of Performance*. New York: PAJ Publications.

───── (1990) 'Are there universals of performance in myth, ritual and drama?' in Schechner, R and Appel, W (eds) *By Means of Performance: Intercultural Studies of Theatre and Ritual*. Cambridge: Cambridge University Press.

Yasemi, S (1965) *Croesus' Treasure*. Iran.

Zeydabadi-Nejad, S (2010) *Politics of Iranian Cinema: Film and Society in the Islamic Republic*. Routledge, London.

PART III

MUSIC

CHAPTER 9

'I AM AN ORIGINAL IRANIAN MAN'
Identity and Expression in Tehran's Unofficial Rock Music

Bronwen Robertson

Tehran's unofficial rock musicians weave complex and exploratory narratives about themselves and the sociopolitical context they live in through their songs, giving listeners insight into their mainly secretive lives. This chapter brings together statements made by the musicians in interviews, excerpts from their lyrics and patterns observed during the year I conducted fieldwork in Tehran (July 2007–July 2008) to formulate a discussion about how notions of 'Iranian-ness' are conceptualised by Tehran's unofficial rock musicians through their compositions, recordings and performances.

The first section of this chapter describes the everyday life of a stereotypical unofficial musician before presenting an overview of the social, cultural and political contexts within which their music is consumed and produced in the Islamic Republic of Iran. I define what I mean by 'unofficial' music and provide a brief historical overview of rock music's contentious status in the Islamic Republic before examining two songs that experiment with thinking about identity. This chapter's title, the poignant opening line from the song 'Koskhol' [Crazy cunt] by Yellow Dogs, firmly establishes the main topics to be explored in this chapter: notions of authenticity and expressions of identity.

Who are Tehran's 'unofficial' rock musicians?

The following typecast is based on observations I made during 365 days (July 2007–July 2008) of participant-observation field research conducted

Figure 9.1 The Beatles watch over Zina (nickname) as he practices with his band Yellow Dogs in their tiny rehearsal studio; sheets of heavy cloth and tightly woven Persian rugs hang on the walls as soundproofing (photograph by author, Tehran, 2008).

in Tehran's unofficial music scene – 365 days, four seasons, and the harshest winter in 50 years. Tehran's unofficial rock musicians are typically male, aged 18 to 30, come from liberal democratic-minded middle to upper-middle class families and speak at least one foreign language. They have either graduated from university or are in the process of completing degrees with majors as diverse as pharmacology and philosophy. Those females who participate in the unofficial rock music scene tend to do so as photographers, graphic designers, filmmakers and writers but, where present as musicians, they are nearly always lead singers. All scene members are technologically literate and have a solid understanding of local and international politics, geography and culture. Due to the Iranian government's strict control over education, media and public life, most of their knowledge has been gained through autodidactic means. Iran's unofficial musicians spend hours on the internet skirting Iran's strict web censorship with proxies and anti-filters in order to be able to gain access to diverse information that may or may not contradict the ideology of the Islamic Republic.

The unofficial music scene constitutes a small minority of Tehran's vast population and its visibility within Iran is limited. It is easier for Tehran's unofficial rock musicians to promote their music to audiences outside Iran than to work within the country's rules and regulations in order to target audiences at home. Despite being financially able to travel, many research participants have not yet ventured outside Iran because after the age of 18 their right to leave the country becomes conditional on their completion of (or exemption from) Iran's mandatory military service. Importantly, due to social and economic pressures, most young unmarried Iranians still live at home with their parents. Crippling inflation, astronomic unemployment rates and firmly engrained social values make it difficult for single young men and women to live on their own.

Since the establishment of the Islamic Republic in 1979 much of social life has retreated into the private domain. The socialisation of unofficial rock musicians, who have been illegitimated by state stricture, continues to take place in the private sphere. In the words of one research participant: 'We have experienced every moment of happiness, love and fun in basements and behind closed doors, just like how our music making has always been secret' ('Obaash,' interview with the author, 11 November 2007). Behind these closed doors are hidden studios, gig rooms and practice spaces, and sometimes in the most unusual places. Tehran's innovative unofficial musicians have converted saunas, greenhouses and oversized storage cupboards into secret practice spaces (see figure 9.2). Musicians have instruments, basic recording equipment and internet connections in their bedrooms, the combination of which enables them to write, record, produce and distribute their own music without needing the mediation of official recording companies. What else do they need? A research participant told me on the way to their rehearsal space, 'In Iran you

Figure 9.2 Marcus, Mehran and Shervin (l-r) of the Audioflows practising in a disused sauna in Pasdaran, Tehran (photograph by author, Tehran, 2008).

need three things to be a proper band. First, you need band mates, then you need a practice space, and then you need a Myspace page' (Siavash, interview with the author, 1 January 2008).

The social, political and historical context of Tehran's 'unofficial' rock music

Whether or not music is acceptable in Islam is a longstanding and ongoing debate that has been examined by many scholars but Shiloah argues there is nothing in the Qur'an that concerns music explicitly (1995: 32).[1] After the 1979 Iranian revolution the new Islamic government cracked down on all art forms, and music suffered the most. Khomeini's desire was to eliminate any remaining residue of the Shah's cultural and social reform policies, anything that the Revolutionary Guard, the keepers of the morals of the Islamic Republic of Iran, labelled 'Westoxification' (*gharbzadegi*).[2] But perhaps the main reason for Khomeini's ban on music was because of its immense popularity, pervasiveness and persuasiveness. Khomeini was well aware of music's power because he had encouraged its use, albeit in the form of revolutionary anthems, to rally the support of Iranians from diverse socioeconomic backgrounds prior to the revolution (Daniel and Mahdi, 2006: 192). One politically-embittered young musician relished narrating the following joke for me during an extended focus group interview (Hossein, focus group interview, 9 July 2008, sarcastic inflection italicised):

> At the beginning of the Islamic Republic they [the new government] announced a total ban on music, but there was a song written for Khomeini's return, called 'Khomeini Ey Imam' that went [singing] 'Khomeini oh Imam, oh fighter, oh sign of honour, oh sacrificer of thine life for the purpose.' We were *all* forced to sing it in school. Then when he said 'music is a sin' and they banned everything to do with music, one famous composer said, 'so how are we supposed to sing 'Khomeini Ey Imam' then? With our farts?' But of course performing that song was ok, because *the government decided* that it *wasn't really a song.*

Hossein's last sentence, a sort of throwaway comment, is the most telling of the whole joke. Music is permissible in Iran as long as it is not deemed to be against the ideals of Islam. Khomeini's anthem mobilised a nation against the monarchy and contributed to the general cohesion of the movement that resulted in the shah's downfall. Khomeini knew music was powerful and when music is censored, the censor inadvertently acknowledges its importance and social significance (Kahn-Harris, 2003: 81). In the early years of the Islamic Republic, during a time when the religious authorities had not totally coordinated their new government, the censorship of music (and other cultural art forms that could potentially be used for anti-regime propaganda) made it easier for them to manipulate the Iranian people.[3] But after months of research, and still not convinced by the explanations academics and music researchers gave concerning the contested state of music in Islam, I decided to ask some of Iran's religious scholars, via their websites, a very specific question. My question was:

> I would like to know what your opinion about rock music (for example, with electric guitar, drums, bass and lyrics) is. What types of music are forbidden and what facets (for example, loud sound, heavy rhythm etc) make it so? How can I know whether a certain song is permissible or not?

Seeing their replies in my inbox surprised me as they responded quickly, even though at that time Iran was in social and political disarray following the 2009 presidential elections. Ayatollahs Ardebili, Gorgani, Sistani and Jannaati gave similar responses to the question and Ardebili's office scanned a handwritten note, stamped with the official emblem of his office, which they emailed to me on 25 August 2009. His reply read:

> Listening to any kind of music that is suited to gatherings for the purpose of amusement and having fun is not permitted and the criteria of this is judged by a religious expert who has been charged with the duty of performing this function.

These responses were all rewordings of Khomeini's decree concerning the perceived futility and intoxicating nature of music that was published in the book *Tahrir al-Vasila* (in Schirazi, 1997: 240).

Among the responses I received there was one remarkable, considerably liberal and very unexpected reply. It was from Ayatollah Saanei, a cleric favoured by young Iranians. Saanei has his own YouTube channel and is the feature of a documentary by Newsweek reporter Maziar Bahari.[4] Saanei's response to my question was, 'If the music is not anti-religious or satanic or futile, and if it is not for a mixed-gender gathering where there will be dancing, then it is not forbidden and there is no decree against it'.[5] While Saanei's religious decrees do prove popular among young Iranians, young reform-minded Iranians are wary of hoping for anything better than their current situation. One musician noted after reading Saanei's statement, 'It is good in principle but the statement's just too general. They can still beat the shit out of any musician just according to that statement' (Pouriya, personal communication, 14 August 2009).

In focus group interviews musicians depicted early post-revolutionary Iran as a fearful and murky place, a place where much of a musician's or music enthusiast's life was forcibly conducted in extreme secrecy. Being a musician in the 1980s and early 1990s was far more difficult than it is today. Musicians spoke of having their instruments confiscated at parties, being lashed by the authorities for possessing illegal cassette tapes, struggling to acquire good quality bootlegged cassettes and having Walkmans confiscated in the street. Many musicians told me their parents burned their entire LP collections out of fear of the new regime who, for a time, would go from door to door checking houses for illicit books, films and records. One young man described the tragic death of a friend who had tried to escape the police during a raid on a party. He was escaping across the neighbour's roof and crawled across a glass panel that shattered; he fell to the bottom floor ('Kamiar', interview with the author, 8 July 2008). But although the regime has stayed the same, Tehran has changed a lot over the last ten years. Cars circle main streets with their windows down and illicit music blaring, girls and boys socialise together in restaurants and cafes, and musicians download MP3s of the latest music with their broadband internet connections. One research participant said, 'Rock was always in Iran, it never got wiped out. Maybe it was in bedrooms for 15, 20 years, but it was always here' (Shervin, interview with the author, 10 July 2008).

Rock music may have always been in Iran but it is becoming increasingly visible. Today musicians carry their instruments, not only classical but rock instruments, proudly along Tehran's streets, an act that was unthinkable before the late 1990s. Shops all over the city, but concentrated mainly along Baharestan Avenue, sell the instruments and equipment necessary for making rock music. Electric guitars and drum kits feature proudly in their window displays. In 2009 on a visit to Tehran I was in a music store in Takht-e Tavoos where a middle-aged man was shredding Metallica riffs on a distorted guitar while a young woman was playing Schubert on an electric piano. Tehran is a city of contradictions and rock music is coming out from the 'underground'.

Underground v unofficial: a call for the renaming of the scene

Researchers and journalists usually call the music that emanates from Tehran's unofficial rock music scene 'underground' (*zir-e zamin*). 'Underground' is a universally recognised genre with associated connotations of rebellion and anarchism (Nooshin, 2005; Jecks, 2009). While much of Tehran's 'unofficial' music is quite literally performed underground, in converted basements and hidden alcoves, I believe that the term 'underground' unnecessarily overpoliticises the genre and that this overpoliticisation works strongly against these musicians who are struggling to gain acceptance and a public platform within Iran through which to disseminate their work. The musicians unanimously agreed in focus group interviews that 'unofficial' (*gheir-e rasmy*) or 'illegal' (*gheir-e ghanuny*) were better descriptors. They collectively agreed that the word 'underground' is more open to misinterpretation because of its strong history of use. The musicians whose songs have been analysed and interpreted within this chapter are not anarchists and they are not going against current trends (as Western underground musicians do). In fact, many of their acquaintances, including filmmakers, painters, writers and photographers, contribute to Iran's current and internationally acclaimed contemporary art movement. It is just that music, which has proved particularly problematic since the establishment of the Islamic Republic, has forcibly illegitimised them and their work.

But my argument that the word 'underground' overpoliticises unofficial rock should not detract from the political nature of what these young musicians are doing. However much they might like to be seen as apolitical, the context in which they are producing music has other ideas. In order to become an official recording artist or band in Iran there is a lengthy application procedure that can take months, even years, and seldom results in a wholly positive outcome. The official application process includes dozens of forms, which must be submitted along with a demo recording and a copy of the lyrics to the Ministry of Culture and Islamic Guidance's Council of Music and Council of Poetry respectively. The twist is that Iran's unofficial musicians do not have time to fill out the application forms, submit them to the Ministry and then wait months for a deliberation and probably rejection. Tehran's unofficial rock musicians cannot fathom enduring a process from which there is nothing to gain. They can, technically, write a song, record and distribute it on the same day.

Following Rodnitsky's lead and considering that the politics of music 'is a product of the politics of its context' (2006: 53) we can deduce that Tehran's unofficial rock music is intrinsically political. Performing rock music in Iran without a permit is to partake in an activity that is vetoed by the ruling powers, and to partake in such an activity, regardless of the content of the lyrics or the philosophies of the performers, is, logically, to be oppositionist. 'King Raam', the lead singer of the Iranian band Hypernova who are now resident and relatively successful musicians in New York, wrote in his 2007 online zirzamin.se article 'The art of selling out' that the traditional definition of 'underground music' dictates that a band must be difficult to access and found through unorganised networks that are 'less reliant upon commercial success'.[6] However, Tehran's unofficial musicians and bands are 'underground' only because the current Iranian government does not sanction their music. They are 'underground' because they have no public profile. King Raam concludes, 'I think that every 'underground' musician is *subconsciously defying the authorities*' (ibid, emphasis mine). Rock music's contested status in the Islamic Republic of Iran has forced its politicisation because music, even if it is lyrically apolitical, becomes politicised as it embodies the political tensions of its immediate sociopolitical surroundings. Performers at a private concert or party in Iran do not look upon the event as a means for rallying support to overthrow the regime; they perform to escape from the rigidity of their outside world and to explore alternate ways of existing in a society of suppression. And they perform to explore and discover themselves and to diversify their identities.

Who are the 'original' Iranian men?

The two songs to be interpreted in the final section of this chapter demonstrate how unofficial rock musicians use their songs to experiment with and question their identities. Each analysis begins with a brief biography of the musicians before analysing the lyrics and musical content of their songs. Although the characters and personalities in the bands studied below are diverse, they share a desire to be recognised as Iranian by their foreign audiences. The first, Yellow Dogs, sing in English and the second, 127, used to adamantly claim that they would never sing in Persian. Whether or not Iranian bands should sing in English is a longstanding debate (see Nooshin, 2007) that is not limited to academia. This debate has also permeated the unofficial music scene. 127 were adamant at the start of their careers that they would never sing in Persian, but they have since released an entire album of Persian-language songs. This raises some questions. What exactly *is* Iran for young Iranians? What makes a song recognisably Iranian? Musicians can use traditional Iranian instruments in their group and still 'sound' Western. But can the use of the Persian language alone make something Iranian? Are lyrics the sole conveyer of identity and intention? Is heavily derivative music, based on the premise that its lyrics are in Persian, any more 'Iranian' than raw and raucous indie rock, sugar-coated with English lyrics but peppered with allusions to contemporary social life in the upper-northern suburbs of Tehran?

Tehran's unofficial rock musicians placed a lot of emphasis on environmental inspiration in our focus group interviews about their music. Shervin said, '[Someone asked me] why everyone in Tehran plays rock. I guess it's just because Tehran is the kind of place that requires you to play rock music' (interview with the author, 10 July 2008). Arya argued, '[The environment that we live in] has a huge influence on our music ... We grew up with the traffic, the *Basij* [a large voluntary militia group under the direction of the IGRC, the Revolutionary Guard], and the pollution' (personal communication via email, 20 February 2009). Unofficial rock musicians do not represent a majority of the Iranian youth population. Research participants unanimously concurred in interviews that Tehran affects their work, but if Tehran demands rock music of its inhabits, then why does not everybody consume it? Ali summed it up most beautifully when he told me, '[Tehran] makes me, and therefore my music, a little angrier and more depressed. Although I must say there's no guarantee that if I was playing music in another country I'd be any happier' (personal communication via email, 2 February 2009). Ali expresses that living in Tehran affects his music in some way, but acknowledges that he has never experienced living anywhere else, so how could he know if things would have been different had he grown up in a different environment? Tehran's unofficial rock music scene encompasses many different types of people and many different styles of musical production and the main point of the following case studies is to introduce two different songs, written by two very different groups of people, all of whom are acquainted with each other in some way and take part in the same social scenes and circles.

Yellow Dogs

Yellow Dogs recently featured in Bahman Ghobadi's feature film *No-one Knows About Persian Cats* (Ghobadi, 2009). They were in Iran at the time I was conducting field research but have since emigrated to New York. At that time their lead singer 'Obaash' (nickname, 'rascal') was 19, a skateboarder who had competed twice in the annual Red Bull skate competition held in Tehran's Enqelab Sports Centre. He sported a large Afro hairstyle when I first met him but always wore a hat or headband when in public so as to not attract any unwanted attention from the authorities. It is not just females who must adhere to the dress code of the Islamic Republic of Iran.

Obaash and his band mates adopted younger teenagers, who whom they would call their 'sons' or their 'little brothers', into their well-established community and they would teach them how to skate board and to play rock music. Yellow Dogs practised nearly every afternoon in a purpose-built soundproofed and air-conditioned 3 × 2 metre studio tacked onto the roof of their drummer's apartment building. When the evening call to prayer rang out they were usually sitting out on the roof railings having a cigarette and watching the next-door neighbour tend to his carrier pigeons. Yellow Dogs performed two concerts in Iran, both underground (literally), in a basement that they converted with their 'brother' band, the Free Keys. They have a strong social network and the audience members were all personal friends of the bands who had been invited personally. These musicians and their peers are well connected. They use social networking sites like Facebook and Myspace, they attend English or French classes and read foreign news media because their own is so censored.

The title of their song is one of the rudest Persian swear words and in it the band appropriate anti-Iranian stereotypes in order to disprove them. The song, which opens with the line, 'I am an original man', poses a humorous challenge to stereotypical preconceptions of what an 'original Iranian man' is exactly.

'Koskhol' [Crazy cunt][7]

I am an original Iranian man
Every day I used to fuck nine camels maybe ten
There's oil in my veins
There's oil in my veins
My daddy was the pilot of an airplane
He had a crash with two towers on September 11
There's oil in my veins
There's oil in my veins
24 hours in each day
Half of it I fuck, half of it I pray
Suicide bomber, 'OUACHHH'
I joined the army the day I was born
Our leader said put it in the hole
20 million 'koskhol'
Hairy asses, bears and opidol
When the God is emperor it's under control
20 million 'koskhol'
Suicide bomber, 'OUACHHH'
Without my daughter, never! 'OUACHHH!'
Axis of evil! 'OUACHHH!'
Conflict, conflict with all the world, republic
Conflict, conflict with all the world, republic.

The stereotypes Yellow Dogs set out to disprove in this song are fairly apparent. They're the stereotypes that depict a typical Iranian as being a 'camel fucker', a terrorist who lives and breathes oil money, a suicide bomber who spends half of his day praying. Yellow Dogs and their friends are very aware of what the outside world thinks of them and they have set out to challenge these misconceptions. In the final verse, where Obaash sings 'without my daughter, never!', he proves just how aware his generation are by referring to Betty Mahmoody's controversial book (1989) that demonises Iranian men by sensationalising a story about her journey to Iran with her husband and daughter. Mahmoody depicts Iran as a backwards nation, where sheep are killed in the middle of the street, she is held captive by her husband, and her daughter no longer belongs to her. Turned into a Hollywood movie featuring Sally Field and used as compulsory reading in my high school at least, the book perpetuates a gloomy and extremely biased perspective of Iran. Obaash, echoing a sentiment that so many of my Iranian friends shared with me (personal communication via email, 7 February 2009), said:

> When I tell a foreigner that I'm Iranian there are a few things that inevitably come into their minds: The Persian Gulf, a vast and magnificent history, and now: terrorist, camel-herder, Muslim extremist, suicide bomber, flying carpets ... but those are misconceptions. Everywhere in the world has both good and bad people, and this anti-Iranian propaganda makes everyone around the world think badly about Iranians.

127

In the eight years 127 had been playing together they released three studio albums via their website. They were in Iran at the time I conducted field research but since that time two members have emigrated to the USA and another two remain in Iran. The Ministry of Intelligence has forced the remaining members to sign a decree stating they will have no further involvement with the group. While in Iran they practised in a converted greenhouse at the back of an apartment complex in the west of Tehran near the airport. The sound of aeroplanes and the surrounding highways provided good cover for their frequent rehearsals. Posters of their musical idols adorned the wall and with the band's six members crammed into the practice room there was not much room to breathe. The double doors and soundproofing made it a hot box, the electric fan cooled the unavoidable sweat that collected on the skin of anyone in the room. Their practice space was heated, as was their music and their history. The greenhouse had been raided before, and they were careful not to take too many people there at one time in case it was raided again. During one particularly bad month their equipment was stolen and they were summoned to the Ministry of Intelligence for questioning. Their latest album *Khal Punk* (2008) mixes Iranian modes and rhythms with Persian lyrics and their new style, which has elicited an array of both positive and negative responses from their audience, is a contemporary reworking of old Iranian folk music genres.

127's new music is clever because it sets socially relevant lyrics to *sheesh-o-hasht* (lit. six and eight), the cross-rhythmic and off-kilter 6/8 beat that pulses through every Iranian's veins, mixes in some *tombak*, a traditional Iranian drum, and adds this to a rock-inspired jazz ensemble. Their first two albums, recorded in English, sounded like odes to Bob Dylan and the band repeated adamantly that they would never sing in Persian because 'English is the language of rock music' (Nooshin, 2005: 483). 127's most recent album frames a distinct departure from this early mindset and it represents a current trend that is emerging for unofficial rock artists to sing in Persian. 127 even omitted English translations of the band name and album name on the first run of promotional material for the album, including the CD cover.

'Man kiyam' [Who am I?] is a through composition of an early twentieth century folk song by an unknown author. Sohrab, the band's singer and guitarist, asks in the song's chorus: 'who am I?' and, more importantly, 'what am I?' These philosophical questions seem to plague young Iranians more than they do young Westerners. During the year I spent in Tehran I witnessed many friends battling depression while struggling to plan their futures. When 127 performed on Valentine's Day, 2008, at the Brazilian Embassy in Tehran, they were drowned out by their audience during the chorus of this song. These words resonate with a generation of young Iranians whose opportunities are severely limited by a government that attempts to control every aspect of their everyday lives. Young Iranians have grown up knowing nothing else. They were born after the Islamic revolution and many of them have only experienced the outside world in a mediated form, through an internet connection or satellite dish. But what if things suddenly changed? The band's pianist Sardar mused (11 July 2008):

> If we suddenly had freedom here, freedom of expression, and could do exactly what we wanted, I don't even think I could be bothered doing something out of the ordinary... A few years ago I wanted it more. We're scarred now.

'Man kiyam'?[8]

Verse 1

Years, years, years
I have laboured years for an education in the arts
I've simmered away for so long that I've stuck to the bottom of the pot
I've had a small role and I've seen scenes
In theatre on ponds[9] and in auditoriums
Sometimes the role of Joseph, sometimes the role of Farhad[10]
I've worn the costumes of both sultans and shepherds upon the stage
I've directed, I've written stories
I've prompted, and for a time I was also a makeup artist[11]

Chorus

Who am I? What am I? Who is that? What is this?
Who am I? What am I? Who is that? What is this?

Verse 2

A time, a time, a time
For a time as a singer I searched the heart's desire
I've lamented and got it all off my chest
I have played jazz and tombak and sometimes I've set the rhythm
I've danced for anyone who played an instrument for me
I wandered aimlessly in search of many cities
I slept with the other actors upon the stage
I spent my whole life on this work
Sometimes smiling and sometimes crying from the pain I'd experienced

Chorus

Who am I? What am I? Who is that? What is this?
Who am I? What am I? Who is that? What is this?

Verse 3

Finally, finally, finally
Finally a distribution deal for an album blindsided me
So I went after that as well
Everyone walked over me and my flailing and rejection
I've heard so many insults; I've been offended so many times
Hey passionate wanderers, I'm not a clown

I've had to live with this for years
From the start my life has been uncertain, it'll be like that until the end
I've twisted around and around myself like a caterpillar for years
Oh gracious God,
Let the legs of anyone who works against us get stuck to this rug I'm sleeping on[12]
Because nobody knows how much effort we've expended
I'm removing myself from the focus of culture and the arts

Chorus

Who am I? What am I? Who is that? What is this?
Who am I? What am I? Who is that? What is this?

The first and second verses of this song describe the conundrum of Iran's young creatives. They expend so much energy on learning a craft that is censored by the state that they have little energy remaining to co-operate with state ideology. But in most of their daily lives they are unable to be their true selves. They juggle numerous different identities simultaneously. At university, in front of their parents, on the streets and with their friends they must be entirely different people. It is no wonder they struggle with questions such as 'Who am I? What am I? Who is that? What is this?' The third verse of 'Man kiyam' is wholly autobiographical. In the first two lines Sohrab describes applying to the Ministry of Culture and Islamic Guidance for permission to distribute their second album. The band's application was denied and they were left feeling disillusioned. He describes holding his head up in the face of adversity and reveals he knows this uncertainty is set to continue: 'From the start my life has been uncertain, it'll be like that until the end.' The fear of the unknown is something that plagued the young Iranians with whom I spoke. Gil, a brooding poet said: 'We don't know even what's going to happen in the next five minutes, so how can we plan for the next five years?' (Gil, interview with author, Tehran, 1 September 2006).

Conclusion

Although this chapter started by introducing the 'typical' characteristics of an unofficial rock musician I hope to have demonstrated the diversity and creativity of Tehran's unofficial rock musicians. The rigidity of the Islamic Republic has invariably politicised unofficial music although musically and lyrically it may be very apolitical. This is something that unofficial musicians struggle with. They do not necessarily want to instigate regime change with their songs and many of them just want to have a good time. Little by little unofficial music is becoming more visible and this is through its representation in feature films, online and by the Western news media. It is however far easier to access this music outside Iran than it is inside the country's geo-political boundaries. In a system where nobody is sure of what is acceptable at any given time, particularly when it comes to music and other art forms, fear of the unknown and uncertainty are very frustrating emotions. Tehran's unofficial rock musicians might feel that their environment requires them to play rock music, but they are in the minority. The two songs presented within this chapter demonstrate that Tehran's occupants experience the city very differently. They also reveal how Tehran's unofficial rock musicians are using their music to experiment with and question their identities. The goal that most of the unofficial musicians I spoke with shared was to leave Iran so that they could perform concerts and live freely as their true selves. Yellow Dogs and half of 127 have attained that goal but are realising that in order to be successful on the outside it is to their advantage to market themselves as 'original Iranian men' ... whatever that may be.

Notes

1 An introduction to this debate, which is beyond the remit of this chapter, can be found in Otterbeck, 2004, Shiloah, 1995, and Leaman, 2004: 118–120.
2 Jalal Al-e Ahmad (1923–69) coined the term *gharbzadegi*, variously translated as 'West struck', 'Westoxification' and 'occidentosis' in his 1962 critique of western influence on Iranian culture (translation printed 1984). The book was published and distributed clandestinely in Iran, because it criticised the shah's policies. Al-e Ahmad came from a clerical family and Khomeini embraced his message strongly.
3 Although pop music remained largely absent from the public domain for the first 20 years after the Islamic revolution, film, classical music and visual arts resurged in popularity and patronage.
4 See Bahari, M (2008) 'Witness Online Ayatollah', Al Jazeera English at www.youtube.com/watch?v=-BoP8aOamyY(last accessed 25 August 2009).
5 Ayatollah Saanei, email, 11 August 2009. Ayatollah Saanei's personal website is available online at www.saanei.net (last accessed 25 August 2009).
6 Zirzamin is a frequently updated online music magazine based in Sweden that has interviews with artists from a broad range of genres, reviews of albums, and other information about Iranian musicians both inside and outside Iran (see www.zirzamin.se).
7 © Yellow Dogs (2008).
8 © Sohrab Mohebbi (2008).

9   Traditional homes and Iranian palaces were built around a courtyard that would have a pond, *hoz*, as the centrepiece. For parties a floating stage would be erected upon the water and the actors would perform on this.
10 Farhad is a masculine proper noun that means 'elation' or 'happiness' in Persian. It is also the name of four kings in the Persian Empire, the name of Farhad Mehrad (1943–2002) a renowned Iranian singer/songwriter and the name of a legendary character who was besotted with Shirin, the wife of Khosro II.
11 Jafar Panahi, the director of the film *Offside*, which was perhaps Iran's answer to Bend it Like *Beckham*, was not only a makeup artist early in his career, but also acted in a well-known Iranian television drama called Sultans and *Shepherds* in which the main character, played by Panahi, enacted both roles.
12 In Iranian poetry the carpet is often used as a sign of wealth or, as it is used in this case, poverty. Dervishes and other worldly people with few possessions are often depicted in literature as sleeping on cheap, worn pile rugs, which are among their only possessions.

References

Al-e Ahmad, J (1984) *Occidentosis: A Plague from the West*. Berkeley: Mizan Press.
Daniel, E and Mahdi, A (2006) *Culture and Customs of Iran Westport*. Ct: Greenwood Publishing Group.
Ghobadi, B (2009) *No-one Knows About Persian Cats*. France: Wild Bunch.
Jecks, N (2009) 'Iran's underground pop gypsies'. *BBC* (http://news.bbc.co.uk/1/hi/world/middle_east/7912952.stm (last accessed 1 June 2009).
Kahn-Harris, K (2003) 'Death metal and the limits of musical expression' in Cloonan, M and Garofalo, R (ed) *Policing Pop*. Philadelphia: Temple University Press: 81–99.
'King Raam' (2007) 'The art of selling out'. *Zirzamin: the ultimate Iranian underground and alternative music magazine* (www.zirzamin.se/?q=node/75 (last accessed 27 March 2007)).
Leaman, O (2004) *Islamic Aesthetics: An Introduction*. Edinburgh: Edinburgh University Press.
Mahmoody, B (1989) *Not Without My Daughter*. London: Corgi.
Nooshin, L (2005) 'Underground, overground: rock music and youth discourses in Iran'. *Iranian Studies* 38(3): 463–94.
Nooshin, L (2007) 'The language of rock: Iranian youth, popular music, and national identity' in Semati, M *Media, Culture and Society in Iran: Living with Globalization and the Islamic State*. Abingdon: Routledge: 69–93.
Otterbeck, J (2004) 'Music as a useless activity: conservative interpretations of music in Islam' in Korpe, M (ed) *Shoot the Singer! Music Censorship Today*. London; New York: Zed Books: 11–16.

Rodnitsky, J (2006) 'The decline and rebirth of folk-protest music' in Peddie, I (ed) *The Resisting Muse: Popular Music and Social Protest*. England/USA: Ashgate: 17–29.

Schirazi, A (1997) *The Constitution of Iran: Politics and the State in the Islamic Republic*. London: I.B.Tauris.

Shiloah, A (1995) *Music in the World of Islam: A Socio-Cultural Study*. Aldershot: Scholar Press.

CHAPTER 10

NEITHER 'ISLAMIC' NOR A 'REPUBLIC'

Discourses in Music

Nahid Siamdoust

At the end of almost every Mohammad Reza Shajarian concert, a scene unfolds that goes something like this: Iran's most popular vocalist of Persian art music[1] intones the last notes of his performance – often in a crescendo – and finishes the show to ecstatic applause. But then – whether in Tehran, London or New York – the imploring audience soon calls out for him to sing the ritual *encore* 'Morgh-e Sahar' ['Bird of Dawn'], a song that urges the bird to summon its powers and finally break free from the cage and fill the air with tunes of freedom. Without much hesitation and with a subdued but pleased smile, Shajarian obliges. As he fills the song's verbal bodice with his familiar sad tenor he embodies the pained bird, dramatising in the limelight the epic struggle of a people. An enraptured audience eagerly accompanies the lyrics that call the powers of the universe to bring about the metaphorical dawn:

> Oh God, Oh Heavens, Oh Nature, turn our dark night into morning again!

'Bird of Dawn', a song originally written in the 1920s, has been rendered by various well-known artists since its inception, but Shajarian has turned its performance into a ritual of engagement, allowing for a discursive community where participants publicly express their desire for justice and freedom from tyranny. At a different end of the artistic spectrum, the *enfant terrible* of new Iranian music, Mohsen Namjoo, also engages in this song's reenactment through his contemporised rendition of it, a more uptempo fusion that is darker in its enunciation of the lyrics, accompanied by riffs on a rock guitar (performed by Kiosk front man

Arash Sobhani). Both Shajarian and Namjoo perform 'Bird of Dawn' as an expression of protest against the Islamic Republic, but Namjoo belongs to a newer generation of musicians whose musical critique undermines the government on a whole different level as well. While continuing the tradition of placing old songs within new signifying contexts and engaging in the discursive national forum mentioned above, Namjoo and his cohorts also sing more explicit songs that attack the Islamic credentials of the state and ridicule its figures of authority. In one song the rapper Bahram tells President Mahmoud Ahmadinejad that his Qur'an needs dusting; in another the rapper Hichkas wonders whether God himself may be susceptible to bribes; and in one of his newer songs Namjoo insults the manhood of the country's supreme leader, Ayatollah Ali Khamenei, by calling him God's favourite wife. In this way Shajarian and Namjoo exemplify the two different but complimentary streams of current critique of the Islamic Republic. Shajarian's classical songs like 'Bird of Dawn' criticise authoritarianism and repression, in part because their musical repertoire antedated the creation of the Islamic Republic. But newer post-revolutionary songs in musical genres like rap, rock or fusion – created by a generation that grew up in the Islamic Republic – attack not just the government's authoritarianism but also its religious credentials, accusing the Islamic Republic of not being 'truly Islamic'. Together, these two rhetorical strands – one criticising the repression and the other the hypocrisy of the religious regime – effectively combine to discursively discredit the Islamic Republic as being neither 'Islamic' nor a 'Republic'.

*

Music has played an important role in Iran's modern history both due to the frequent absence of a free public sphere, as well as the harsh retribution of dissenters. It has provided space for what James C Scott (1990) calls 'public and hidden transcripts' to be declared, undermined, or opposed, acting as a mnemonic of sorts, rekindling and sustaining political sentiments that dwell in the national psyche.[2] According to the music historian Ruhollah Khaleqi, music took on this function less than 100 years ago when a poet/singer by the name of Abol-Qasem Aref Qazvini (henceforth referred to as Aref) became the first to 'cloak criticism of his time's circumstances in the mantle of song and music and turned music into a publishing and advertising medium for his revolutionary beliefs and liberal opinions' (2002, 325).[3] Over the course of the first decade of the twentieth century, as Houchang Chehabi richly narrates, 'a type of metric song known as *tasnif* (sometimes translated as 'ballad') became a vehicle for mobilising the supporters of the constitutionalist cause' (1999, 144). By 1923, when an adolescent Khaleqi finally managed to attend one of Aref's highly popular concerts, Iran was again in a state of uncertainty following Reza Shah's 1921 *coup d'etat* of the Qajar government. Khaleqi recalls (2002, 322):

> At that time I still didn't fully grasp the real reasons behind the power of the song-maker. But I understood this much, that the majority of audience members had a hidden secret in their hearts, and without revealing it, when they would see others of the same mind, with one look alone, would share that secret. That same secret that wasn't expressed in front of strangers, but in burning hearts lit a luminous fire.

Hence, the public performance of some music – such as Aref's – had evolved into a medium and a forum through which people shared ideas and showed allegiance to certain political beliefs. This seems to have been unprecedented, as Aref remarks in his memoir: 'At the time when I started composing *tasnif* and made national and patriotic songs, people thought songs were meant to be made for the courtesans or 'Babri Khan', the cat of the martyred Shah [Naser al-Din Shah]' (Qazvini 1977, 331).[4]

The lyrics of many contemporary classical songs either hail from centuries ago or from the time of the constitutional revolution. Both because they are older and because they were written before the Islamic Republic, their critique is usually more allegorical and directed more generally at injustice and oppression. The poem 'Bird of Dawn', for example, stems from the 1920s, when the poet/educator/politician Malek o-Sho'ara Bahar[5] wrote it in an apparent criticism of Reza Shah's rising authoritarian measures.[6] Throughout the twentieth century, artists as varying in style as the pioneering female vocalist Qamar ol-Moluk Vaziri and the pre-revolutionary rock/folk singer Farhad Mehrad have sung their renditions of the 'Bird of Dawn', attesting to the song's appeal. But the song's arguably most popular version is Shajarian's cover, which he first performed publicly at his first concert tour in the USA in 1990, in commemoration of the song's composer Morteza Neydavud, who had just passed away. Shajarian performed this song a couple of years after the devastating Iran–Iraq war (1980–8) and following a dark decade of social restrictions and political repression. It soon turned into a celebrated yet subdued protest song, so that – as mentioned above – almost two decades later, Namjoo decided to give it his own interpretation following the controversial 2009 Iranian presidential elections.

For nearly 100 years then, the 'Bird of Dawn' has retained a particularly broad, timeless capacity for reflecting desires for a free Iran. The poet and scholar Mohammad Reza Shafi'i-Kadkani points out that 'talk of freedom' and the enunciation of this word 'in its meaning synonymous with Western democracy' starts with the constitutional era, and that it 'did not exist [in this context] before' (2001, 35). 'The poetry of the constitutional period is full of the word *freedom* in its new sense, but the best praises to this freedom are to be found in Bahar's work', Kadkani adds (*ibid.*). Set to Persian art music in the relatively upbeat *Mahur* scale with a swinging rhythm and a rolling crescendo as the song progresses and the bird builds up the resolve to break free, this song further enables participation as it is not only a known song but also – more broadly – as it is couched in this genre of music, with which most Iranians are at least acoustically familiar.

The creation of this politically conscious poetry early in the twentieth century developed along with a changing relationship of the poet to his social context, which 'seems to have been affected by the emergence of a cultural entity named Iran' (Karimi-Hakkak, 1995, 114). The role that these poets/singers had carved out for music continued. Throughout the current century political groupings have made strong use of poetry and song for their cause. The 1979 revolution itself was aided in no small part by songs – some of them inherited from the constitutional era – that inspired people by encouraging solidarity, calling 'brothers' to arms to avenge slain blood, conjuring up images of a just society, and declaring a new dawn to be within reach. Thirty years on, during the campaigns for Iran's 2009 presidential elections and in the ensuing unrest, music once again played a prominent role in giving form to the many sentiments that accompanied what is now called the Green Movement. Once again, many of those songs borrowed heavily from currents that had led to the country's two twentieth century revolutions. The repertoire and what Derrida refers to as its 'iterability' meaning the 'repeatability of certain textual fragments [...] and citation in its broadest sense', (Porter, 1986, 35) function as a reflecting pool of collective memories and allow for overlapping interpretations of the past and engagement in a national discourse.

Both the content and the form of these songs allowed for a benign, politically less risky way of partaking in these communities of protest. The most widely used segments of these songs are the more subtle and allegorical verses as opposed to the more overtly political ones. For instance, Aref's 'Hengam-e mey' ('Season of wine'), better known in common parlance as 'Az khun-e javanan laleh damideh' ('From the blood of youth tulips have sprouted'), was first written and performed at a time when hundreds of mostly young men were killed in their efforts to institute a constitution and establish Iran's first parliament. In the winter of 1978, Shajarian revived this lamenting slow-paced song with his grieving voice:

> From the blood of the motherland's youth, tulips
> Yes my dear, tulips, oh God, tulips, have sprouted
> From the cypress-sized sorrow, like a cypress my dear
> Oh god, like a cypress, the leaves are all bent too
> In the shadow of the rose the nightingale is hiding in grief
> [...]

Some of the song's less used verses are far more explicit in their political meaning:

> The lawyers are asleep, and the ministers are corrupt
> They have stolen all of Iran's silver and gold

And:

> If there is a man in you, now is the time for battle

Aref has taken typical tropes of Persian literature – the *gol o bolbol* (the rose and nightingale) – to signify loss and mourning, not for the lover but for a political struggle. Karimi-Hakkak brilliantly elucidates this appropriation of old poetic signifiers for use in a new semantic field at the time of Aref, and points to this important shift in the poetic voice: 'The poet's function is thus transformed into a demonstrably social one: guiding the collective memory of his community' (1995, 87). This *tasnif* became once again one of the most popular tunes leading up to the 1979 revolution, and tulips became the quintessential emblem for the martyr. Chehabi credits 'Az khun-e javanan' with being 'probably the main origin of the symbolic charge of the tulip in contemporary Iranian political culture' (1999, 152).

Another constitutional-era song, Bahar's 'Bird of Dawn' – as discussed earlier – calls for a 'new dawn' or, translated into political rhetoric, revolution:

> Bird of Dawn start wailing, refresh my anguish
> With your scintillating sighs break this cage and mess up everything
> Wing-tied nightingale emerge from the cage corner, sing of freedom of a human kind
> And with your breath fill the arena of this earth with rage

> The cruelty of the oppressor, the callousness of the hunter, have destroyed
> my nest
> Oh God, Oh Heavens, Oh Nature, turn our dark night into morning again!
> [...]

Here again, the poet has taken the traditional nightingale and woven it into the new, politically conscious poetic context. On one level, the metaphor of the caged bird – a possibly universal symbol of repression – heightens the song's emotional impact. Nightingale the lover, usually at home among beautiful roses, is wing-tied and resigned to a cage corner. On another level, the immediate following of the next verse, which urges the bird to sing of freedom of a *human* kind, also gives it a human kind of agency. 'Bird of Dawn' was already available on record in 1927 in two different renditions,[7] and had been sung by several other famous musicians.[8] Hence, 'Bird of Dawn' was already a famous song with various renditions when Shajarian decided to cover it. In a 2004 interview he explained why he uses old songs for his creations (Shajarian 2004, 79–80):

> That I reach back to the past sometimes is because I have no alternatives, meaning I don't have any music or song at my disposal that is appropriate for the conditions of the day. That's why I have to reconstruct old works. [...] Unfortunately we currently don't have artists like Aref [...], songwriters like Aref and Malek o-Sho'ara Bahar who could write songs like that for their own time.

In the tumultuous decade of the 1970s, music made its comeback to the political arena. Leftist political groupings were particularly skilled at making revolutionary songs, so much so that several of them were later appropriated by the Islamic Republic itself, such as 'Baharan Khojasteh Bad' ('May the Spring be August') and 'Qasam Be Esm-e Azadi' ('The Pledge in the Name of Freedom'), and later by Mir Hossein Mousavi's presidential campaign in 2009, such as Aftabkaran (Sun planters). One group that was instrumental to reviving the political *tasnif* at the time of the revolution was the Chavosh Culture and Arts Society, formed in 1978 by some of Iran's most accomplished young musicians, including Mohammad Reza Lotfi, Hossein Alizadeh, Parviz Meshkatian and Shajarian, who was the voice behind some of the most popular songs of the time. These musicians – all of whom worked for state radio – resigned *en masse* the day after what was later called Black Friday (8 September 1978), when the Shah's forces killed dozens if not hundreds of demonstrators[9] in Jaleh Square. They formed Chavosh and soon started creating political music out of Lotfi's basement. Lotfi, the main founding member thus describes the necessity of Chavosh and its creations (Ranjpur, 2008):

> When the revolution happened, I realised everyone was in the streets and an affectionate warmth and excitement was current everywhere. People were no longer interested in the music of that time, neither the pop music of that time nor any other music.

Considering the political nature and musical form of constitutional era *tasnifs*, it is no wonder that these virtuosos of classical Persian music reached back and revived that particular genre after several decades. Following Reza Shah's takeover in 1925, there had been a big rupture of some 50 years when the *tasnif* had been replaced by the *sorud*, a cross between a march and a hymn with nationalistic overtones. During Reza Shah's period of modernisation (1920s–1930s), the state promoted Western classical music while the Persian *radif*, an elaborate music system unique to Iran, was almost entirely neglected. Chehabi narrates this process and reckons that the, 'transition from the libertarian and patriotic *tasnif* to the nationalistic and monarchist *sorud* illustrated an authoritarian turn that Iranian politics took after World War I' (1999, 151).[10] By the same token, the comeback of the *tasnif* in the 1970s signaled a return to the political spirit of the constitutional era, along with the longing for cultural authenticity and independence away from the alienating Westernisation of the Pahlavi regime.

The musical form that carried these songs is widely referred to as *musiqi-ye asil-e* or *sonnati-ye Irani* (authentic/traditional Iranian music) in Persian, and is variously called Iranian classical, traditional or art music in English. In brief, this music is based on the Persian *radif* – a series of modal scales and tunes that must be memorised – and is recognized by many as a quintessential Iranian heritage that is beyond ideological or political reproach. Most political *tasnifs* of this kind are a combination of this music with poetic verse placed within a new signifying context. Hence, the nightingale and rose 'come to signify concepts on a plane distinct from the cultural spaces wherein they have been inscribed traditionally' (Karimi-Hakkak, 1995, 87) while defying government condemnation based on the usual charges of Westernisation and moral corruption. However, at the peak of political passion, some songs couched in this metaphorical language also entailed more explicit verse such as 'Tofangam ra bede' ('Give me my gun') in *Shabnavard*, where Shajarian calls his brothers to arms:

> It's night and the motherland's visage is black
> Sitting in blackness is a sin

> Give me my gun so I can get going
> Because every lover is underway
> Brother is agitated
> Brother is in flames
> The brother's heart is a valley of tulips
> [...][11]

Once the revolution succeeded and the new state was established, even Chavosh – whose creations had arguably aided the revolutionary movement that brought the Islamic Republic to power – got caught up in the new regime's conflicted stance toward music and suffered from a lack of government support. Today, Islamic Republic officials acknowledge the impact of Chavosh. Babak Rezayi, the executive director of the governmental Fajr Music Festival, remarked in early 2009, 'Music had a great role in the victory of the revolution. The Chavosh songs reflected the people's feelings about the revolution' (Broughton, 2009). Still, the religious government's uneasy relationship with music was soon revealed and, at first, even Persian art music was not going to be an exception. Revolutionary leader Ayatollah Ruhollah Khomeini set the tone already in the summer of 1979 (*Ettela'at*,1979):

> [...] One of the things that intoxicates the brains of our youth is music. [...] There is no difference between music and opium. Opium brings a sort of apathy and numbness and so does music. If you want your country to be independent, from now on you must transform radio and television into educational instruments – eliminate music.

In spite of government neglect, a few artists such as Shajarian and Shahram Nazeri were able to continue creating their music, although it would be another decade before public concerts were allowed. Ironically, while other kinds of music such as pop and rock were banned and many pre-revolutionary stars emigrated, the majority of *Chavosh* artists – who happened to have produced some of the most political songs of their era – remained inside Iran and continued their work. Already in 1995, Shajarian wrote a letter to Ali Larijani, then director of the Islamic Republic of Iran Broadcasting (IRIB, Iran's state radio and television), to forbid them from airing his music, and when the IRIB frequently aired his song 'Sepideh' ('Dawn') – a proud patriotic song that bestowed the epithet 'house of hope' (*Saray-e Omid*) on Iran – at the time of the 2009 elections, Shajarian angrily forbade the government from playing his songs altogether.[12] In a telephone interview with the BBC Persian TV on 18 June 2009, an audibly disturbed Shajarian complained:

> Every time I hear my own voice in these media, my body shakes and I feel shame [...] These songs that I sang in the years 1979 and 1980 were for the uprising that people achieved then, it was for that movement, but now I see that they are making a mockery of these songs in my face and others like me and the face of people who I sang these songs for. That's why I no longer allow them to broadcast these songs because they have no right over my songs and my voice.

Thirty years after the revolution, at the height of the anti-government protests in Iran, it was once again Shajarian's work that best embodied the sentiment of the new movement of dissent. Despite a flurry of new songs by younger musicians, Shajarian's 'Zaban-e Atash' ('The Language of Fire') was one of the most popular at the time.[13] Iranian audiences across Europe entreated him to sing this new song in his Autumn 2009 tour of the continent. This *tasnif* is based on contemporary poet Fereydun Moshiri's verse by the same name, and directly addresses the perpetrators of violence:

> Lay down your gun
> As I am disgusted by the sight of this abnormal blood shedding
> That gun in your hand means the language of fire and metal
> But I, in front of that evil instrument of destruction
> Have nothing but words of the heart, a heart brimming with love for you
> For you, an enemy friend.
> [...]

In part due to his own legacy and in part due to the internet and satellite television, an artist like Shajarian enjoys such wide popularity that he is no longer able to continue his craft without getting either political, politicised, or both. His prominent position has angered pro-regime *apparatchiks* who have attacked him viciously in their press. In various outlets such as *Kayhan* newspaper and *Fars News Agency*, Shajarian has been reminded that he owes his 'fame, wealth and artistic position' to the Islamic Republic, accused of being a non-believer and a traitor, 'a peddler singer' who in old age is selling himself to America, and addressed in terms that an art music vocalist like Shajarian would find insulting, such as *motreb* (entertainer) as opposed to *ostad* (master). In 2010, all state radio and television channels stopped broadcasting his rendition of the pre-*iftar Rabena* prayer, which had been broadcast since 1979 and had for fasting households become as much a part of Ramadan as *iftar* itself. State media no longer broadcast his work, but his immense popularity shields him from serious harm. He continues to live in Tehran and in the summer of 2011 even received a permit from the Ministry of Culture and Islamic Guidance for his new album *Morgh-e Khoshkhan* [*Songbird*].

*

While Chavosh and Shajarian did much to revive the political *tasnif* of the constitutional period, the new state's stance on music and the devastating years of the Iran–Iraq war put an end to the protest song. In the first years of the war when thousands of young men were dying on the frontlines, the only music state television would broadcast were marches, patriotic hymns and songs (Youssefzadeh, 2000, 57), as well as religious songs and chants. Sadeq Ahangaran's lamenting voice chanting of heroism and martyrdom came to embody those years more than any other. His 'Ey Lashgar-e Saheb-Zaman, Amade Bash!' ('Army of the Savior of Times, Get Ready!') tells of soldiers tying red martyrdom bands around their foreheads, readying their firearms, tying shoelaces 'fast like male lions,' giving each other's cheeks 'last kisses' and heading to Karbala, where Imam Hussein was martyred, invoking their readiness to die. Much of the authorised discourse's essential themes were already visible in the early days of the Islamic Republic: Islam, Karbala, war, martyrdom, sacrifice, and defence of *namus*.[14]

With the election of the more liberal President Mohammad Khatami in 1997, the government eased restrictions on the cultural sphere – including music – and the possibility for an authentic music scene once again emerged. In her article about underground rock music in Iran, Laudan Nooshin says this space allowed for 'a grassroots popular music for the first time in Iran since 1979' (2005, 463). Young Iranians looking for musical role models outside religious, traditional or the recently budding state-sanctioned pop music had to look beyond Iran's borders because government bans on other forms of music had led to the absence of a homegrown, non state-sponsored musical vocabulary. Rock and fusion bands mushroomed around Tehran, with the pioneering rock band O-Hum's first public concert in the capital's Russian Orthodox Church early in 1999 marking a watershed moment.[15] Another big sensation to break into the Iranian 'underground' music scene was Mohsen Namjoo in 2006 with his melancholic yet angry 'Zolf bar bad madeh' ('Don't Give your Tresses to the Wind'), Hafez poetry rendered in an unusual musical style, part contemporised Persian *avaz* (classical vocals), part sarcastic declamation and part folk. For Namjoo, who was trained in the vocals of the *radif*, but 'felt a great urge to break free from the patterns of traditional music' (personal interview, 2 October 2009), the biggest concern was to 'initiate dialogue with the music of the West' (Naseri, 2007). But Namjoo also has a burning political tongue that does not confine itself to Iran's tradition of allegorical poetry. Having come of age during the most repressive years of an Islamic government, the language of '*gol o bolbol*' no longer sufficed. His critique explicitly targets religious sanctities, even when he makes use of Hafez poetry, such as in 'Yek cheshmi o sad nam' ('An Eye and One Hundred Tears'):

> Of ascetics... we've repented ourselves
> Of pious deeds also... God forbid!
> They have fooled us, those slyboots
> Those ignorant seniors, those lost sheikhs

The lyrics to this song are beyond transgressive or subversive; they openly reject the leadership of what is, within the song, presented as a horde of corrupt, greedy old men. Since the Islamic Republic claims to derive its authority in great part from religious as well as popular legitimacy, the most powerful way to debunk that claim to legitimacy is by exposing religious authorities as neither religious nor popular. Namjoo admitted in a personal interview (2009, Treviso, Italy) that he was fully aware of the poem's current-day relevance when he selected it. What seems culturally and politically most irreverent is Namjoo's usage of Qur'anic phrases that the Islamic Republic promotes in its religiously saturated rhetoric. Namjoo takes those expressions and, in combination with his portrayal of religious men as crooks, turns them upside down. These phrases, overused by the regime and those who want to demonstrate allegiance to it, are presented as a smoke screen of holiness to an effectively morally rotten essence, hollow of meaning. Namjoo's prominent and wolf-like howl of the phrase *al-hamd-ul-allah* calls into question not only the hypocrite but also the concept of the God that such men adhere to. However, the piece that finally turned Namjoo into a *persona non grata* in Iran[16] was a song in which he sings verses from the Qur'an in an unusual and almost mocking manner interspersed with a rhythmic 'ooh ooh ooh'. It emerged on the internet after his emigration from Iran in 2008, and led to him being sentenced in absentia to five years' imprisonment. The impact went beyond Iran's borders though. In early 2011, he had to cancel a concert in Kuala Lumpur – where a large number of Iranian expatriates reside – because Malaysian authorities denied him a visa due to his Qur'an song.

On a different front, Iranian rappers have been leading the way in creating socially and politically critical lyrics. With his song 'Qanun' ('Law'), the rapper Hichkas (Nobody) highlights the injustices and corruption of a society in which the law means nothing, and where it seems as though even God may be susceptible to bribes:

> Here the bottom is asphalt
> It's a post where even the constitution can be trampled upon
> [...]
> The child's soul isn't black when he's born
> I'm that same child but the child within has perished
> I'm innocent and God's my witness
> Or do you think it's possible someone will bribe God too?
> [...]

Hichkas describes a world of total moral depravity in which even the highest sanctity, the ultimate arbiter of justice, may be susceptible to corruption. In the last three years younger rappers have appeared who have been even more forthright in their direct critique of power and of the government. In early 2008, Bahram's song 'Nameh-i be rais jomhur' ('A Letter to the President') hit the underground rap scene and was soon widely distributed. He put his finger on the pulse of sentiments at a time when President Mahmoud Ahmadinejad's populist promises of economic justice and national pride seemed like mockery in the face of people's worsening economic circumstances:

> I never imagined things would turn into this
> That we'd have millions of youth who run away from religion
> [...]
> People go to the mosque, but to steal shoes
> By God, this much pretense deserves mockery
> Iran exports 18-year old girls
> You sit on the floor and think you're the pinnacle
> [...]
> By God, the Qur'an on your shelf needs dusting
> It's only empty slogans that you're after

Other young musicians have expressed similar critique. In her song 'Nakonim ab ra gel' ('Let's not Muddy the Water'), female rapper Kalameh [*Word*] equates the current regime to 'Cain, Goliath, Pharaoh and Yazid', evil rulers that the Islamic Republic itself decries as the height of corruption and immorality. Her song starts with female cries of *Allah-o Akbar*, (God is great!) reminiscent of the rooftop protest at the time of the revolution and again following the June elections, thus drawing a line from 1979 to 2009.

Although the internet had already offered a space where non-sanctioned musicians were able to distribute their oftentimes critical music, it was again at the time of Iran's recent presidential elections in June 2009 that music took on the important role it had slowly carved out for itself over a century. There was a burst of musical activity outside of the official realm. On YouTube, a dozen or so old revolutionary songs[17] were adapted to those days' political context, forming the soundtrack to video footage of street protests and state violence. At the same time, a number of new songs were created in sympathy with the Green Movement. The lyrics of the new songs were either based on modern Persian poetry or were newly written, referencing the recent events, highlighting in particular the names of the new victims, or 'martyrs' (*shahid*), and appropriating the state's Islamic rhetoric and thus contesting the state's use of the same terminology. The names of those killed in the protests were the subject of several songs, especially Neda, the name of the young woman whose tragic death was vividly captured on a cell phone video. One song that was widely shared was 'Neday-e Sohrab' ('Sohrab's Message', a word play that joins the names of the two most prominent protest victims) by Mazdasht Gerami (alias), who is said to be residing in Iran:

> News came that winter was leaving
> Silence was fleeing the dark city
> Look how toward this land's freedom[18]
> The most beautiful flowers are dying
> [...]
> News came that Neda is rolling in blood
> So she won't let freedom perish easily
> [...]
> News came that Sohrab's heart became blood
> And Taraneh was burned by the hand of injustice
> Rain, oh heavens, on this dark night
> When they shower lovers with bullets

Using the designation 'martyr' for these young people was a subversive move on par with shouting *Allah-o Akbar* from the rooftops at night. When young and old climbed rooftops to shout 'God is great!', they engaged in an act that was symbolically important on three levels. Firstly, they connected their action to actions taken 30 years earlier, thereby implying that the revolution's goals had not been reached and that the people were still seeking freedom and independence. Secondly, they were claiming back Islam for themselves, away from the monopoly of the state. Finally, they were calling for the help of God, the highest power, and hence differentiating their spiritual and religious beliefs from those of a self-righteous Islamic government.

Conclusion

Thirty years into the Islamic Republic, the state that benefitted at its inception from the works of the likes of Shajarian suffers from a poverty of credible, popular musical creations. Following the June 2009 protests, it was again Shajarian's work that most widely reflected popular sentiment, championing the cause of non-violence and humanism. While Shajarian's classical work still allows the most benign form of political alignment and dissent, younger and more brazen artists have composed a number of songs over the past few years, a great many of which tend towards open protest. Whereas older revolutionary songs are concerned with decrying injustice and calling for political freedom, post-revolutionary songs by younger artists are also concerned with condemning religious hypocrisy. There are a few clear trends in the newer songs. They rely less on Islamic lingo and symbolism and more on humanistic values. When Islamic signifiers are used, they are appropriated in contradistinction to the religious state and outside of the government-sanctioned realm to imply that Islam is on the side of the unjustly oppressed – in this case the Iranian people. Together, old and new *tasnifs* as well as newer songs by the young generation of Iranian musicians combine to insinuate that the people's democratic demands remain unrequited. Through the main message of these songs, which charge that the Islamic Republic is neither Islamic nor popular, the state is discursively stripped not only of its legitimacy, but also of its name.

Notes

1 I refer to *musiqi-ye asil-e* or *sonnati-ye Irani* variably as Persian art and Persian classical music.
2 James C Scott terms that which is sanctioned by the dominant authority as the 'public transcript,' and 'hidden transcript' that which represents a 'critique of power' (1990, xii).
3 All translations from Persian are my own unless otherwise noted. The volume I have cited here was first published in its current form in 2002, but the original text was published in 1955.

4   Aref became very popular for imbuing songs with sociopolitical meaning and he crafted some of the most enduring songs, a few of which resurfaced during the Iranian revolution of 1979 and again in 2009.
5   The poet's actual name was Mohammad-Taqi Bahar. He inherited the honorific title 'Malek o-Sho'ara' from his father Mohammad Kazem Sabouri, who was a court poet laureate.
6   The year of the poem's creation is not known, but it first appeared in print in the 7th anniversary edition of the magazine 'Nahid' in 1927 without attribution to its creator (Parvin, 2007). Throughout his life, Bahar was incarcerated or internally exiled several times due to the critical nature of his writing, and banned from publishing a collection of his poetry. Mohammad Ali Sepanlu comments on the dual nature of this poet's writing whereby he would publish seemingly neutral verse under his own name and critical ones anonymously (1995, 11). At the 'Nahid' anniversary celebration, a singer by the name of Iran o-Dowleh performed this *tasnif* (Parvin, 2007, 174).
7   They were by the female singers Iran o-Dowleh and Moluk Zarabī (Sepanta, 1998, 222).
8   Nader Golchin, Hengameh Akhavan, Farhad Mehrad.
9   The numbers are contested.
10 Ironically, the officially sanctioned genre *sorud* of the first Pahlavi era was used heavily again as a blanket term for a whole variety of kinds of songs in the first decade of musically strict Islamic Republic officialdom due to the term's tame connotations.
11 Most agree that this song was written by Aslan Aslanian in remembrance of the Marxist Fedayeen activist Amir Parviz Pooyan. See http://zohrehyaddashtha.blogspot.com/2009/02/blog-post_1754.html.
12 He made an exception for his 'Rabena' (Arabic, 'our God') a prayer broadcast right before the break of the Ramadan fast, *iftar*. In 1979, when Shajarian was training *qaris* (Qur'an reciters) at state radio, he sang his famous 'Rabena' as a demonstration to the students, which was not meant for recording or broadcast. But then state radio decided Shajarian's demonstration 'Rabena' was better than all other recordings and started airing it, along with state television, at the time of *iftar*. For 16 years, it was not even public knowledge that the voice behind this national 'Rabena' was Shajarian's. While banning IRIB from broadcasting his music, he specifically excluded 'Rabena' as he believes it to belong to the people (personal interview, 10 October 2010, Tehran).
13 Personal observation; I was in Iran at the time. In addition, there are more than 200,000 YouTube viewings on the different uploads of the song: see for example: www.youtube.com/watch?v=64PPDrnJ7BA (last accessed 23 August 2011).
14 *Namus* translates into honour, and is a gendered cultural umbrella term that covers all the 'honours' a man must protect, such as his homeland and family. *Namus* is something that men possess and must protect, while women *are* the *namus* belonging to their male family members.

15 Those 300 or so lucky to attend witnessed not just a fusion of an unprecedented kind, Hafez poetry sung unconventionally to a fusion of Persian and rock music, but also raucous head banging in the audience (personal interviews). However, as Nooshin explains, although most rock music lyrics were quite innocuous, 'rock is problematic as much because of what it represents as a genre as because of the specific sounds and lyrics musicians use' (2005, 478).
16 After all, his first album was published by none else than the artistic branch of the Islamic Propaganda Organisation, Hozeh Honari, which is overseen by the supreme leader himself.
17 The most well-known were *Az khun-e javanan laleh damideh* ("From the blood of youth, tulips have sprouted"), *Baharan khojaste bad* (May the spring be august!), and *Qasam be esme azadi* (Pledge in the name of freedom).
18 Freedom (*azadi*) is both the word for 'freedom' as well as the name of the square where the largest post-election demonstration of 2–3 million people happened on 15 June 2009.

References

Aref Qazvini, Abol-Qasem (1977) *Kolliyat-e Divan-e Mirza Abol-Qasem Aref Qazvini*. Tehran: Amir Kabir.

Broughton, S (2009) 'Something inside so strong'. *The Guardian*, 16 January, 10.

Chehabi, HE (1999) 'From Revolutionary Tasnif to Patriotic Surud: Music and Nation-Building in Pre-World War II Iran'. *Iran* 37: 143–54.

Karimi-Hakkak, A (1995) *Recasting Persian poetry: Scenarios of Poetic Modernity in Iran*. Salt Lake City: University of Utah Press.

Khaleqi, R (2002) *Sargozasht-e Musiqiy-e Iran (Seh jeld dar yek jeld)*. Tehran: Moassesseh-ye Farhangi-Honari-ye Mahur. Original edition, 1954.

Naseri, M (2007) '*Mohsen Namjoo: Muzik dar tadabir-e shadid-e amniyati*' Radio Zamaneh, 14 September (last accessed 3 May 2010) www.radiozamaneh.info/music/2007/02/post_120.html.

Nooshin, L (2005) 'Underground, overground: Rock music and youth discourses in Iran'. *Iranian Studies* 38(3): 463–94.

Parvin, N (2007) '*Sher-e Morgh-e Sahar*' Bokhara: Majjaleh-ye Farhangi va Honari 55: 171–6.

Porter, JE (1986) 'Intertextuality and the discourse community'. *Rhetoric Review* 5(1): 34–47.

Ranjpur, A (2008) '*Ma hamisheh amade-ye taghyirim: Goftegu ba Mohammad Reza Lotfi*'. *Etemad*, 7 December, p. 9.

Scott, JC (1990) *Domination and the Arts of Resistance: Hidden Transcripts*. xviii, 251 p.; 25 cm. ed. New Haven, CT; London: Yale University Press.

Sepanlu, M (1995) *Shahr-e sher-e Bahar: zendegi va behtarin ashar-e Malek o-Shoara Bahar.* Chap-e 1. Tehran: Elmi.

Sepanta, S (1998) *Tarikh-e tahavvol-e zabt-e musiqi dar Iran.* Tehran: Mahur.

Shafii-Kadkani, MR (2001) *Advar-e Sher-e Farsi.* Chap-e 3. Tehran: Sokhan. .

Shajarian, MR (2004a) *Latifeh-ye Nahani: Gozideh-ye goft-o-guha va goftarha-ye Ostad Mohammad Reza Shajarian va naqd va nazarhayi darbareh-ye u va asarash.* Edited by Z. Habibnejad. Tehran: Moassesseh-ye Farhangi-Honari-ye Māhur.

Youssefzadeh, A (2000) 'The situation of music in Iran since the Revolution: The role of official organizations.' *Ethnomusicology Forum* 9(2): 35–61.

PART IV

REPRESENTATION

CHAPTER 11

DIGITAL HEROES

Identity Construction in Iranian Video Games

Vít Šisler

An Iranian teenager deciding which game to buy in one of Tehran's ubiquitous game shops is no longer limited to *Bioshock*, *Oblivion* or *The Sims*. Games of US or European origin are increasingly subject to competition from Iranian domestic producers. This production ranges from governmental games developed in accordance with the official communications policy of the Islamic state to independent games produced by various private entrepreneurs, the latter of whom encompass multi-faceted cultural and historical backgrounds. Therefore, the above-mentioned teenager can choose whether he or she will spend hours of virtual game play as Mohamad Marzoghi, an elite member of the Lebanese Hezbollah commando, sneaking through an Israeli military base on a mission to rescue a kidnapped Iranian scientist in the game *Resistance* (Tebyan, 2008b); be a member of the *Pasdaran* (Revolutionary Guards) attacking and finally subduing Iraqi forces in the fierce battle of the Fao Peninsula in 1986 in the game *Valfajr 8* (Tebyan, 2007); or be Garshasp, an ancient Persian hero saving the world from the army of darkness in the game *Garshasp* (Fanafzar, 2011), which is based on Persian mythology. All of these characters can become the player's virtual identity, one of many possible McLuhanesque 'extensions' of his or her body (McLuhan, 1964).

Video games constitute a form of mainstream media for Iranian youth and they have become a popular leisure time activity. Unlike other audiovisual media, video games immerse consumers in action and engagement, rather than inaction and passive reception. At the same time, they provide youngsters with a convenient source of cultural symbols, myths and rituals, all of which help them to form their own identities. The question of identity construction is thus central to video games, since they enable a risk-free and socially acceptable way of engaging in virtual role play (Murphy, 2004: 224). Besides personal computers at homes, the so-called 'game nets' facilitate access to the latest products of the gaming industry to a younger generation. Until recently, games of European, US and, to a lesser extent, Japanese origin have almost exclusively dominated the Iranian market. As Sreberny and Khiabany (2010: 24) note, US embargoes prohibit many software companies from doing legitimate business in Iran. This factor contributes to widespread software piracy in the country, which is helped by the fact that Iran is not a signatory to international copyright conventions. Thus, a typical US or European game can be bought for $2–5 in most Iranian cities. Moreover, these games usually appear on the local market soon after their release in the USA or Europe, if not even sooner.

Unsurprisingly, the Iranian authorities are concerned about the negative influence of Western games on Iranian youth. Some games have even been banned, usually due to their explicit display of sexuality or violence, like in *Grand Theft Auto: San Andreas* (Rockstar Games, Inc., 2005). Others, like *Call of Duty 4* (Infinity Ward, Inc., 2007), have been criticised for misrepresenting Islam. Alongside this censorship, the Iranian authorities strive to provide young audiences with alternative domestic production. Therefore, the government approved the establishment of the National Foundation of Computer Games (NFCG) in Tehran under the supervision of the Ministry of Cultural and Islamic Guidance in 2006.[1] The aim of this foundation is twofold: first, to boost economic growth in the video game industry; and, second, to subsidise the development of games in Iran, ie those conceived in accordance with Iranian and Islamic values. The foundation particularly focuses on 'the indication, improvement and promotion of cultural bases and Iranian-Islamic identity by this industry with a special attention to the children and adolescent' (NFCG, 2011). Consequently, a variety of independent producers have become involved in this emerging industry.

This chapter analyses contemporary Iranian video games and explores how they communicate different concepts of identity to players in multiple ways. It is based on content analyses of more than 20 games developed in Iran between 2005 and 2011 and interviews with major Iranian game producers. Substantive portions of the materials reviewed in this chapter were gathered during a fieldwork trip to Tehran in 2008 and many of the games that were then in production were obtained for analysis later on. The interviews were made in Persian and/or English in November 2008.

Essentially, this chapter argues that while the Iranian government perceives games as a new semiotic language for youth and therefore utilises them to promote Islamic values and foster national pride, many independent or semi-independent producers manoeuvre within and around the state's interests, presenting instead their own, oftentimes quite different, concepts of identity. Therefore, contemporary Iranian games encompass a broad variety of topics, ranging from the Islamic revolution (1979) through to popular soap operas and ancient Persian mythology. The resulting concepts of identity are achieved through sensitive negotiations between the demands, funding and restrictions of the Islamic state and the visions and engagement of private entrepreneurs. Nevertheless, this chapter demonstrates that, despite varying ideological backgrounds, independent and state-directed producers both share a common belief: that Iran and Iranians are misrepresented by global video game production and they should strive to present unique and relatable Iranian heroes to their audiences.

Paradoxically, the establishment of the NFCG and the support it provides resulted both in the production of games directly asserting the official concept of Iranian Muslim identity, as well as games whose particular elements directly challenge this identity. The Ministry of Culture and Islamic Guidance often remove controversial elements from games during the pre-approval process. In other words, video game production in Iran is, similar to other digital environments, subject to friction and competition between factions within the regime, the institutional interests of various agencies, and the tensions between the state and the private sector. Therefore, beyond analysing the different concepts of identity as constructed and communicated to the players by Iranian video games, this chapter aims to provide case studies enhancing our understanding of the contentious nature of cultural politics in Iran, particularly related to the youth culture, Western cultural production, and the emerging Iranian digital entertainment industry.

Procedural rhetoric: Video games as media

Unlike film or other audiovisual media, video games are interactive. Thus any content analysis has to cover three intertwined levels: audiovisual signifiers, narrative structure and game play, which stems from the system of rules governing the players' interaction with the game. On all three levels cultural, social, or even politically relevant messages can be communicated to the players. The hidden system of rules governing game play is particularly important, because it shapes and limits the choices and decisions player can make in the game.

In this respect, Bogost (2007: ix) argues that games open up a new domain of persuasion. He calls this new form 'procedural rhetoric', the art of persuasion through rule-based representations and interactions rather than the spoken word, images, or moving pictures. Bogost suggests that in addition to becoming instrumental tools for institutional goals, video games can also disrupt and change fundamental attitudes and beliefs about the world, leading to potentially significant, long-term, social change. According to him, this power is not equivalent to the content of games, but rather to their above-mentioned ability to put forward arguments through procedural rhetoric. Thus, 'all kinds of video games, from mass-market commercial products to obscure art objects, possess the power to mount equally meaningful expression' (Bogost, 2007: x).

To give a particular example of what is meant by procedural rhetoric, I will briefly mention the two, probably most prominent, examples of 'persuasive' games in existence today, *America's Army* (US Army, 2002) and *Special Force* (Solution, 2003). The former is a US army, next-gen public relations and recruitment tool and the latter is a promotional game of the Lebanese Hezbollah Movement. Both games have been consciously conceived as persuasive and both utilise the procedural rhetoric of a first-person shooter game in a very similar way, albeit to different ends. The former stresses the courage, professionalism and high moral profile of US soldiers (Nieborg, 2006) whereas the latter emphasises resistance, martyrdom and Hezbollah fighters' obligation to a higher spiritual whole (Sisler, 2008).

Another game successfully using procedural rhetoric in the political domain is *Assault on Iran* (Kuma, LLC, 2005). It is part of the so-called Kuma\War series, which are downloadable for free. These first-person shooter games are based on real US army campaigns, mainly from the wars in Iraq and Afghanistan, and advertised as 'playable recreations of real events in the War on Terror' (Kuma\War, n.d.). Yet, *Assault on Iran*, the first fictitious game in the series, anticipates the US's potential further engagement. It features Iranian soldiers as enemies in a story depicting US special commandos who are sent to Iran to terminate its nuclear programme.

The game triggered some harsh criticism from the Iranian side as well as condemnations from Iranians living in diaspora (Ransom-Wiley, 2005). Moreover, it probably inspired the first full-fledged Iranian game developed with governmental support. This game is called *Special Operation* (*Amaliyat-e Vizhe*) and was published in July 2007 by the Iranian Student Union. This first-person shooter game narrates a fictitious story about an Iranian nuclear scientist, who was kidnapped by US security forces in Iraq while visiting the tomb of Iman Hussein. The player takes the role of a Special Forces commander, Bahman Nasseri, who is appointed to rescue the scientist. Muhammad Taqi Fakhrian, one of the authors of *Special Operation*, stated in an interview with Al-Manar TV on 17 July 2007, 'The game is based on cultural and religious principles. It encourages the culture of martyrdom and defence of rights.'

Iranian and Islamic values: Video games as official communications policy

Soon after the release of *Special Operation*, a number of other games appeared on the Iranian market. A substantial amount of them have been conceived of or directly developed by Tebyan Cultural and Informative Institute. The institute was established as an independent legal entity affiliated with the Islamic Propaganda Organisation (*Sazman-e tablighat-e eslami*) in 2001.[2] Its main aim is 'to explain, develop and promote Islamic culture and educate the new generation religiously, socially and practically by the means of information technology' (Tebyan, 2008a). As Hamid Roustaie, the PR manager of Tebyan, told me:

> Tebyan Institute has a cultural and religious mission. It aims simultaneously to fill the gap in the contemporary digital production in Iran as well as inform the world about the Iranian culture. Therefore, we started by producing religiously and culturally oriented online software and, later on, games.

Tebyan currently employs around 100 people and has published more than 20 games (NFCG, 2011b). Prominent among them is a series called *Memorable Battles* (*Nabardehaye Manadekar*), which aims to foster national pride by virtually reconstructing key victorious battles from throughout Iranian history. For example, *Valfajr 8*, mentioned in the introduction (see figure 11.1), is based on Dawn 8, an Iran–Iraq war operation during which Iranian forces captured the Fao peninsula in 1986. *Saving Harbor* (*Najat-e Bandar*) retells the story of defending the Bandar-e Pahlavi port, today known as Bandar-e Anzali, against the Soviet invasion in 1941. All these games fall under the third-person shooter genre and have a relatively simple game play that revolves around tactical combat. Despite their low technical quality, they emphasise the Iranian and Muslim identity of the hero and communicate it to the players on all three of the content levels delineated above through graphics, music, in-game sounds, narrative and game play.

In 2008 Tebyan Institute published *Resistance* (*Moqavamat*, see figure 11.1), a newer and more technologically advanced action game. In the game,

Figure 11.1 The game *Resistance*. Courtesy of Tebyan (2007–8).

set in the year 2015, the player controls Hezbollah commandos sent to Israel to seek and destroy a secret military programme focused on the development of an unknown weapon of mass destruction. The game utilises a classic first-person shooter framework, with Israeli soldiers as enemies. Instead of realistic video clips mimicking actual Hezbollah operations, such as in the above-mentioned Hezbollah-based game, *Special Force*, the introductory video for *Resistance* adopts science fiction, cartoon aesthetics portraying Hezbollah commandos as superheroes. *Resistance* is another example of a domestic game produced in clear response to US military games.

Figure 11.2 The game *Valfajr 8*. Courtesy of Tebyan (2007–8).

Computer games can be used for positive or destructive means. The latter represent games preparing the public for military campaigns, such as attacks on Iraq or Afghanistan, and misrepresenting Muslim forces. [Authors of these games] misuse their monopoly for developing and publishing games. [...] Therefore we aim to develop games in accordance with Islamic and Iranian values. (Tebyan, 2008)

Games like *Resistance* and *Special Operation* utilise the procedural rhetoric of first-person shooters for expressing a political stance and thus directly participate in an ideological struggle with the USA and Israel by simply reversing the polarities known from the above-mentioned US war games. Yet, particularly in comparison with the US game *Assault on Iran*, it is important to note that all the Iranian games from the *Memorable Battles* series are based on the concept of *defa* (defence) rather than attack. The rhetoric of defence runs deep in Iranian culture and is used most often in reference to the invasion of Iran by Iraq, which culminated in eight years of war between the neighbouring countries (1980–1988) and is commemorated in the public transcript as *defa-e moqqaddas* (sacred defence). *Resistance*, the only game in the series in which the player is sent to carry out a military operation on foreign soil, the only game in which the player must attack rather than defend, deliberately uses Lebanese Hezbollah fighters as the player's virtual representations rather than Iranian soldiers. Moreover, when I confronted Hamid Roustaie about what I perceived to be a discrepancy in the concept of *defa*, he argued that *Resistance* is essentially about defence as well, since in the game 'the Zionists are developing a weapon which could destroy the whole world'. Although the game takes place in Israel and features Hezbollah fighters as heroes, its meta-narrative directly deals with an identity concept that could be relevant to the Shi'ite Islamic state. As Hamid Roustaie told me:

> We wanted to show that Hezbollah includes people who care, people who fight for their own country. We wanted to correct the wrong point of view on Hezbollah some people have here in Iran, that they're old-fashioned guys with big beards and guns. In our game, they have modern weaponry and outlook. More importantly, they sacrifice their lives for their country.

Finally, other games, which are now in development by Tebyan, promote Islamic and family values. The game *Islamic Sims* openly appropriates a successful Western pattern and recasts it in an Islamic fashion.

Iranian mythology and culture: Video games as private enterprise

The previous games, like *Saving Harbor* or *Valfajr 8*, have been directly designed and produced by Tebyan. Yet, the emerging mechanism of official game production is that some governmental institutes, like Tebyan or *Sepah* (The Army of the Guardians of the Islamic Revolution), produce a concept or script which is then contracted to individual software studios. These software studios then develop the game relatively independently, using a game engine, the core component of a game, which is freely available online (like *Torque*) or by developing their own. This was the case with *Resistance*, which was in fact developed for Tebyan, who produced the script, by the studio *Tahlil Garan Tadbir*. When I conducted interviews with designers and programmers in these various software studios, it became clear that besides the governmental concerns about the political and ideological implications of such games, the people working on them have other, more personal and professional motives. These stem from their desire to design and produce games that are technologically and conceptually advanced and that do not pale in comparison with mainstream European or US production.

Oftentimes, these software studios, beyond developing games for the governmental institutes, also design and develop games on their own. These can differ significantly from the governmental production. For example, in *Tahlil Garan Tadbir* there is currently a game in development called *Norouz*, which aims at teaching children about various aspects of Iranian culture by engaging them in an adventure quest, similar in a sense to Western 'edutainment' games (Egenfeldt-Nielsen, 2005). Yet, the ambitions of Farshad Samimi, one of the authors of this game, are higher. He told me that he wants to 'change the way children in Iran play games and let them contemplate why they are playing' in order to foster a yearning for knowledge among them. 'We accepted everything [that we were taught] without any questions. I don't want the kids of today to be like this. I want them to question everything.'

Beyond the above-mentioned companies, there are also independent video game producers on the Iranian market. An example of an independent game that clearly stems from the needs of its authors to articulate their Iranian identity through the media, which they perceive to be of utmost relevance to their generation, is *Quest of Persia*. *Quest of Persia* is a series of action-adventure games covering different periods of Iranian history, ranging from Qajar times to the Iran–Iraq war. Thus far two games have been published within the series, *Quest of Persia: The End of Innocence (2005) and Quest of Persia: Lotfali Khan Zand* (2008). As the author Puya Dadgar told me, he was disturbed by the way his university colleagues in the USA had perceived Iran:

> The way they were thinking about Iran was a place of desert and camels. They thought that there is no technology there, no history and civilisation. That kind of bothered me, because that was the view of most people in the US and Western countries. So, I was thinking, if we could have a game that would show the nature of our country, our history and civilisation, that would help people understand about Iran.

In fact, a similar concern was expressed by Farshad Samimi, who told me that they are not producing *Norouz* for an exclusively Iranian audience, but also 'want to export it to other countries, so not only Iranian but also foreign people can understand the Iranian culture and see that Iran has two thousand years of history'.

Quest of Persia is also a response to a US game, not the above-mentioned *Assault on Iran* but *Prince of Persia* (Brøderbund Software, Inc., 1989), which is a very popular adventure game exploiting typical Orientalist imagery reminiscent of the realm of *One Thousand and One Nights* (Šisler, 2008: 206). As Puya Dadgar says:

> We haven't got anything against *Prince of Persia*; it's a great game after all. But as you know, *Prince of Persia* uses mostly Arabic and Indian themes, textures, and music, not Persian. With *Quest of Persia*, we wanted to show what the land of Persia is truly all about. *Quest of Persia* is one hundred percent Persian, from music to environments, up to characters.

Quest of Persia was very positively received by the players and won several awards.[3] Puya Dadgar described the game: 'People bought it in big numbers because it's an Iranian game with an Iranian story. We got emails from places in Iran where you don't even think computers exist, but people there played the game and they liked it.' Yet, economically speaking, the game was not particularly successful. Given the rather flimsy state of copyright protection in Iran, the first *Quest of Persia* game suffered heavily at the hands of illegal copying and distribution and did not recover its high development costs. As Puya Dadgar notes, 'After six weeks or something the copies were all over the place.' Therefore, the sequel, *Lotfali Khan Zand*, as well as most Iranian games currently available on the market, use an unusually sophisticated copyright protection system, which includes double codes and registration over the internet. According to Puya Dadgar, within a few weeks of its release, *Lotfali Khan Zand* (see figure 11.2) sold more than 20,000 copies. This is a remarkable success given that, as Iranian gamers have almost free access to Western video game production, they tend to be very critical and selective towards what they buy and play. As Puya Dadgar observed:

> Even if the game features an Iranian hero, it has to have a game play that people enjoy. If the game sucks, no one is going to buy it, even if it's Iranian. There are other Iranian games out there, and they are not selling at all.

In this respect, I should mention another ambitious, independent game, which is based on ancient Persian mythology and is distinguished by both conceptually well-developed game play as well as high graphical and

Figure 11.3 The game *Lotfali Khan Zand*. Courtesy of Puya Arts Software (2008).

technological quality. The fantasy action game, *Garshasp*, was developed under the original name, *Soshiant*, by the Iranian company Fanafzar. It was released in 2011 in co-operation with Dead Mage Studios, which is based in Pasadena, Texas. This game deliberately challenges the Anglo-Saxon mythological canon that has dominated the fantasy game genre by translating an ancient Iranian epic poem into the realm of virtual entertainment.

> The treasure trove of Persian mythology contains within it some of humanity's oldest and most profound myths. They recount a rich and ancient culture, meaningful literature, and exciting legends that bring to life the excitement of Iranian civilization in all its glory - an experience often lost

Figure 11.4 The game Age of Pahlevans, Courtesy of Rezana Afzar Sharif (2009).

in the daily travails of modern life. This video game, *Garshasp*, is a symbolic recreation of the spirituality, grandeur and mythical atmosphere of ancient Persia, derived from the epic poem, *Garshasp Naame*, written by Asadi Tousi. [...] Most of the images and scenes depicted in this game are drawn from or based directly upon historical resources and ancient stone carvings found throughout Iran, and a chain of thought that goes back thousands of years to the dawn of Western and Eastern civilizations alike. (Garshasp, 2011)

Garshasp is a third-person action adventure, revolving around melee combat, puzzle-solving and exploration in a way typical of the fantasy genre. As Fanafzar's director Arash Jafari told me, the game 'is something like *The Lord of the Rings*, but based on Persian mythology and Persian characters'. The game even appropriates an ancient Iranian mythological map, one that was associated with Tusi's epic poem. The game was generally well-received by Iranian gamers, as was shown by the high amount of attention it attracted at the Second Digital Media Festival held in Tehran in 2008, where its preliminary version was exhibited.

Another recently released, independent game is *Age of Pahlevans* (*Asr-e Pahlevanan*, see figure 11.2), which was developed by the Rezana Afzar Sharif Company in 2009. This game is also based on ancient Iranian mythology and retells the story of a hero struggling to save his city against the forces of doom in a fairly typical fantasy-genre manner. And again the question of the hero's specific Iranian identity is important to the authors. It is emphasised by the game's background, its story, locations and textures. Moreover, Bahram Borghei, the author of the script, told me: 'In foreign games, like *Grand Theft Auto*, you can play a hero who kills people and steals cars. In *Age of Pahlevans* the hero is Pahlevan, which means not only is he a hero but he follows a moral code.'

The concept of Pahlevan is deeply entrenched in the Iranian culture. Pahlevan, literally meaning champion, could be a combat hero, a national athlete, or a cultural icon. More importantly, he or she has to be distinguished by his/her humanity and moral integrity (Sheibani, 2009). In fact, an emphasis on the hero's high moral profile, ie on the virtual representation of the player's self, can be found in most contemporary Iranian games, including those produced by the government. Oftentimes this emphasis is directly embodied in the game rules. As Hamid Roustaie from Tebyan told me:

> In our games we of course can't omit the action factor of the game, because it's the main interest of the youngsters. So in our games we have fights, but we don't give scores or award bonuses to a player when he kills someone.

Similarly, violence is not emphasised by the game graphics. In comparison with Western production, the use of blood and gore is significantly limited. By the same token, Arash Jafari from Fanafzar mentioned the ethical dimensions of their games:

> We bring a lot of new concepts to the game, like forgiveness and ethics. For example, when you meet a character which you would probably kill in a normal fantasy game, but you do not kill him, you perhaps meet this character later on in the game and he can help you with a different quest. So, indirectly, our games can have positive educational effect because of this underlying moral logic.

The emphasis on a hero's moral profile could be in many cases the result of the authors' genuine motivations as well as of the necessity to ensure that the game will get the approval of *Vezarat-e Ershad* (The Ministry of Culture and Islamic Guidance). Essentially, all cultural production in Iran has to be approved by the Ministry of Culture in one way or another to be officially published. As Sreberny and Khiabany (2010: 24) note, the Islamic state that came to power after 1979 defined itself predominantly in a cultural sense. The twin aims of the cultural policy of the new state were based on destruction of an imposed Western, alien culture and its replacement with a 'dignified, indigenous and authentic Islamic culture' (Alinejad, 2002), which was said to have declined under the previous monarchical regime. Because of such broad cultural aims, the state began to develop a whole range of institutions to implement and safeguard the Shi'ite Islamic culture of Iran. The Ministry of Culture and Islamic Guidance was then given the specific tasks of managing and running the press, the Iranian News Agency, as well as charities and religious endowments (Sreberny and Khiabany, 2010: 25). Recently, the Ministry has also been charged with overseeing the development of a rating system for foreign games and, more importantly, approves all domestic Iranian game production. Puya Dadgar's first game *Quest of Persia* did not have to undergo any approval procedure in 2005, since the process was non-existent at the time. Nevertheless, after the establishment of the NFCG in 2006, the need for guidelines for such approval became obvious. This is because many independent producers started to submit their games to the NFCG, regularly seeking financial help in the costly development process.

According to Puya Dadgar, the NFCG's granting of such aid is based on scrutinisation of set criteria relating to both the technical quality as well as cultural content of the game in question. Nevertheless, the content of every game meant to appear on the Iranian market has to be approved in advance by the Ministry of Culture and Islamic Guidance, even if the authors do not seek financial support from the state. In such a case, a summary of the screenplay, the story of the game, and its characters all have to be submitted to the Ministry before development starts. In the case of a few fantasy games, as I was informed, the authors had to remove all indirect references to Zoroastrianism and radically change the concept of magic in the game in order to get even preliminary approval. At the same time, a strong level of self-censorship seems to be in play. As Puya Dadgar puts it, 'In Iran, nobody is going to make a game with lots of bloodshed, or lots of sex. I don't think anybody is stupid enough to do it. Overall, everybody follows the rules in their mind, anyway.'

The issue of approval leads us back to the question of financing. Even though many of the Iranian games are developed independently and do not result from a governmental contract, at the end of the day most producers get at least some financial support from official institutions. Given loose copyright enforcement in Iran and the low prices of copied Western games, commercial development of a new game is a seriously risky business unless the producers have at least part of the development costs paid by another source.[4]

Most of the independent companies mentioned above started to produce their games on their own, working in their free time or alongside other activities, such as the development of webpage applications. As Arash Jafari told me:

> It was more passion and personal interest than business. The greatest challenge was that you hoped that the Iranian youngsters and teenagers would buy this, because this is something different than other Iranian or Western games, it has a fascinating, unique story. We tried to bring Eastern values into the game, not just, you know, the violence that you can see in Western games.

In interviews I got very similar responses from all of the independent producers, confirming that their primary motivation for developing games was a deep personal interest in and desire to produce a high quality Iranian game. Yet, understandably, all of them have been seeking further possible options for co-financing their projects from the state. The Rezana Afzar Sharif Company, the authors of *Age of Pahlevans*, obtained several technological grants from governmental institutions, which covered approximately half of their development costs. In other cases, like *Quest of Persia* or *Age of Pahlevans*, the authors finalised the games on their own and then submitted them to the NFCG to get additional support. Obtaining this support has been eased by the fact that several ancient Iranian cities have been digitalised and virtually recreated in these games. The cities of Kerman and Bam have been preserved in *Quest of Persia* and Zabul appears in *Age of Pahlevans*; these games are vehicles for preservation of cultural heritage. This 'virtual preservation' is particularly relevant to the city of Bam, which was largely destroyed by a massive earthquake in 2003. The team at Puya Arts had been doing fieldwork there just two weeks before the earthquake and they took literally thousands of high resolution pictures of the city's unique architecture, walls and entrances. In turn, according to Puya Dadgar, the Ministry of Culture bought approximately 3,000 copies of *Quest of Persia* for promotional purposes.

It has to be emphasised once again that developing a fully-fledged game is a costly and risky endeavour anywhere, with less than 50 per cent of started projects being successfully finished (Klima, 2011). The fact that Iranian producers compete on a domestic market with copied, and thus remarkably cheap, Western games, combined with the US technological embargo on Iran, makes the situation even more difficult for them. In this situation, state support can make the difference between survival and oblivion in the realm of digital entertainment. Yet, as Puya Dadgar notes:

> They are not giving money to just anyone, I mean, you show the sample work, and after that they do some interviews, and they have a rating system, they give you points if you qualify, and then you produce a demo of the game. If this demo is close to what they want to do in terms of their games, if you're lucky, they give you like ten thousand, twenty thousand. It is not much, I mean, but it's good...

Conclusion

This chapter has discussed key video games produced in Iran between 2005 and 2011 and explored how these games communicate the concept of identity, ie the virtual representation of the player's self, to the gamers. The games analysed in this chapter range from official governmental production to independent games developed by private entrepreneurs. They differ significantly in their aims, quality, and background. As mentioned above, the Iranian government perceives games primarily as a new semiotic language for youth and utilises them to promote Islamic values and foster national pride. At the same time, many independent or semi-independent producers manoeuvre within and around the state's interests, presenting instead their own, oftentimes quite different, concepts and ideas.

As Sreberny and Khiabany (2010: 25) point out, Iran's digital environment is controlled through complex legislation and non-legal ploys, including the setting up of a variety of regulatory bodies. The digital environment is therefore subject to friction and competition between factions within the regime, the institutional interests of various agencies, and the tensions within the state as well as between the state and the private sector. By the same token, Siavoshi (1997: 513) argues that the plurality of the institutions and agencies involved in the process subjects cultural development and policies to power struggles among many factions within the state: 'Although every faction declared its commitment to Islamic cultural ideals, all consensus vanished when it came to the question of what these ideals were and which policies were required to achieve them.' The domain of video game production is similarly subject to the above-mentioned tensions, including economic competition on a specific entertainment market.

Contemporary Iranian games encompass a broad variety of topics and the resulting concepts of identity are achieved through sensitive negotiations between the demands, funding and restrictions of the state and the visions and engagement of private entrepreneurs.

Nevertheless, this chapter demonstrates that despite varying ideological backgrounds, independent and state-directed producers all believe that Iran and Iranians are misrepresented by global video game production and thus strive to present unique Iranian heroes to their audiences. The success of *Quest of Persia* suggests that there is a huge potential demand for local games and local heroes among Iranian gamers. At the same time, where most of the independent producers avidly use ancient Iranian mythology, history and contemporary popular culture as a background for constructing their heroes, the official production utilises the iconography of the Islamic Republic, the concept of martyrdom, and the sacred defence.

It is important to note, that both the developers from the official institutions (such as *Tebyan* or *Sepah*) as well as the independent designers aim, albeit arguably for different reasons, to transcend the schematising conflictual framework dominating Western mainstream video game production. As Hamid Roustaie told me,

> We don't try to portray the Americans, or any forces which came to Iraq, as bad people, as they do in most of their games with Iranians. Rather, we try to show the cultural and religious richness of Iran, provide a more historically accurate picture of Iran, and construct positive Iranian heroes.

In some cases, the desire of the developers accurately to represent Iranian culture has even influenced the choice of the game genre, ie the fundamental framework which ultimately shapes and limits the eventual player's interaction with the game. As Bahram Borghei, one of the authors of *Age of Pahlevans*, told me:

> We have chosen the role-playing game genre because we wanted to get some added value into our game. *Age of Pahlevans* is based on Iranian cultural background and we have some great stories and great characters in Iranian culture. These concepts can be best communicated through a role-playing

game, since it allows for communication with non-player characters and various interactions other than fighting. At the same time, by producing something different from other games we can more easily succeed on the international market.

In fact, most of the Iranian producers, including state-directed and private ones, aim to get their games to the international market. *Garshasp* is currently available for download in Persian, English and German versions for $9.99 payable via PayPal (Garshasp, 2011). Similarly, *Quest of Persia: Lotfali Khan Zand* is available for download in English for $15 (Quest of Persia, 2009). Another Iranian game *Mir Mahna* (Espris Studio, 2011), dealing with the liberation of Iran from colonial forces, will be, according to the managing director of the NFCG, Behruz Minai, distributed in Indonesia and Turkey (Payvand, 2011). As I have demonstrated above, the motivations of the producers to succeed on the international market entangle the economic needs with the desire to present the technological aptitude and cultural richness of the contemporary Iranian game production to the outside world. Nevertheless, given the novelty of the Iranian game industry, we have no data available yet on how successful are, or will be, these games on the highly competitive global market.

Finally, utilising games for delivering messages to the young audience opens up a new domain for persuasion, the domain of procedural rhetoric. The Iranian authorities are apparently aware that their message, in order to be heard, has to be recast in accordance with the new cultural and media environment. Yet when we examine the games produced by Tebyan and other governmental institutes so far, they actually fail to utilise the full potential of the media's procedural rhetoric. They pale in comparison with Western production and their game play is mostly unappealing. The games produced by independent game producers, on the contrary, are mostly comparable to similar Western production, including the quality of graphics, music, and level design. Moreover, they consciously utilise frameworks established by Western games of a similar genre. So, for example, *Age of Pahlevans* appropriates the pattern of *Oblivion* (Bethesda Game Studios, 2006) whereas *Garshasp* uses the pattern of *God of War* (Sony, 2005). On a structural level these games are Western, which in fact clearly corresponds with the aims of the developers, who wish to simultaneously express their Iranian identity and compete with Western games, reaffirming their belonging to a global cosmopolitan gaming community. While the games may use Western frameworks, we can conclude that on a symbolic level these games are clearly Iranian, with Iranian heroes, mythology and culture.

Acknowledgements

This study was partially supported by a research grant No. DF11P01OVV030 financed by the Ministry of Culture, Czech Republic and investigated at the Charles University Faculty of Arts in Prague, 2011. I would like to thank Hamid Roustaie, Farshad Samimi, Puya Dadgar, Arash Jafari and Bahram Borghei for the interviews and Ebrahim Mohseni Ahooei, Rioushar Yarveysi, Hamed Rajabi and Houman Harouni for the invaluable help.

Notes

1 The statute of the NFCG was ratified in the 584th session of the Supreme Council of Cultural Revolution (Shoraye Enghelabe Farhangi) on 21 June 2006. The foundation was subsequently founded on 10 July 2006. More information can be found on the foundation's website (NFCG, 2011).
2 The statutes of Tebyan were approved on 10 December 2001 (Tebyan, 2008).
3 *Quest of Persia: The End of Innocence* won five awards in the First Digital Media Festival held in Tehran in 2007. The awards included: Best achievement in Animation, Graphic Design, Game Programming, Screenplay, and The Professional Game (Quest of Persia, 2007).
4 As for August 2011, most of the Iranian games available on the market cost 50,000 riyals ($5), whereas copied Western games cost 20,000 or 30,000 riyals ($2 or $3). See Forooshgah Bazi Shop, 2011.

References

2K Games (2007) *Bioshock* (DVD).
Alinejad, M (2002) 'Coming to terms with modernity: Iranian intellectuals and the emerging public sphere'. *Islam and Christian-Muslim Relations* 13: 1: 25–47.
Bethesda Game Studios (2006) *Oblivion* (DVD).
Blizzard Entertainment Inc. (1996) *Diablo* (CD-Rom).
Bogost, I (2007) *Persuasive Games: The Expressive Power of Videogames*. Cambridge: MIT Press.
Brøderbund Software, Inc. (1989) *Prince of Persia* (floppy disk).
Egenfeldt-Nielsen, S (2005) *Beyond Edutainment: Exploring the Educational Potential of Computer Games*. Dissertation thesis, University of Copenhagen (http://egenfeldt.eu/blog/my-research (last accessed 20 June 2011)).
Espris Studio (2011) *Mir Mahna* (DVD).
Fanafzar (2011) *Garshasp* (http://garshasp.com (last accessed 20 June 2011)).
Forooshgah Bazi Shop (2011) (http://shop1.bazyshop.com/ (last accessed 9 August 2011)).

Garshasp (2011) (http://garshasp.com/about-garshasp (last accessed 20 June 2011)).
Infinity Ward, Inc. (2007) *Call of Duty 4* (DVD).
Iranian Student Union (2007) *Special Operation* (DVD).
Klima, M (2011) Re: *prosba citace*, email to V Sisler (vsisler@gmailcom), 24 June (last accessed 9 Aug 2011).
Kuma, LLC (2005) *Assault on Iran* (www.kumawar.com (last accessed 20 June 2011)).
Kuma\War (n.d.) *What is KUMA\WAR?* (www.kumawar.com (last accessed 20 June 2011)).
Maxis Software Inc. (2000) *The Sims* (DVD).
McLuhan, M (1964) *Understanding Media: The Extensions of Man*. New York: McGraw Hill.
Murphy, SC (2004) 'Live in your world, play in ours: The spaces of video game identity'. *Journal of Visual Culture* 3, 2: 223–38.
National Foundation of Computer Games (NFCG) (2011) *About Us* (http://ircg.ir/index.php?sn=aboutUs&pt=&&lang=en (last accessed 9 August 2011)).
National Foundation of Computer Games (NFCG) (2011b) *Cultural and Information Institute of Tebyan Noor* (http://ircg.ir/sn/producers/pt/full/lang/en/id/134 (last accessed 9 August 2011)).
Nieborg, D (2006) 'We want the whole world to know how great the U.S. army is!' in Santorineos, M, Dimitriadi, N (eds) *Gaming Realities: A Challenge for Digital Culture*. Athens: FourNos.
Payvand (2011) *Iran Seeking to Enter International Market for Computer Games* (www.payvand.com/news/11/apr/1203.html (last accessed 9 August 2011)).
Puya Arts Software Inc. (2005) *Quest of Persia: The End of Innocence* (DVD).
Puya Arts. Software Inc. (2008) *Quest of Persia: Lotfali Khan Zand* (DVD).
Quest of Persia (2007) (www.questofpersia.com/eoe (last accessed 20 June 2011)).
Quest of Persia (2009) (www.questofpersia.com/lotfali/buy.html (last accessed 9 August 2011)).
Ransom-Wiley, J (2005) 'Assault on Iran is not a game to some'. *Joystiq* (www.joystiq.com/2005/10/25/assault-on-iran-is-not-a-game-to-some (last accessed 20 June 2011)).
Rezana Afzar Sharif (2009) *Age of Pahlevans* (DVD).
Rockstar Games, Inc (2005) *Grand Theft Auto: San Andreas* (DVD).
Sheibani, K (2009) *Authorship in Performance in the Post-Revolutionary Iranian Cinema*. Paper presented at the MESA 2009 conference.

Siavoshi, S (1997) 'Cultural policies and the Islamic Republic: Cinema and book publication'. *International Journal of Middle East Studies*, 29: 509–30.
Sisler, V (2008) 'Digital Arabs: Representation in video games'. *European Journal of Cultural Studies* 11, 2: 203–20.
Sreberny, A and Khiabany, G (2010) *Blogistan: The Internet and Politics in Iran*. New York: I.B.Tauris.
Solution (2003) *Special Force* (DVD).
Sony (2005) *God of War* (DVD).
Tebyan (2007) *Valfajr 8* (DVD).
Tebyan (2008a) *About Us* (www.tebyan.net/index.aspx?pid=58430 (last accessed 20 June 2011)).
Tebyan (2008b) *Resistance* (DVD).
Tebyan (n.d.) *Saving Harbor* (DVD).
US Army (2002) *America's Army* (DVD).

CHAPTER 12

SATIRE IN THE IRANIAN MEDIA

Development and Diversity

Katja Föllmer

Introduction

Despite, or perhaps because of, the new cultural orientation and the political climate that followed the Iranian revolution of 1979, satire in the Islamic Republic has undergone a series of specific developments since 1984, which is when the first satirical column, *Do Kalame Harf-e Hesab* (two proper words) was published in the newspaper *Ettela'at*. The more moderate political atmosphere that prevailed in Iran following the conclusion of the Iran–Iraq war in 1988 resulted in a greater variety of print media. This played an important role in the development of Iranian satire as it shifted from the social into the political sphere. Since then, a range of satirical works have been published. After President Khatami's election in 1997 and the ushering in of what came to be called the reform movement, various political factions used the press as their battlefield. The liberal atmosphere in the Iranian media enabled a public dispute between conservatives and reformers and greatly influenced the work of Iranian satirists. They developed individual and recognisable satirical styles to express a relatively wide range of opinions concerning reform ideas.

At the end of the 1990s, satire reached a high degree of directness and criticism in the reform press. This was demonstrated by the blossoming of publications such as the satirical magazine *Gol-Agha*, the literary magazine *Donya-ye Sokhan*, the reform newspaper *Jame'e*, and its successors. Since 2000, satire has enjoyed immense popularity in other media, such as TV, cinema and especially the internet. For various reasons, the print media seem to have lost much of their importance in this field. This chapter analyses the relationship between politics, media and satire, demonstrates the characteristics of officially tolerated satire in the different media in Iran and reveals how satire has shifted from being a textual medium into a visual one.

Satire's development in post-revolutionary Iran

Despite the strong restrictions on Iranian media since the foundation of the Islamic Republic, over the course of the past three decades, humour with critical overtones has become increasingly present in the Iranian public sphere. In the years following the revolution the Iranian media was charged with protecting revolutionary ideals and, especially during the eight-year war with Iraq, did not allow space for any kind of humour and public criticism. With the close of the war, Khomeini's death, the new leadership of Ayatollah Khamenei and the presidency of Ayatollah Rafsanjani, in 1989 came the beginning of a more moderate media policy and public criticism laced with humour and irony emerged gradually in parts of the Iranian press. This mode of communication was called satire (*tanz*). The first step in this development was the emergence and popularity of the satirical column *Do Kalame Harf-e Hesab* (two proper words), written by Kioumars Saberi Fumani in the newspaper *Ettela'at* since 1984. Fumani developed a unique style of satirical communication, which was accompanied in the press by a discourse on an Islamic conception of Iranian satire.

In Islamic countries, and especially in Iran, satire is often construed as a rhetorical form of humour. Its function may be to entertain, but its aims are didactic. In Iran, satire has the aggressive intention of exposing, ridiculing or framing somebody. In classical Persian the words *hazl* (jesting or comical) and *hajw* (ridicule or invective) were used to describe satire and the meaning of these words is perhaps better comprehensible through an examination of their opposite meanings. *Hazl* is always a humorous mode of expression and is thus considered the opposite of *jedd* (seriousness). *Hajw* is, by definition, never a panegyric (*madh*), even though it can found in the works of Iranian classical poets like Ferdowsi, Sa'di and Rumi. Although the word *tanz* is now commonly used to describe satire, Javadi (1988: 13) points out that the term *tanz*, in the sense of mockery or irony, was never specifically a genre of satire. This term was not used extensively in classical literature but is used in Iran as a direct equivalent to the European term satire. There is really no clear distinction between these three terms and their form and function can often overlap. The terms are even sometimes interchangeable. In fact, as I have argued previously (2008: 45–53), they differ only partially from each other.

The most important factors for the Iranian understanding of the satirical mode of communication are their entertainment function, their moral and social message, the directness of their criticism and aesthetics. For *hazl*, entertainment is the most important factor, whereas *hajw* focuses on critique rather than entertainment. Direct criticism is more important for *hajw*, but less so for *hazl* and certainly not for *tanz*. The most dominant characteristics of *tanz* are the didactic aims and aesthetic criteria, which are of minor importance for *hazl* and distinctly unimportant for *hajw*.

Until the latter part of the twentieth century, Iranian satire as a mode of communication was hardly a subject of research and academic discussion either inside or outside Iran. Academic interest in satire arose parallel to an increase in the importance and social influence of the press after the Iranian revolution in 1979 and parallel to the growing popularity of the satirical column *two proper words*. During the Pahlavi era (1925–79) satirical texts in the Iranian press seemed to be largely ignored by Iranians. The only exceptions to this were the satirical images published in *Towfigh*, a popular newspaper published from 1927–71.

First steps towards defining Iranian satire in an academic context

The popularity of the satirical column *Do Kalame Harf-e Hesab* (discussed below) and the *Gol-Agha* magazines is an indication of the growing importance of satire in Iran after 1979. The satirists recognised the social and political tensions in Iranian society and made them the subject of their texts. Their intention was not to strengthen the existing conditions but to encourage necessary changes and improvements corresponding to the social, economic and political needs of the people in post-war Iran. Thus, Saberi's style of satire could be construed as the initiation of the political reform process that reached a climax during the first years of Khatami's presidency.

This newly established form of written satire forced Iranian satirists to think generally about what satire was and what its future role in Iranian art was to be, but detailed analyses and definition of Iranian satire were rare. Zarru'i-Nasrabad's structural analysis of the satirical column *Do Kalame Harf-e Hesab* in *Ettela'at* (1995) is the only exception from this time. Accompanied by the broad popular appeal of satire, these first analytical steps generally encouraged further historical and literary research on this subject by Iranian scholars, journalists and writers. When examining academic and journalistic interpretations of satire, one finds a common basis for the general Iranian understanding of the medium, which is formulated around a set of main criteria: humour and entertainment, aesthetic criteria and social aims, and masked criticism. The terms *hajv* (in the sense of mockery and ridicule), *hazl* (humour) and *tanz* (irony), are the main subcategories of Iranian satire (*tanz*). Humour and entertainment are the main characteristics of *hazl*. The entertaining function is lesser significant than aesthetic criteria and moral social aims in *tanz* and direct criticism in *hajv*.

At about the same time the country's Ministry of Culture and Islamic Guidance entered the public discussion about satire by developing mandatory guidelines for an officially acknowledged form of satire, which they called *tanz-e matlub va sazande* (desirable and constructive satire). In 1999–2000 the ministry's quarterly magazine *Resaneh* [*Media*] published an article outlining the 'requirements and properties' of 'desirable satire' (*Esma'ili* (1378/1999–2000): 81–6). The text emphasises the entertainment value and didactic function of satire and argues that satire should divert the attention of the public away from grief, worry and exhaustion and make people forget their troubles. 'Desirable satire' should avoid lies, discrimination, indecency and disturbing subject matter, and uphold social morals and the principles of Islam. The article also states that media have a legal duty to function as a 'university for the common people' (*daneshgah-e bozorg-e omumi*) and with these words the official function of satire became limited to didactic entertainment and moral instruction.

As far as the production of satire was concerned, the purpose of the text and the style of the satire were key considerations that determined the conditions of its publication. For Iranian theorists such as Halabi (1998/1377) and Behzadi-Anduhjerdi (1999/1378), a key aim was to establish links between theory and practice, at least as far as modern satire was concerned, and to develop a system of classification that corresponded to current social aspirations and expectations. Naturally, theoretical treatises focused only on those aspects of satire that were considered to be the most relevant to Iranian society: the construction of a history of Iranian satire, the determination of relevant terms and their meaning, aesthetical criteria, entertainment and didactic function. Importantly, treatises on Iranian satire generally avoided transparent analyses of satire and focused primarily on classical literary texts (Föllmer, 2008: 45–72).

The success of *Do Kalame Harf-e Hesab*

Research on Iranian satire, when it eventually appeared, was motivated by the enormous success of the post-revolutionary satirical column *Do Kalame Harf-e Hesab* (two proper words), which was first published in the daily newspaper *Ettela'at* in 1984. It was the first time since the closure of many periodicals in Iran following the revolution that such a column had appeared in the press. The column was a sensation at a time when the country was in the midst of war with Iraq and topics such as the need for adequate food supplies, accommodation, health care and formal education were discussed from behind a shield of humour. The column was both humorous and critical and it highlighted the needs of the Iranian people in an indirect way after years of deprivation and geographical isolation.

The success of the column's author Kioumars Saberi Fumani (1941–2004) after 1979 was based on the particular method of satirical writing he developed, which enabled him legally to criticise recent social and political deficiencies and manoeuvre around prevailing taboos. Saberi created fictional characters named Shahgholam, Ghazanfar and Gol-Agha. Their authentic actions and vivid speech formed the permanent link across the columns, while the characters were depicted as being from the lower stratum of society and as simple-minded and naïve, thus fulfilling their satirical role as intended by the author.

Another factor contributing to Saberi Fumani's success was his moral character. He was an upstanding citizen in the eyes of the Islamic Republic, a good example of a moral, religious man who was a defender of the Islamic values of the Iranian revolution. Saberi also moved within the highest political circles and had a career as politician for a time (Sadr, 2005: 5–6). He was the government's consultant for Culture and Media until 1983 and had made a pilgrimage to Mecca and Karbala in 1984. Furthermore, Saberi later received the full approval of famous and important persons such as the prominent Iranian short-story writer Mohammad-Ali Jamalzadeh (c. 1892–1997) (*Haftenameh-ye Gol-Agha*, 1991/1369: 12–13). Saberi began using the name Gol-Agha as his pseudonym and conferred some of his own characteristics onto his character. Before long the satirist was known only as Gol-Agha and he positioned himself as the mediator between his contentious fictional characters and the reader. In Saberi's satire, fiction and reality were masterfully combined. He created satirical slapstick, a serial comedy in a press column that witnessed unprecedented popularity.

In 1990, Saberi began editing the weekly satirical magazine *Gol-Agha*. Its numerous contributions aimed to entertain the people with humorous and comical lyrical and prose texts, caricatures and cartoons, which often implemented criticism of contemporary sociopolitical circumstances. The monthly and annual omnibuses of *Gol Agha* focused more on highbrow critique while the weekly editions continued the already established and customary entertainment of the masses. Saberi and his team of authors (a number of whom were former contributors to *Towfigh*) and caricaturists developed a variety of textual and visual forms of satire in the Iranian press. Textual satire, which Saberi had developed, had already reached a high artistic level, whereas the progress of caricature artists still lagged behind. Lyrical expression was increasingly being replaced by short prose texts such as jokes, anecdotes and news stories. Furthermore, the number of illustrative figures (e.g. drawings, caricatures, cartoons or even advertisements) and photos with captions increased notably, especially in the weekly edition of *Gol-Agha*.

Other examples of satire in the press

Gol-Agha magazine's strict observance of the official criteria for satire meant that the sociopolitical criticisms expressed by its writers were quite vague and were often masked by the use of complex style. A key example is Saberi's creation of a frame story with different fictive characters with whose function Saberi played at will. One of them, usually Gol Agha, was the moral actor who had to mediate between opponents (Föllmer, 2008: 73–138). Specific subjects such as religion or the Iran–Iraq war were avoided entirely in their satire. There were also some other satirical magazines such as *Tanz-o-Karikatur* and *Keyhan-e Karikatur*, but none of them were as popular as *Gol-Agha*. Satirical pieces or columns that were printed in journals or magazines with a small specialised readership and little public interest, such as Salahi's *Hala Hekayat-e Mast* (now for our story), which was published in the literary journal *Donya-ye Sokhan*, could be more direct in their satirical criticism. Salahi's columns focused on literary criticism. They also included social and political issues concerning the problems of Iranians. The method and style of Salahi's texts were not as sophisticated as Saberi's texts. It was sufficient enough to use self-irony and to presuppose the reader's special knowledge (Föllmer, 2008: 139–90).

Even during Khatami's more liberal presidency, the tolerance for certain subjects in satirical criticisms was limited and the satirical style only changed gradually. The relevant references in Saberi's satire were less confused than before, even though method and style were not modified strikingly. When Salahi spoke about current political events after 1997 he refused contextual references and turned his satire to good comprehensible allegories. Satirist Ebrahim Nabavi, whose column *Sotun-e Panjom* (the fifth column) was published in the reform-oriented daily newspaper *Jame'e*, did not need to conceal his political opinions as much as Saberi and Salahi did. In his columns he portrayed the behaviour of the conservatives, the political opposition at that time, in a remarkably open and direct manner. This was unprecedented in post-revolutionary Iran. Nabavi was persecuted and imprisoned many times due to his outspokenness.

When Nabavi went into exile in Europe in 2002 after the closure of the liberal, reform-oriented periodicals (*Jame'eh*, *Toos*, *Neshat*, *Asr-e Azadegan*) this did not spell the end of Iranian satire. However, I would argue that the increase in censorship after 2000, especially following Ahmadinejad's election in 2005, and the development of the internet as a new communication platform for Iranians, brought an end to the importance of satire in the Iranian press. After the deaths of Saberi and Salahi and the emigration of Nabavi, satirical texts in the Iranian press lost popularity. However, other satirical papers such as *Tanz-o-Karikatur* or the conservative *Keyhan-e Karikatur* continued publication. These primarily contained cartoons, caricatures and comics and were published monthly (Sadr, 2006).

The development of caricatures and cartoons and the stifling of satirical press

The vacuum left by the absence of the aforementioned satirists accelerated the development of some alternatives in satirical communication such as caricatures and cartoons in the Iranian print media. The popularity of these satirical forms had increased during the first ten years of the *Gol Agha* publication. A survey of the weekly edition from 1990 to 2000 reveals that written contributions reduced in length over time (Föllmer, 2008: 96–8). Poems were soon reduced from 12 lyrical contributions per issue in the first year to three after ten years. These were replaced by short prose texts, such as anecdotes and jokes, as well as by illustrations and caricatures. While in 1990, the magazine printed an average of 19 caricatures per issue; ten years later, that number had risen to 31.

In addition, the Gol-Agha Institute, founded by Saberi in the first half of the 1990s, regularly organises caricature competitions and hosts seminars to foster the artistic development of those with a talent for drawing caricatures. The caricatures produced through these competitions and workshops generally critique social habits. Absolutely excluded from criticism are internal political issues, religion, sexuality and depictions of Iranian clerical politicians. Exceptions to this include the yearbooks of caricatures published by Ebrahim Nabavi and the caricaturist Nik Ahang-Kowsar who have been living in exile since 2003. Their books, published in Tehran in several editions, are collections of social and political caricatures, cartoons and witty anecdotes. The publication *Dar Sal-e 79 Ettefagh Oftadeh*

[*Something Happened in the Year 2000*] was so popular that it reached a second edition of 5,000 copies in the same year.

The Gol-Agha Institute continued to support the publication of other visual art forms such as comics, comic strips, animation art and photographs with humorous captions, offering a good deal of creative space to capable artists. Since 2001 the Gol-Agha Institute has organised Tehran's International Cartoon Biennial and Iranian cartoonists have been successful in international competitions, with artists like Kambiz Derambakhsh, Bahram Azimi, Javad Alizadeh and Touka Neyestani winning many awards. And since the beginning of the twenty-first century the internet has played an important role in the evolution of the field of visual satire. Iran's satirical cartoonists present their work on their own websites or weblogs. Magazines like *Gol-Agha* or *Irancartoon* have established an online presence and special websites for Iranian caricatures; www. Persiancartoon.com (est. 2003) and *The House of Caricatures*: http://iran cartoon.ir provides space for artists to show their work. In general, the visual forms of satire presented on the internet and at international competitions are highly skilled and creative, representing the awareness and the critical attitudes of the artists towards global issues.

A certain development in the depiction of Iranian politicians in caricatures is observable through an examination of *Gol-Agha* magazine over the years. The first issues contained stylistically simple and non-controversial caricatures of some non-clerical ministers and members of parliament, which were often published days or weeks after the related political event. Later, Karbaschi, Tehran's mayor, various members of parliament and former Vice President Habibi became the favourite subjects of the magazine's caricatures. Habibi was often depicted instead of the clerical Presidents Rafsanjani and Khatami, as it is more controversial to critique the clergy. In later editions, photos of clerics with humorous captions began to appear in print and, since 2005, Ahmadinejad, the non-clerical Iranian President, has himself been the subject of many of *Gol-Agha*'s caricatures. The delay between the actual event and the publication of its satirical comment and the taboo of exposing clerics in satirical drawings still remains.

Despite the popularity of caricatures and cartoons the scope for these in the Iranian press these days is very small. In an interview with *Eja* (2009), Javad Alizadeh, caricaturist and editor of the magazine *Tanz-o-Karikatur*, points out that there are striking differences between caricatures that comment on daily issues (*karikaturha-ye matbu'ati*) and caricatures without references to specific events (*karikaturha-ye namayeshgahi*). Whereas Iranians have been very successful in international caricature exhibitions, the caricatures published in the Iranian press have lost their importance as a source for social and political criticism. Takjou (2009) confirms that recently there has only been a narrow scope for *karikaturha-ye matbu'ati* in Iran.

Iranian satire on the internet

By the end of the 1990s the internet had become a growing platform for communication and satirical expression in Iran (Rahimi, 2008: 37–56). In the beginning of the 2000s, with increasing public access to the internet, internet space became an alternative for reformist and dissident voices in particular. The online presence of independent Persian news agencies offered a lot of raw and diverse information for the Iranian people, provoking both thought and discussion. Many Iranians also took advantage of the opportunity to create personal websites and weblogs to comment on current events and express themselves. Some of them published satirical comments or jokes on their own websites and Iranian satirists and caricaturists also began using the internet as a platform for their profession. Some of them gained popularity in Iran solely through the internet, including the Iranian writer Roya Sadr (http://bbgoal.com/) and the popular cleric Mohammad Ali Abtahi (http://www.webnevesheha.com/weblog/). Their exceptional statuses as a woman and an Iranian cleric respectively make these satirists worthy of scholarly attention. In 2003 the state made its first efforts to block unwanted websites (Sadr, 2003: 88; Rahimi, 2008: 47) and the extension of state control over the internet motivated some Iranian satirists like Nabavi to work outside Iran. After his emigration from Iran he wrote a satirical column for BBC Persian and the Iranian online journals *Rooz* and *Gooya*; in 2011 he was working for the Amsterdam-based radio programme *Zamaneh*.

Iranian satire's presence on the internet makes it a more global phenomenon than a specifically Iranian one. It facilitates communication between Iranians in exile and diaspora and those at home. The most beneficial aspect of satire on the internet is the interactive flow between authors and their audiences, which the print media cannot offer. Satirist and writer Manuchehr Ehterami reasoned in an interview in 2005 that the differences in satirical communication partly derive from the generation of those concerned and partly from the medium used. Ehterami is not able to work with the new communication platforms that the younger generation preferably uses; his age and the more personal satire distance him from the youth (2005: 33).

Satire's appearance on television

While satire in the Iranian press has stagnated since 2000, it quickly expanded into television a more popular medium. Comedy serials have been broadcast on state television since the early 1990s. In 1993, for example, Mehran Modiri acted in and directed his own first comedy programme. However, his first wide-reaching success came in 2002 when the satirical serial *Pavarchin* (*On Tiptoes*) screened on Iranian television for the first time. Even those who usually watched programmes on satellite television switched to the state's network (Alikhah, 2008). Why was this satirical serial so popular? Modiri did not follow the conventional Iranian comedy guidelines and he also avoided moral messages in the episodes. In order to get the audience to laugh at social matters relevant to Iranian society, the director played around with social clichés and stereotypes. *Pavarchin* picked up on various issues of daily urban life, including humorous scenes depicting marital and workplace relations, as well as creating contrasts between urban and rural life. It also parodied the elaborate rituals of Iranian etiquette (*ta'arrof*). *Pavarchin's* criticism of social conventions and behaviour was realised mainly through an accentuation of imperfections and exaggerations in the performance as well as in the use of language.

Modiri's subsequent serials *Noghtechin* (*Dots*, 2004) and *Jayeze-ye Bozorg* [*The Grand Prize*, 2005] were also humorous portrayals of primarily sociocultural issues. Yet even though these serials were popular, they were unable to attain the same level of success as *Pavarchin*. Modiri again achieved widespread acclaim with *Shabha-ye Barareh* [*Nights of Barareh*, 2005–6]. The director created a fictional historical and rural town that he called Barareh, which had already featured in *Pavarchin* and links both stories. The allegorical satire of the *Night of Barareh* takes place during the time of Reza Shah and criticises recent Iranian sociopolitical problems and cultural issues through an historical façade. Not only was this programme immensely popular, it divided Iranian society. While conservative newspapers such as *Resalat* denounced the serial, the liberals' newspaper *Shargh* defended it (Golpari, 2005).

Modiri's next serial, *Mard-e Hezar Chehreh* [*Man of a Thousand Faces*, 2008] departed from the historical setting that had been a feature of his previous creation. This time the programme parodied the gangster film genre. It provided sociopolitical criticism on many different realms of recent Iranian society and became a hot topic of discussion on Persian websites. Some claimed that the serial's criticism was superficial and humorous (*fokahi*) rather than satirical (*tanz*) while others felt so personally insulted that they sued the serial. In contrast to the previous programmes, the *Man of a Thousand Faces* linked the criticism of the administration system directly to the district of Shiraz. The administrative director sued those responsible for insulting him and his administrative apparatus. The charge did not result in a conviction and Modiri continued his programme the following year with the story of the *Man of Two Thousand Faces* (*mard-e do hezar chehreh*).

In contemporary Iran, every television channel has its own satirical programme. Even though Modiri's serials developed from simple social humour to allegorical sociopolitical criticism, satire on TV tends to be general and inoffensive, a characteristic that was criticised in the *Gol-Agha* year book of 2002/1381 (Shahidi, 2002). The magazine explains that the popularity of satirical TV shows has resulted in a form of satire that was mainly entertaining rather than an intellectual reflection on relevant sociopolitical and sociocultural issues. Before 2005, critical comments to the serial did not have crucial consequences for a further production of such satirical serials. This was seen for instance in the series of *Noghtechin*, as discussed by *Gol-Agha* (Asemi, 2005: 66). The journal approves Modiri's professionalism and the serial's deeper meaning, comparing it with *Pavarchin*, while avoiding the jokes about the people of the city Qazvin and the 'mistakenly' (*badrang*) satirised police service. Modiri's serials after 2005 alluded even to political issues, such as the elections, but this was rather exceptional. Satire on TV has generally shied away from thought-provoking satire and focused on entertaining humour instead, to attract the greatest possible number of viewers and to avoid conflicts with the administrative and political establishment. As will be discussed in the next section, Iranian cinema has not followed this trend towards inoffensive humour in such a pronounced way.

Satire in Iranian cinema

The public broadcasting of Iranian comedies in film and on television resumed slowly after the conclusion of the eight-year Iran–Iraq war when laughter and humour were almost entirely absent from the public sphere.

Between 1991, when the Gol-Agha Institute organised an event to honour the best Iranian comedy and comedians from the satirist's point of view, and 2008, there is little documentation about satirical films or comedies. Since movies are seldom produced with the intention of making satire, and since comedies do not automatically imply satirical messages, the best way to determine satirical movies in the period from 1992 until 2008 is through the effect they have after being screened.

Iranian cinema production is different from TV production and a lot depends on the status of the producer. Because television is a state-controlled institution, producers do not need to apply for licences to produce each individual work. The key difference between television and film is that film directors and producers have to pass through a permission-seeking process for the filming and release of their films, which is dictated by the Ministry of Culture and Islamic Guidance. This begins with obtaining a licence for the screenplay and lasts until the ministry has determined the place and time for public broadcasting. If a semi-private or public institution appears as producer, its special status allows more freedom from censorship. For example, the Arts Centre, which produced the film *The Snowman*, did not need to seek permission for the production of their screenplay from the Ministry of Culture and Islamic Guidance (Devictor, 2002: 73). However, just before the film was to be released for screening the ministry banned it. In addition to the constraints imposed by the application process described above, films also have a smaller potential audience than television serials. The costs of tickets, the extremely varying places and screening times, as well as the limited number of cinemas where a particular film is screened, all constrain the size of audience for any film (Farahmand, 2002: 90).

There are many Iranian cinema productions with critical content. Directors such as Mohsen Makhmalbaf, Amir Naderi, Bahram Beyzaei, Dariush Mehrjui and Masoud Kimiai have worked on socially critical films both before and after the Iranian revolution, but among their work there are a few outstanding satirical films. One of these films is Mehrjui's *The Lodgers* (also translated as *The Tenants, Ejarehneshinha*, 1987). The film parodies Iranian society and administration and has political implications that, at the time of release, were not recognised by the ministry (Esfandiary, 2011: 345). An apartment block on Tehran's periphery is in bad repair but its property status is unclear. The lodgers of the house need to restore their apartments which are all in various stages of dilapidation so they have to convince the landlord, who is also living in the house, to take action. Since the lodgers are at odds with each other over payments and the course of action, the house becomes more and more decayed until its residents are in danger of losing their lives and livelihoods. Sadr (2006: 200) calls this film a 'comedy of extremes.' He notes, '*The Lodgers* brimmed with satirical allegories concerning ownership, class differences, and the general life of the middle classes in the 1980s.' This film became a commercial success and was the highest-grossing film in 1987 (Javdani,

2002: 187). Sadr (ibid.) says that the film's imposition of order on a naturally chaotic subject, its good humour, and its outstanding actors were the reasons for its success.

Some ten years later another satirical film, *The Snowman* [*Adam-e barfi*, completed in 1994 but released in 1997], made by Davoud Mir-Bagheri reached Iran's cinemas. This bitter comedy was banned for three years for its undeniable political implications and representation of taboo subjects, such as the desire to travel to the USA and the highly controversial cross-dressing male protagonist (Sadr, 2006: 217, 238). Although many had already seen the film by purchasing or renting it on the black market between 1994 and 1997, the film became the most successful film of the year at the box office when it was finally released (Javdani, 2002: 278).

The war with Iraq became the subject of satirical criticism in the anti-war film *Leili Ba Man Ast* [*Leili is With Me*, 1995], which was directed by Kamal Tabrizi. A TV journalist goes to the front to film a documentary but his fear of war creates comic effect. He tries to escape but finds himself in several dangerous situations before finally becoming a hero. By critiquing the Iran–Iraq war Tabrizi broke a longstanding taboo and he distanced the film from what is typically known as a war movie in a humorous way. Tabrizi's second and deeply satirical film *The Lizard* (*Marmulak*, 2003) was outstandingly popular and highly significant for Iranian society. The film's depiction of a charismatic cat-burglar who escapes from jail by dressing in the clothes and turban of an ayatollah brought the issue of the relationship between people and religion into Iranian public discourse for the first time. It pushed at the boundaries of satire by using another taboo, socioreligious issues. The director made this viable through humour, as the film's sensitive wit is never blasphemous. *The Lizard* was criticised in its preliminary stages, was screened after a delay of a few months, and was very quickly banned from cinemas after its immense popularity and thought-provoking nature became apparent. Since its first screening in 2003, no other film has been of such importance and its release marked the first occasion since the instigation of the Islamic Republic that social attitudes towards religious issues were represented humorously as a way of expressing criticism.

Conclusion

The development of the mass media has contributed to the expansion of satirical communication under the cultural and sociopolitical circumstances that have existed in Iran since the revolution in 1979, broadening its variety and diversity. The mode of expression has shifted from textual to visual and the only exception to this development is found where text intersects with technology, as in the Iranian weblogs where satirical poetry is occasionally found. Visual forms of satire, especially caricature, comics and films, have increasingly replaced written satire and this has had many repercussions for Iranian satire in general. The control of media by the state as well as a desire to cater to a broad audience have both impacted on the modes of satirical communication. Humour on Iranian television currently focuses more on entertainment, tending towards a more social and private comedy while maintaining a certain seriousness and criticism, in particular in the serials of Modiri. On the other hand, cinematic satire is more critical, as the above-mentioned examples have shown. These films flirt with the red line of officially permissible content and can gradually break taboos, as Tabrizi's films have demonstrated. However, even cinematic satire is carefully articulated in an easy and humorous manner as directors exercise self-censorship so as not to be banned.

In summary, even though satire's official definition and its social function, meaning and mode of communication may vary from its Western counterpart, satire is an important part of public communication and society in Iran. The degree of public interest in a certain medium often determines the degree of state control and self-censorship, especially in satirical contributions to Iran's cultural corpus. Despite the several limits imposed through censorship and state control, Iran still offers a certain scope for creativity in satirical expression. Satirists, for instance, adapt their modes of expression and communication alongside the rules of the Ministry of Culture and Islamic Guidance, or find new mediums for publication. Thus, Iranian satirists have persistently found alternatives, circumventing existing limits, leaving restrictions behind and publishing their satirical works with remarkable success.

References

Alikhah, F (2008) 'The politics of satellite television in Iran' in Semati, M (ed.) *Media, Culture and Society in Iran. Living with Globalization and the Islamic State.* London: Routledge: 94–110.

Asemi, M (2005/1384) 'Hasht al-haft: Negahi be haft majmu'e-ye komedi-ye televiziyun-e sal-e 1383. Noqtechin – shoor-o-shirin'. [A glance at seven TV comedy serials of 2004. Noghtechin – bitter and sweet]. *Mahname-ye Gol Aqa* 161: 66–8.

Behzadi-Anduhjerdi, H (1999/1378) *Tanz va tanzpardazi dar Iran. Pazhuheshi dar adabiyat-e ejtema'i, siyasi, enteqadi – 'elal-e ravani va ejtema'i* [Satire and Satirical

Art in Iran. Research on Social, Political, and Critical Literature – Psychological and Social Reasons]. Tehran: Saduq.

Devictor, A (2002) 'Classic tools, original goals: cinema and public policy in the Islamic Republic of Iran (1979–97)' in Tapper, R (ed.) *The New Iranian Cinema. Politics, Representation and Identity.* London: I.B.Tauris: 66–76.

Esfandiary, S (2011) 'Mehrjui's social comedy and the representation of the nation in the age of globalization'. *Iranian Studies* 44.3: 341–58.

Esma'ili, M (1999–2000/1378) 'Tanz-e matlub va sazande: zarurat va vizhegiha' ['Desirable satire: Requirements and properties']. *Rasane* 4: 81–6.

Farahmand, A (2002) 'Perspectives on recent (international acclaim for) Iranian cinema' in Tapper, R (ed.) *The New Iranian Cinema. Politics, Representation and Identity.* London: I.B.Tauris: 86–108.

Föllmer, K (2008) *Satire in Iran von 1990 bis 2000.* Wiesbaden: Harrassowitz.

Golpari, E (2005) 'Negahi be majmu'e-ye janjal-barangiz-e *Shabha-ye Barareh*', ['A glimpse to the disturbing serial Barareh Nights'] (www.bbc.co.uk/persian/arts/story/2005/11/051103_pm-el-barareh-nights.shtml (last accessed 28 April 2010)).

Halabi, AA (1998/1377) *Tarikh-e tanz va shukhtab'i dar Iran va jahan-e eslami ta ruzegar-e Obeyd-e Zakani* [*History of Satire and Humour in the Islamic World until the Time of Obeyd-e Zakani*]. Tehran: Behbahani.

'Harf tu harf ba Manuchehr Ehterami az *Towfiq* ta *Gol Aqa*' (2005/1384) *Mahname-ye Gol Aqa* 161: 28–33.

Javadi, H (1988) *Satire in Persian Literature.* London and Toronto: Associated University Press.

Javdani, H (2002/1381) *Salshomar-e tarikh-e sinema-ye Iran Tir 1279-Shahrivar 1379* [*Annual Historical Survey of Iranian Cinema from 1900 to 2000*]. Tehran: Qetre.

'Karikaturist bayad risk konad' ['A caricaturist has to take a risk']. Interview about caricature, an art of criticism, with J Alizadeh (http://eja.ir/category/cartooneiran from 19 January 2009/30 Dey 1387 (accessed 28 April 2010)).

Rahimi, B (2008) 'The politics of the internet in Iran' in Semati, M (ed.) *Media, Culture and Society in Iran. Living with Globalization and the Islamic State.* London: Routledge: 37–56.

Sadr, HR (2006) *Iranian Cinema – A Political History.* London: I.B.Tauris.

Sadr, R (2002/1381) *Bist sal ba tanz* [*Twenty Years with Satire*]. Tehran: Hermes.

——— (2003/1382) 'Tanz-e weblogi' ['Satire of weblogs']. *Salname-ye Gol Aqa*: 87–96.

——— (2005/1384) 'Bayad rahash ra peyda konam' ['I should find the way'] *Tanzpardazan-e mo'aser: Kiyumars-e Saberi-ye Fumani – Gol Aqa* [*Recent Satirists: Kiyumars Saberi-Fumani – Gol Aqa*]. Tehran: Gol Aqa.

——— (2006/1385) *Bardasht-e akher: Negahi be tanz-e emruz-e Iran*. Tehran: Sokhan.

Salahi, E (1993/1372) 'Mo'arefi-ye yek nashriye: *Towfiq*' ['Introduction of a publication: *Towfiq*']. *Salname-ye Gol Aqa*: 46–85.

Semati, M (ed.) (2008) *Media, Culture and Society in Iran. Living with Globalization and the Islamic State*. London: Routledge.

Shahidi, S (2002/1381) 'Tanz dar televiziyun' ['Satire in TV']. *Salname-ye Gol Aqa*: 28–31.

Takjou, J (2009) 'Karikatur az aghaz ta emruz. Peydayesh, gostaresh va shakhebandi-ye karikatur va anva'-e an dar Iran' ['Caricature from the beginning until today. Manifestations, prevalence, and classification of caricature and its varieties in Iran'] (http://eja.ir/category/cartooneiran from 19 January 2009/30 Dey 1387 (accessed 28 April 2010)).

Tapper, R (ed.) (2002) *The New Iranian Cinema. Politics, Representation and Identity*. London: I.B.Tauris.

Towfiq, F (2005/1384) *Ruzname-ye Towfiq va Kaka-Towfiq* [*The Newspaper Towfiq and Kaka-Towfiq*]. 3rd edn, Tehran: Nashr-e abi.

Zarru'i-Nasrabad, A (1995/1374) 'Moqaddame'i bar sabk-shenasi-ye 'Do kalame harf-e hesab' ['Introduction to the stylistics of the "Two proper words"']. *Salname-ye Gol Aqa*: 100–30.

CHAPTER 13

GENDERED TABOOS IN IRAN'S TEXT MESSAGE JOKES
Naghmeh Samini

Do you know the phone number of the perfect girl?
0020908560
Do you know what it means?
IQ: 00, Age: 20, Hips: 90, Bust: 85, Waist: 60

The sound of an SMS being received breaks the silence, alerting someone to his or her mobile phone. They download the message and see the above, which is typical of the many SMS jokes circulating in Iran these days. Because of the character limit imposed on SMS messages (140 characters), the receiver of the joke has inadvertently read it before consciously deciding whether or not to be its audience. If he or she finds the joke funny, barely any time passes between a laugh and forwarding the message on. This brief chapter will describe the different genres of SMS jokes in Iran and explain why they are so popular.

Iran's cellular network was launched in 1994, but it was only incorporated extensively into Iranian life about ten years ago (Ghodsizadeh and Parvin, 2010) Today, there are more than 40 million handsets in Iran, which means that one in two people have access to a mobile phone. This communication tool rapidly changed from a mechanical appliance into an integral part of everyday Iranian life and culture, and it adapted accordingly. The requirements of each culture reveal new functions for media, as people adapt technologies to suit their needs. I label these non-standard usages of standard technologies 'marginal functions'.

SMS capabilities are a standard feature of mobile phones, but over the last six years the sending of SMS messages has become very popular in Iran. Through its popularisation it has also adopted some marginal functions. While the sending of news, advertisements and personal messages are all primary functions of SMS technology, sending and forwarding jokes can be labelled a marginal function. This 'marginal function' is fast becoming one of the most universal applications of SMS in Iran today.

There are very few important current events that have not been subject to the sharply mocking tone of an SMS joke. When Iran launched a satellite into space, when fuel was rationed, and when Obama was elected US president, SMS jokes raced from phone to phone. This chapter reveals why SMS jokes are spreading wildly in Iran through an investigation of their place within contemporary Iranian culture.

A majority of SMS jokes circulating within Iran clash with social, moral, political and religious taboos. Taboos are rife in Iranian society, and the deeper that taboos run through the veins of a culture, the easier it is to create objectionable jokes out of them. While it is unsafe to tell jokes of this calibre in public, SMS technology provides the satirist with safe cover; most of the time an SMS joke is received, the original author remains anonymous. Jokes making fun of political events are subject to a very particular social context at a point in time and thus have a limited shelf life but jokes clashing with sexual and religious taboos are more deeply rooted and also circulate for much longer. This is why the majority of jokes cited in this article are of a sexual nature.

The formal culture and widely accepted conventions engrained in Iranian society have a general taboo against any public revelation of sexual issues. This culture is well ingrained, a lens through which many of the social behaviours and even historical changes of Iran can be examined. In addition, official laws reinforce sexual taboos by supporting the tradition of hiding every issue related to sexuality. In the traditional, official and monopolistic culture, the concept of sexuality is strongly linked to the concept of 'woman'. The Islamic government veils sexual issues as comprehensively as they veil women. In the official and ancient literature of Iran, women are defined as being empty of sexual qualities, or depicted through a veil of mysticism, piety and virtuousness. Or she may be placed in a position of 'symbolic mortality', where metaphors and allusions transcend the reality of the dominant culture (Strinati, 2001: 243). In instances of symbolic mortality, words are translated into symbols in order to circumvent traditional and religious norms (ibid.). Women characterised as the divinely beloved in classic Iranian literature or, contrarily, as the incarnation of earthly temptations, have all been depicted through the same symbolic mortality.

In this monopolistic culture, truth is a predetermined issue towards which there is no possibility for critical approach. It contrasts starkly with 'conversation culture', informal and unofficial, in which reality is an inconsequential issue (Ghazi-Moradi, 2008: 243). The omission of sexual dialogue from 'official' Iranian culture, particularly in ancient literature, has left no possibility for the instigation of critical discussion. We wonder why most Asian myths are integrated with sexual discourse, while in post-Zoroastrian Iran, Anahita, the most significant Iranian goddess, lacks all signs of sexuality.

However, while official culture leads the nation in one direction, public and conversational culture pulls the people in the other. Richards (2009: 21) believes that great historical and cultural narrations cannot deny the instinctual needs of people and says these needs will eventually be revealed in some context, as they cannot and must not be suppressed. They are just like weeds, uncontrollable and unpredictable. In Iran SMS jokes conflict with the dominant culture. These jokes reveal this conflict in two ways – firstly, by confronting sexual taboos and, secondly, through the use of satirical humour, they transform their observations on reality into a sort of analysis. Sexual jokes are in conflict with the dominant monopolistic culture. In the Islamic Republic of Iran, where obviously female mannequins, suggestive clothing and women's underwear are banned from public display and physical contact between men and women is banned from television, film and theatre, sexual jokes play a special role.

To understand this concept, let us analyse some examples of SMS jokes being exchanged in Iran:

> A Rashti man tells his wife, 'The 'Night Bat' is raping women in Tehran.'
> His wife replies, 'Damn it! How come he's only raping Tehrani women?!'

What kind of a woman is being depicted in this joke? Is it not the same familiar picture of woman that traditional beliefs are trying to propagate, that a woman wants to be used as a sexual object even if this occurs in the form of rape and is perpetrated by one of the most violent serial murderers of Iran, the 'Night Bat'?

Let us compare this joke with another example.

> The wolf stops by Shangool and Mangool's house and knocks at the door. Their mother replies, 'The kids aren't home, come on in.'

This SMS joke has a classic structure. It states first a familiar subject, which connects the reader to a collective childhood memory. All Iranians have heard the original story of *Shangool and Mangool* during their childhood. In this popular folk story, which is similar to *The Three Little Pigs*, the wolf tricks three lambs into letting him into their house by imitating the voice of their mother. He subsequently eats them. The impact of this joke comes from its broad appeal to the collective memory of its audience. In this joke, the lambs' mother, whose sexual temptation dominates her motherly affection, calls him in. She sexually objectifies herself, in a similar manner to the female character in the 'Night Bat' joke.

The following joke is an example of an SMS joke that must be read rather than spoken. In this imaginary advertisement, it is the man who is humiliated, and the woman is empowered through being positioned as a femme fatale.

> Marriage advertisement: I am a nice lady, educated and pretty, with blonde hair, blue eyes, a toned body and narrow waist. I am fully communicative and financially rich, but I'll never marry a silly and cowardly man.

Generally speaking, SMS jokes can be divided into four categories.

- jokes satirising the specific qualities of Iran's various ethnic groups;
- jokes using fables, folklore and famous stories;
- jokes dealing with daily issues and tasks;
- jokes conflicting with dominant sexual taboos.

The jokes presented above belong to the final category and, through their confrontation of sexual taboos, conflict with the ideals of the monopolistic dominant culture. In this dominant culture, reality is a predetermined and unchangeable issue. The solutions may be different but the results are the same. In both jokes and the dominant cultural discourse women are perceived as sexual objects. However, while these ideas create further reason to oppress sexual dialogue in traditional culture, the same hidden thoughts about sexuality move into the rhetoric of sexual jokes and perpetuate the same beliefs. In other words, jokes act as the subconscious mirror to the anti-sexual moral culture in Iran. The dominant discourse in literature never speaks of sexuality but the marginal discourse does. Here the hegemonic sexual culture holds the reins of marginal discourse, in the form of SMS jokes, firmly in its hands. These jokes may be explicitly taboo-classed, but they are implicitly in a position of servitude to these same taboos.

It is also important to examine the medium through which these jokes are expressed. At first glance, it may seem as though SMS jokes are similar to other jokes and that mobile handset and SMS technology has only facilitated their exchange, thus having a minimal effect on their meaning and function. However, this is not the case. As Marshall McLuhan (1972: 70) has argued, 'the medium is the message'. The fact that these jokes are circulated by SMS is of great significance and the medium itself has impacted strongly upon the content of the jokes. These impacts can be categorised as follows:

Jokes that rely on the format of SMS to impart their humour

Some jokes are only funny when read – the very particular format of an SMS. In other words, they exploit the specificities of the medium. The joke presented below belongs to this category.

> honey, sweetie, sugar, salt, peach, candy, gold, silver, copper, zinc, scrap iron, valves, broken samovars [Iranian tea pots], household appliances... we buy all those things!

The joke is displayed in such a way that the reader must scroll through the text in order to find the punch line at the end. At first, it seems that the sender is attempting to be romantic but at the end, it becomes clear that the narrator of the joke is a street peddler (*Kaseh-boshghabi*). This joke has clearly been designed for the specific format offered by mobile phone technology and it loses all meaning and function in oral form. This joke also explores sexual taboos. Rhetoric used to describe a love object are also used to describe commodities, and through this metaphor the woman becomes objectified and relegated to the realm of products a street peddler may buy or sell; she is compare with the broken samovar, for which there is no longer any use. The following joke is also an example of a joke that is only successful in SMS format.

> Are you masculine or feminine? Look down to find out ...
> ...
> ...
> I don't mean down here, you idiot!

Again, the reader of this joke has to scroll down the SMS in order to receive the whole joke, and again the joke makes fun of the physical differences between men and women.

Standard jokes that have been condensed due to format restrictions

In order to fit within the space provided by the SMS format, standard oral jokes must be condensed into a minimised form before circulation. This minimisation seems to be accidental, a purely practical consideration, which does not influence the meaning and theme of joke. However, Adorno and Horkheimer (1972/2001: 80) have argued, 'The more clearly and purely words transfer the narrator's purpose, the more ineffective they become.' In fact, the constraints of the text message format reduce all florid prose, imparting the message (in this case sexual jokes) far more strongly and almost in a penetrating way to the audience. The next category clarifies how this ineffectiveness influences the process of receiving jokes.

Omission of the traditional roles of speaker and audience

Traditionally there is a live and direct confrontation between the speaker and their audience when a joke is told. According to Ahmad Okhovat (2005: 15), the relationship between speaker and audience constitutes a crucial part of a joke's structure. The audience, by smiling, acting indifferently, or even expressing disdain, reveals their opinion about a speaker's joke in the simplest form. The usual process of joke telling can link dialogue with protest. However, in SMS jokes, the active and critical audience is omitted, and something happens which Habermas calls a 'communicative action loss' (in Ghazi-Moradi, 2008: 246).

The audience of an SMS joke is a fairly passive assembly and in consuming the joke they acquire a mass identity rather than individual identity (ibid.). The recipient of an SMS joke knows that their individual identity is not addressed; they know that this joke has been forwarded to many other individuals, thus creating the mass identity of the collective audience. On the flip side, the recipient does not assume any responsibility while taking part in this collective audience, and remains a passive acceptant. In the end, nobody is responsible for the joke, as everybody assumes that the sender they received it from was merely forwarding the message.

Both the joke teller and their audience remain anonymous to some extent through the circulation of SMS jokes. The joke teller's identity is virtual and becomes, in a sense, the mobile phone itself. An important characteristic of protest is the risk of endangerment through action, with the protestor assuming the responsibility of the danger. In the case of the SMS joke, the sender (protesting against the dominant cultural discourse) is only a mobile number. Even if a name has been ascribed to that number and appears alongside the message on the recipient's handset, it is assumed that he or she simply received the joke and forwarded it. Therefore, nobody must accept responsibility for the confrontation of taboos in SMS jokes; the original joke teller becomes completely hidden in the virtual space.

As the hidden speaker of SMS jokes does not carry the responsibility of their own words, the audience is also selected far less carefully than it would be if the joke was being told face-to-face. When jokes are forwarded, they are sent to most of the contacts in someone's phonebook without much thought. The audience cannot react to or interact with the hidden speaker. Global communications technologies have made the circulation of predigested material so simple that the recipient barely thinks about the content of the joke before deciding whether or not to forward the message to their friends. Richards believes (1994/2003: 24), 'If an experience is not satisfactory, then the public does not continue it collectively.' One who receives a sexual joke and sends it to someone else is taking part in a collective activity, without any critical action or participatory dialogue occurring. In fact, unwittingly, the senders and recipients of SMS jokes have contributed to a debate on the responsibility of discourse. Today, traditional forms of joke telling in Iran are waning. Even in parties and gatherings, those previously known as the 'jokers' take out their mobile phones and read jokes aloud from their handsets. Most commonly, the reaction of their temporary real life audience is, 'Forward it to me!' And thus begins the cycle of sending and receiving.

Neither traditional culture nor the law attempts to stem the flow of SMS jokes. Perhaps one reason why the authorities are not so concerned is because if every one of Iran's 40 million mobile phones sent an average of only one SMS message per year, the annual net profit for the Iranian Telecommunications Company would be huge. That might be the biggest joke of all.

References

Adorno, TW and Horkheimer, M (1972) 'Saanate Farhang Sazi' ['The culture industry']. Translation from English by Morad Farhadpour (2001). *Organon Quarterly* 18, Autumn: 35–83.

Ghazi-Moradi, H (2008) *Estebdad dar Iran*. [*Despotism in Iran*]. Tehran: Akhtaran Publication.

Ghodsizadeh, P and Parvin, M (2010) *Ashnaii ba Tarikhche eie Tekefon dar Iran* [*An Introduction to the History of the Mobile in Iran*], Hamshahri (www. hamshahrionline.ir/news/?id=64485 (last accessed 15 May 2010)).

McLuhan, M (1967) 'Resaneh Paiam Ast' ['The medium is the message: An inventory of effects']. Translation by Mohamad Taghi Maieli (1972). *Farhang o Zandegi* 8, Spring: 65. 77.

Okhovvat, A (2005) *Latifeh ha az koja miaiand?* [*Where do Jokes come From?*]. Tehran: Ghesseh Publication.

Richards, B (1994) *Ravankavi-e-Farhang-e-Ammeh*. [*The Psychoanaysis of Popular Culture, Disciplines of Delight*]. Translation from English by Hossein Paiandeh (2003). Tehran: Tarhe.

Strinati, D (2001) *Moghadame ii bar Nazarie haie farhange Ammeh* [*An Introduction to Theories of Popular Culture*]. Translation from English by Soraya Pak-Nazar. Tehran: Gam-e.

CHAPTER 14

IRANIAN MURAL PAINTING

New Trends

Alice Bombardier

In this study on mural painting in Iran,[1] I highlight the 'performed dimension' (Boissière, 2010) of space in contemporary cities of the country, which is constituent of a particular sensory–perceptual feeling experienced daily by a population that is now predominantly urban. The development of Iranian murals from the Islamic revolution (1979) particularly enunciated a scenario based on a non–figurative concept: self–sacrifice by martyrdom (Khosrokhavar, 1995). The extension of the rhetoric of martyrdom in Iran has undergone significant changes over the past few years, with scenarios increasingly linked to the Israeli–Palestinian conflict and not only to the Iran–Iraq war (1980–8). By retracing the steps and the context inherent in the construction of this plastic space, then examining the constant renegotiation of these murals developed 'in palimpsest' (Corboz, 2001), whose superimposed layers cover the walls of major cities, I question the issues raised by artistic 'spatialisation' in Iran. I also indicate the different directions being taken by the movement.

The origins of mural painting in Iran: Between revolution and war

It is interesting to consider how the figure of the martyr was lexicalised in the Islamic Republic and became the driving force behind the mural painting movement in the country.

The surveys that I conducted in 2008 and 2009 among Iranian painters in Tehran (Bombardier, 2012) have shown that the movement of Iranian mural painting began at the time of the revolution, with graffiti and rough paintings, most often with the help of stencils. At night, the entire population and especially artists went all over town and covered walls with slogans or portraits of their leaders. Thus, the walls of the capital reflected the intense struggles between the main revolutionary factions: Islamist, communist and nationalist. Mr T, interviewed in 2009, stated that during this period – because his work was each time fully covered up with red paint – he painted three times in one month, always in the same place, a portrait of Imam Khomeini. According to the painter Hosein Khosrojerdi, the walls of the houses adjacent to the avenues that connected Mehrabad airport to the city centre of Tehran were filled with slogans, hand prints and caricatures, representing the shah as a puppet or as a raptor with bloody claws (Cuomo, 2011: 263).

The return of Ayatollah Khomeini to Tehran in February 1979 coincided with an escalation in the use of the means of expression. The Islamist faction was growing on and marched through the streets with monumental mobile paintings several metres high representing Ayatollah Khomeini. These paintings were carried at arm's length by demonstrators, much as the effigies carried during the religious processions of Ashura.[2] The author of some of these works, Mr S, interviewed in 2009, was 23 years old at the outbreak of the revolutionary events, 'having worked for the revolution' as an artist: his moving portraits were made from photographs. Son of a carpet salesman from the province of Khorasan, this painter was destined to create carpets designs and he initially followed a traditional apprenticeship in a local workshop. Then, he entered the Faculty of Decorative Arts in Tehran and was received at the Ecole des Beaux–Arts in Paris, staying six months in France between March and August 1979, before returning to Iran. In addition to portraits of Khomeini, he is the author of many mural paintings in Tehran.

Before leaving for France in March 1979, Mr S had witnessed the formative steps of the movement of Iranian revolutionary art. The members of this movement, most students in painting at the Faculty of Fine Arts of the University of Tehran, organised a painting exhibition, on 11 February 1979, in the basement of the mosque *Hoseiniyeh–ye Ershad* (where Ali Shariati had taught before the revolution), the day of the abolition of the Pahlavi monarchy. They called their group *Salman*, named after one of the first supposed companions of the Prophet of non-Arab origin, Salman the Persian. According to Mr R interviewed in 2009, this first exhibition of Islamic–revolutionary art was a success. With the loan of two jeeps from IRIB, the Iranian state broadcaster, a tour of the exhibition started throughout the country and led to the creation of the Centre of Thought and Islamic Art (*Howzeh–ye andisheh va honar–e eslami*) (Khosrojerdi, 1999).[3] This Centre, bringing together several disciplines, became the source of the aesthetic credo of the Islamic regime, based on the idea of martyrdom. Made up of a university, workshops and exhibition spaces, it has marked contemporary artistic productions by its edicts on the definition and the value of Islamic–revolutionary art and by subsidising exclusively artists who adhered to the creed.

The painters who submitted works in this founding exhibition were Kazem Tshalipa, Hasan Mohammadi, Mahmud Imani, Habibollah Sadeghi, Hosein Khosrodjerdi, Ali Nowruzitalab, Morteza Haydari, Ali Rajabi, Hosein Sadri, Naser Palangi, Mr Ruhani, Mrs Bargh, Morteza Katuzian and Mohammad Ehsa'i (who presented a work entitled *La–elaha el–Allah*) (Khosrojerdi, 1999). One of the only books devoted in Iran exclusively to revolutionary painting *Dah sal ba naqqashan–e Enqelab–e Eslami 1357–1367 [A decade with the revolutionary Iranian painters 1979–1989]* (Gudarzi, nd) quotes the principal artists of this movement, that included some of the same names: Ali Sani Wazirian, Mustafa Naderlu, Mostafa Gudarzi, Abdolhamid Ghadirian, Habibollah Sadeghi, Hosein Khosrodjerdi, Kazem Tshalipa, Naser Palangi and Iradj Eskandari.

The movement of Iranian mural painting as such was initiated soon after this exhibition by other students in painting from the Faculty of Fine Arts of Tehran University, alongside the professors Alkhas and Sadeddin. According to testimonies collected by Camilla Cuomo in her documentary *The Factory of Martyrs* (Cuomo and Vozza, 2009), the first mural was originally painted by these art teachers and their students in the University of Tehran, on the walls of the Faculty of Fine Arts. It represented the epic imagery of the revolution: before, during and after. Then, other murals were done in the streets of the capital, in schools and factories. The artist Nilufar Ghaderinejad, who participated in the movement as a student, says in the documentary that she had made at that time a mural on the walls of the Worker's Union in Tehran and relates that passers–by stopped in the street to admire her vast composition. These artists tell today that they had in mind as a reference the Mexican muralists such as Rivera, Orozco and Siqueiros. As evidenced by this mural dedicated to workers, the socialist realism theorised in the Soviet Union had also influenced those painters close to the Marxist faction, who also used this means of expression and popular mobilisation in the Iranian revolution of 1979 (Chelkowski and Dabashi, 2000).

The internal struggle that began in May 1979 between the Islamists and other revolutionary factions, including the powerful Marxist faction, resulted in late Autumn 1979 in the total neutralisation of the walls of the capital. In December 1979, when the constitution was being adopted, the Ayatollah Khomeini ordered the cleaning of the walls and the restoration of neutrality in public space (Yavari d'Hellencourt, 1987).

This neutrality has been thrown back into doubt after the offensive of the Iraqi army in September 1980. The Iran–Iraq war has been the real trigger of the mural movement in Iran. The Organisation of Islamic Propaganda (*Sazeman–e tablighat–e eslami*) experienced a considerable period of development. The Centre of Thought and Islamic Art, at first non-governmental, was attached in 1982 to this organisation despite opposition from some artists, who left the institution (Jalali-Naini, 1998). Similarly, the Foundation of Martyrs (*Bonyad–e shahid*) has been mobilised, involved in the war effort and gradually, this Foundation has occupied the front of the public arena by establishing the cult of the martyrs (Marzolph, 2004). Founded in 1979 by a decree of Ayatollah Khomeini, its original mission was to identify the victims of the previous regime to financially support their families (Gruber, 2008). The Foundation of Martyrs has acquired in a very short time an influential power that it would be useful to study accurately. Researches on its founding members, the events that marked its creation and its early years, the development of a network in the provinces and on the institutions attached as the Museum of Martyrs (*Muzeh–ye Shohada*), finally on its current decline, are still lacking. Indeed, the cultural section of the Foundation of Martyrs has become, since 1981, the instigator of a movement (especially regarding Tehran but also other major cities in Iran) of murals dedicated mainly to the themes of war and martyrdom. The mural painting has now been contributing to Iran's official propaganda. According to Mr S – who reported he had been posted to wall paintings during his military service in the 1980s – the Foundation has commissioned artists, students or professionals, or non-artists as young conscripts,[4] to paint these large murals, which have had a considerable impact on the population and are now considered as characteristic of the Iranian capital and of revolutionary art in the country.

The movement of mural painting today

Thirty years after the revolution, the restoration and/or the renewal of this pictorial heritage is in progress. Murals dating from the beginning of the 1980s that have not been replaced at least once are rare. Over the past few years, there have been many replacements. The archives of Ulrich Marzolph allowed me to identify three different murals painted successively on a same wall, reflecting the current changes of mural painting in Iran.

A mural painted on the theme of the martyr Djamshid-e Zardosht and his daughter – whose original model had been applied in 1981 to the wall of the Foundation of Martyrs. Following its great success, it generated many variations across the country (Bombardier, 2011). Located in 2001 on the expressway Modares in Tehran, it was modified twice in a short period, in 2003 and 2004. Significantly, the two following murals no longer refer to the Iran–Iraq war, but to the Israeli–Palestinian conflict.

The painting, photographed in 2003, responded to a particular structure, a 'zigzag' bottom-up composition, which allows parallelisms (see figure 14.1) (Marzolph, 2004 and 2013). The foreground begins on the right. Indeed, the right of the painting is occupied by an anonymous face of a Palestinian, whose features are distorted by a cry of pain. The rest of the foreground is striated of red tulips, a symbol of martyrdom often used by the Foundation of Martyrs. In a balancing effect, on the second level located far left, the bust of the current supreme leader, Khamenei, is represented with a scarf – *keffiyeh* – on his shoulders and with an injunctive finger. The *keffiyeh* is one of the main symbols of the Palestinian struggle. Another *keffiyeh* unfurls like a flag or a shroud. The third level can be seen at the centre of the painting and shows the holy Dome of the Rock in Jerusalem. Finally, on the fourth level, back to the left end, the face of Imam Khomeini is outlined in the sky, while on the right side, a slogan, a quote from Imam Khomeini, is written in Persian and English. According to Ulrich Marzolph, this quote is one of the first bilingual slogans that appeared in Tehran; these have increased over the past few years: 'The Islamic ummah (nation) will always stay alongside Palestinians and be opposed to their enemies.'

Figure 14.1 View 1. Photo: Ulrich Marzolph, Highway Modares, Tehran, 2003.

In 2004, this mural was once more changed but the pro-Palestinian atmosphere and the slogan still remained (see figure 14.2). The reason for this change seems to have been the assassination of Sheikh Ahmad Yasin, leader of the Hamas, by the Israeli army on 22 March 2004. Thus, the portrait of the Palestinian leader appears in a little frame in the middle of the painting. The left part, tinged with cold colours, represents a Star of David striated with the colors of the US flag, torn. The right side, dominated by warm colors, is occupied by a medallion showing the faces of the two supreme leaders who have succeeded as the head of the Islamic Republic, Khomeini and Khamenei. At the top, between colored curves, the Dome of the Rock still appears, topped left by the Kaaba in Mecca and right by the mosque of Imam Hosein in Kerbala. The bilingual slogan is the same, repeated on both sides of the painting. The same curves can be identified on a colorful mural located upstream of the highway Modares, indicating the relay forged between different murals geographically separated, here connected with an intermittent ribbon.

Therefore, the general semiotics of the movement of mural painting underwent transformations. The discourse of the Foundation of Martyrs is evolving. Today, the mural movement seems, 20 years after the end of

Figure 14.2   View 2. Photo: Ulrich Marzolph, Highway Modares, Tehran, 2004.

the Iran–Iraq war, to feed on another conflict, the Israeli–Palestinian conflict. It uses the rhetoric of martyrdom to support the Palestinian cause and rekindles at the same time the flame and the memory of its own struggles.

These recent changes are following a long period of stagnation. During the 1990s, after the war's end in 1988, the mural movement in Iran seemed to run out of steam. However, attempted reforms had already taken place at that time. Some paintings were commissioned in the 1990s from professional artists who made murals in a style that was no longer directly revolutionary either in form or in content. A woman has for example painted a mural on the Square of the Mother (*Meydun–e Madar*) in Tehran. This mural represents a woman in a white *chador*, with a halo of light, her hands raised. This 'mother' overlooks the metal tips of the effigy carried in Iran during the processions of Ashura. The whole drawing is surrounded by foliage (see figure 14.3). This artist is also the author of a mural in this style on Vali'asr Square.[5]

Various attempts have been made to halt the decline of the Foundation of Martyrs. But many Iranians have considered that these efforts were too

Figure 14.3 Attempted Reforms. Photo: Alice Bombardier, Madar Square, Tehran, 2009.

cautious and the fact is they have not renewed popular attention. The Municipality of Tehran and its Office of Beautification [of the Public Space] (*Zibasazi*) has now become associated with the Foundation of Martyrs and is currently implementing new procedures, more audacious, to orchestrate a fundamental reform of the mural movement, whose potential remains unchallenged.

The development of new genres

In 2008, the Municipality of Tehran brought together various stakeholders, the Foundation of Martyrs – the Museum of Contemporary Art in Tehran, University of Tehran and the University of Art – leading to the formation of a new committee within the Foundation of Martyrs. This committee is composed of artists from each institution. They were instructed to set 50 new murals designed by professional artists and responding to the artistic requirements newly defined. Many commissions have been initiated. As reported by some of these artists, a project proposed by Mustafa Naderlu, a professor at the University of Art, has already been commissioned (Bombardier, 2012).

However, the initiatives taken directly by the Office of Beautification [of the Public Space], in the Municipality of Tehran, were the most significant. Paintings were commissioned this time from young designers. The drawings of Mehdi Ghadyanlu have caught the attention, met great success and have been widely reproduced on the walls of Tehran since 2007 (Cuomo and Vozza, 2009). This young artist is the author of murals of a new kind, where he plays with the details, the effects of perspective or shadow. He includes the mural in its context by combining representation and reality. These new murals catch the eye in a humorous way and lead one to consider at the same time the work, its message through different symbols, and the landscape in which it is built. These superimpositions give to his murals an undeniable poetic dimension, which increases the ways of reading and goes into the meaning in greater depth.

Thus, the city undergoing radical transformation is reflected in a composition of the young graphic designer (see figure 14.4). On Vanak Square in Tehran, on the whole front of a glass-walled building, a city under construction is symbolised by carpets put together by men and women launched into space. They fly in an upward movement with propellers. Traditional symbols, such as carpets, are associated with futuristic elements. Mehdi Ghadyanlu also strives to represent various

Figure 14.4 Changing City. Photo: Alice Bombardier, Vanak Square, Tehran, 2009. Attributed to Mehdi Ghadyanlu.

classes of Iranian society (see figure 14.5). At the crossroads of the avenues Enqelab and Vali'asr, on the walls of Azad University, young students in blue robes greet passers-by and show off their diplomas from the bridges linking different parts of the building, suspended in space. A nearby building displays two plastic logos, hanging on its facade, representing the same young graduates in blue dress. These logos are included in the painting, which gives them life. It deals mainly with the idea of success at school and presents educated young people as life models. Another recurring theme of this new kind of mural refers to nature (see figure 14.6).

On the walls of a schoolyard, on Mirdamad Avenue, a country-style painting can be seen: a wilderness without human life is framed by the structure of a futuristic building. A man on the edge of the frame, walking up stairs, is a whisker away from going through a door opening into the void. The mountainous landscape could be that of Tehran in a pre-urban idyll. The nature is green, not barren at all but proliferating in an atmosphere of paradise. This nature is represented by strata: in the foreground, shrubs and a dark green plain, then a light green valley, a violet

Figure 14.5 Inhabitants of Tehran. Photo: Alice Bombardier, at the crossroads of Enqelab and Vali'asr Avenues, Tehran, 2009. Attributed to Mehdi Ghadyanlu.

forest, blue mountains and a sky of white and grey clouds. A round hole appears at the top of the painting, at the juncture of the building structure. This hole leads to the sky. But what sky? The sky of the painting, the sky of the reality or the divine heaven? The practice of *mise-en-abîme* is impressive. It leads through a spatial representation to a questioning that can rest on many levels: aesthetic, real or metaphysical.

This new kind of wall painting, which puts the emphasis on unusual and imaginative worlds but which also uses new techniques such as 3D and *trompe l'oeil*, no longer refers directly to war, the suffering, the emblematic figure of the martyr or the self-sacrifice. However, if we look closer, the war and its corollaries, the martyr and the afterlife, remain present in a metaphorical way. They are depicted by symbols like the dove, the butterfly or the rainbow; by stairs or the upward movements of the characters to the sky, and finally by the passageways (holes, doors, bridges) between several dimensions: real or beyond the real. Inserted in reality, the city and daily life, these murals use the two fundamental registers of human reality: life and death, reality and beyond. The quintessence of war and martyrdom's ideology remains the relationship between life and death (Bombardier, 2011).

Figure 14.6 Pre-urban Idyll. Photo: Alice Bombardier, Mirdamad Avenue, Tehran, 2009. Attributed to Mehdi Ghadyanlu.

In conclusion, the city of Tehran is undergoing changes in its aesthetic and political experience of mural painting while asserting symbolic and semiotic particularities. One of these particularities still falls in line with the revolutionary ideology but from external driving forces. As Christiane Gruber (2008) argues in her article 'Jerusalem in the visual propaganda of post-revolutionary Iran', there is a resort to the archetype of the Dome of the Rock, used as a rhetorical sign urging political mobilisation and 'as a visual metaphor of freedom against tyranny'. The Dome of the Rock 'plays a central role in the Iranian state propaganda and to promote Islamic solidarity beyond the borders of the state while symbolizing the universal uprising against oppression' (Gruber, 2008). The Israeli flag and the Star of David are also signs commonly used in the movement of the Iranian mural, which had first commemorated the martyrs of the Iran–Iraq war before opening up also to the Israeli–Palestinian conflict. But more recently, there is another interesting feature to highlight, a sense of 'beautification' (as institutionalized in the Office of Beautification [*Zibasazi*] in the Municipality of Tehran) has been introduced in the practice of mural painting, allowing a current renewal of the visual language in the Iranian public sphere.

Notes

1. I thank Ulrich Marzolph, Professor at the University of Göttingen in Germany, for giving me access to his photographic archives of murals.
2. An extract from a film archive of these processions is shown in the documentary of Camilla Cuomo and Annalisa Vozza (2009) *The Factory of Martyrs*, Documentary Film. Switzerland: Fabrica and RTSI Production.
3. More precisely, the Cultural Society of the Islamic Movement was created first, but quickly replaced by the Centre of Thought and Islamic Art. See Khosrodjerdi, H (1999) 'The Islamic revolution in contemporary Iranian art', *Tavoos* 1, Autumn.
4. A young painter that I interviewed in Tehran in 2008 said he had also been commissioned to paint murals in the area of Zabol during his military service in the late 1990s. This activity determined his vocation as an artist.
5. The mural on Vali'asr Square appears in the documentary of Camilla Cuomo and Annalisa Vozza (2008) *The Factory of Martyrs*, Documentary Film. Switzerland: Fabrica and RTSI Production.

References

Boissière, A (ed.) (2010) *Activité Artistique et Spatialité*. Paris: L'Harmattan.

Bombardier, A (2012) *La Peinture Iranienne au XXème Siècle (1911–2009): Historique, Courants Esthétiques et Voix d'Artistes. Contribution à L'étude des Enjeux de L'art en Iran à L'époque Contemporaine*. PhD, EHESS Paris and University of Geneva.

——— (2011) 'La peinture murale iranienne: genèse et évolution. Enjeux de la spatialisation artistique dans le processus d'affirmation et de pacification des pays du Moyen-Orient' in Etienne, N and Bernardi, B (eds), *Standing on the Beach with a Gun in my Hand – Eternal Tour 2010 Jérusalem*. Geneva/Paris: Labor et Fides/Black Jack Edition.

Chelkowski, P and Hamid Dabashi (2000) *Staging a Revolution. The Art of Persuasion in the Islamic Republic of Iran*. London: Booth–Clibborn.

Corboz, A (2001) *Le Territoire comme Palimpseste et Autres Essais*. Besançon: Edition de l'Imprimeur.

Cuomo, C (2011) *Images Sacrées et Représentations dans les Traditions Islamiques*. PhD, University of Lyon 2.

Cuomo, C and Annalisa Vozza (2008) *The Factory of Martyrs*, Documentary film, Switzerland: Fabrica and RTSI Production..

Gruber, C (2008) 'Jerusalem in the visual propaganda of post-revolutionary Iran,' in Mourad, S and Mayer, T (eds) *Jerusalem: History, Religion, and Geography*. London: Routledge.

―――― (2008) 'The message is on the wall: Mural artists in post–revolutionary Iran,' *Persica* 22: 15–46.

Gudarzi, M (ed) *Dah sal ba naqqashan-e enqelab-e eslami 1357–1367* [*Une Décennie avec les Peintres Révolutionnaires Iraniens 1979–1989*] Tehran: Art Center of the Organisation of Islamic Propaganda.

Jalali-Naini, Z (1998) 'L'art islamique révolutionnaire. Naissance et agonie', 'L'élection de Khatamy. Le printemps iranien?'. *Les Cahiers de l'Orient. Revue d'Etude et de Reflexion sur le Monde Arabe et Musulman*, Paris, n°49: 125–8.

Khosrodjerdi, H (1999) 'The Islamic revolution in contemporary Iranian art'. *Tavoos* 1, Autumn.

Khosrokhavar, F (1995) *L'Islamisme et la Mort*. Paris: L'Harmattan.

Marzolph, U (2004) 'The martyr's way to paradise: Shiite mural art in the urban context', in Bendix, R and Bendix, J (eds) *Sleepers, Moles and Martyrs*. Copenhagen: University of Copenhagen.

―――― (2013) 'The martyr's fading body: Propaganda vs. beautification in the Tehran cityscape', in Gruber, C and Haugbolle, S (eds) *Rhetoric of the Image: Visual Culture in Modern Muslim Contexts*. Bloomington: Indiana University Press.

Yavari d'Hellencourt, N (1987) 'Les murs ont la parole' in Hourcade, B, Richard, Y (eds) *Téhéran. Au-Dessous du Volcan. Autrement Revue*, HS n°27, Paris: 85–9.

CHAPTER 15

FROM THE PEN TO THE ROTARY PRESS

Women Book Publishers in Post-Revolutionary Iran

Anna Vanzan

One of the most unexpected outcomes of the Islamic revolution in Iran is the proliferation of women's literature (especially prose, fiction and non-fiction) written by women, so much so that their annual production has reached levels that are higher than that of their male counterparts. Women have become the *avant garde* of literature not only as writers, but also as publishers as the number of women entering this field has increased tremendously since the 1990s. The remarkable growth in the last three decades of women's writing is also due to the changing principles of publishing. Some scholars have remarked that women's increasing and multifaceted activities in the Iranian cultural arena is somehow a partial compensation for their absence from the political scene.[1] Nevertheless it is a common opinion that the rise in women's contribution to economic, scientific and cultural production in the arts, literature and cinema has necessarily been a crucial instrument in increasing Iranian women's awareness and participation in the field of social and political change.[2]

The remarkable presence of women as writers in the field of literature can be seen to be in part responsible for encouraging women to enter the world of books on its more business-focused and entrepreneurial side.

This chapter seeks to examine the challenges that women face in the publishing industry in Iran. Although they have reached a high level of visibility and action in the cultural arena, one would suspect that Iranian women would find serious challenges to their position from the asymmetrical and hierarchical gender relations which in part afflict their society. However, the majority of women publishers I met in Iran stated that gender issues do not seem to constitute a significant source of impediment or hindrance to their activities.

I will present a brief overview of the state of women's publishing in Iran, using both archival material and the information directly provided by some of these entrepreneurs and businesswomen whom I interviewed at recent May book fairs of Tehran (2009, 2010 and 2011).[3]

In Iran, as elsewhere, publishing has been predominately a male monopoly as men have always enjoyed greater access to capital and other productive resources and marketing networks. However, during the last three decades opportunities for women publishers have improved as their access to education has expanded. In the Islamic Republic education has improved considerably, especially for women. In the last 30 years the literacy gap between women and men has narrowed, and currently about 65 per cent of the university population is female. As a result, the number of women working in the sphere of education has increased and feminist awareness has grown. And as a further consequence, the development of women's education has been accompanied by the entry of more women into the labour market and the acquisition of entrepreneurial skills required by a complex industry such as that of publishing.

Before the revolution there were no women working in the production of books except those involved in clerical work. After the revolution the Ministry of Culture and Guidance (*Ershad*) introduced new rules, such as the necessity for publishers to have a university degree and to obtain a permit in order to work. At first and probably in order to limit women's access to the profession, the Ministry tried to issue some discriminatory rules against women publishers, such as the requirement to be married and to have a male representative whenever they needed to hold discussions with the Ershad representatives. However, these last two requirements were never fully implemented.

In the first years of the revolution, the business of book publication encountered several challenges, due to both external problems (the war against Iraq had worsened economic conditions and paper was almost unavailable or extremely expensive) and internal tensions. Moreover, the state had taken control of most publishing houses. Nevertheless, in that difficult period at least one woman managed to venture into publishing: in 1981, in fact, Sima Kuban, after being expelled from her position as a university teacher of fine arts, published a collection of essays from some of the most prominent intellectuals on the Iranian scene. This anthology and its successive issues known under the title of *Ketab-e Cheragh* [*The Light Books*] were published by the *Entesharat-e Damavand* (Damavand Publishing), the first female-directed publishing house, which Sima Kuban founded with the help of another two women intellectuals, Partou Nuri 'Ala and Monir Raminfar. The enterprise published both national and international books for four years, until it was closed down by the government. After a while, Sima Kuban and her companions left the country.

By the early 1990s the general situation of publishing in Iran improved as the government lowered the rates of foreign exchange and controlled the price of books. That was also the period in which Mohammad Khatami was in charge of *Ershad*, which showed some degree of tolerance towards intellectual production and, as a result, more and more women started to enter the hitherto male-dominated industry of publishing. In 1991 there were five book publishers that were headed by women. By 1995 – although Khatami in the meantime had resigned as the head of the *Ershad* – there were 40 women who had acquired a publishing permit and were running their own businesses. Some of them had the idea of organising the first women's book fair, which took place in Tehran in 1997 and saw the participation of about 50 women publishers out of the 100 who had been registered.[4]

The accession of Mohammad Khatami to the presidency of Iran in 1997 encouraged many more women to follow suit. In 1999, a book fair for women publishers was held in Abadan (85 women participated) and since then the number of women publishers has grown progressively. According to a survey carried out in 1999, at that time there were more than 2000 publishing firms in Iran and 10 per cent of these were run by women. In November 2001, a round table conference on questions of concern to women publishers was attended by about 70 women, a further sign of the importance that these women assigned to their position within the publishing world and the future of women in the publishing industry in Iran.

It was in those years that women publishers decided to form a professional organisation and the *Jam'e senfi-ye farhangi-ye zanan-e nasher* (Cultural Guild of Women Publishers) was therefore born. The association had the main aim of being a flexible forum within which women could meet others who shared the same concerns about the everyday problems they had to face and discuss them in an open and honest manner in their meetings.[5] After some time, however, the association ran into some difficulties due to several factors, including internal disagreements among the members, and another guild was launched with the help of government offices – thought by many to have been established to create chaos and rivalry among the publishers. And so in 2007, the *Kanun-e farhangi-e zanan-nasher* (Cultural Association of Women Publishers) was formed. Its organisers established a website and regular meetings on the first Thursday of each month. Many of its members have maintained their link with the Senfi-ye farhangi, because it is their trade union, while the Kanun is more a cultural association, which occasionally hosts literary events, seminars and the like.

In the 2000s more than 150 women publishers attended the International Book Fair in Tehran, participation in which requires a catalogue of at least 15 books, a discriminating boundary that automatically excludes newcomers or very small publishers. Nevertheless, the number of women who have entered this field has grown and the total number of licences given by *Ershad* is now more than 500, although less than half of these publishers are currently active.[6]

Like any other aspect of Iranian politics and society, publishing does not enjoy steady progress, as the volatile political leadership of the country deeply influences the business and everyday practicalities of publishing in many respects. For instance, a couple of years ago the government suddenly discontinued the distribution of paper at a subsidised price. Since then the price of paper (mostly imported from abroad) has quadrupled, severely impacting the publishing houses' bottom lines. There is also the issue of censorship, the rules of which are predictably unpredictable and the whimsical policies of which often block the procedures that lead to the publication of a book. Regarding these two aspects – financial constraints and rigorous but erratic censorship – there is no discrimination between women and men publishers: they both suffer from the same hindrances.

This was borne out by the survey I carried out during the 22nd International Book Fair in Tehran. The 20 female publishers I interviewed agreed that the main difficulties they face everyday they share with their male counterparts. These include: censorship applied by the *Ershad*, in whose offices a book would linger from about a minimum of six months to one/one year and a half; the price of paper; the cost of the distribution system which equates to 35 per cent of the book price. The economic crisis which has been affecting the country for a long while aggravates this situation, as distributors now accept small quantities of books and negotiate harshly over their price. Less money means fewer books bought and, as a result, publishers have to reduce print runs: up to a couple of years ago, they would print an average of 2–3,000 copies per book, now they do not exceed 1–1,500 copies.

As expected, these issues mainly concern independent publishers, as state and institutionally subsidised companies do not face the same problems. In addition, institutional publishers have the best booths at the fairs, while independent publishers have to struggle for small places. Space at the book fair can constitute a way of measuring how a publisher is regarded by the authorities: two women publishers I spoke with could not participate in the Tehran Fair – one because she had been directly refused the space, the other being offered the share of a narrow booth with another nine small publishing houses. Furthermore, the latter confessed that she had managed to publish just one book in the past four years, as all the books she had proposed had been 'lost' in the *Ershad* office, or been bluntly rejected. She suspected that she had probably incurred the *Ershad's* anger after printing a collection of poems explicitly dedicated to Mohammad Khatami and his tolerant politics. It must be stressed again that a publisher must print at least four titles a year in order to maintain his/her licence, a requirement that implies much organisation, careful planning of resources and alternative provisional solutions at the publishing house's disposal. Consequently, a constant rejection by the *Ershad* of the books proposed by a publisher could be seen as either a formal or informal strategy to force the publishing house into an increasingly difficult position.

What women publishers publish

Gender ideology clearly plays a critical role in deciding what is published. However, a survey of Iranian women publishers reveals that few of them are engaged in printing titles that primarily concerns women. There may be several explanations: either they do not want to enter the somehow contested and limited (according to some critiques) territory of 'women-who-write-and-talk-only-about-women'; or this is a sensitive topic that would attract too much attention from the *Ershad*; or simply it is not their key interest. At any rate, women publishers deal with a variety of subject matters. Many women publishers produce books exclusively for children and young adults, quite a rewarding field in a country where 70 per cent of the population is under 35 years of age, but also dangerous territory where censorship is concerned, as the regime keeps a steady eye on the sociocultural formation of its future adult citizens. Nevertheless, these women publishers prefer to have a more varied publishing list, ranging from adult literature (both Persian and foreign in translation), children's books, sociology, history and 'how to' books. These latter have become a major source of income for publishers, who often support the cost of other what could be deemed more intellectually worthy books with the profits gathered through these more popular manuals.

The independent women publishers' decisions on what to publish often depend on their background: the women I interviewed have university degrees in literature, foreign languages, sociology, art and political science and their personal interests are often reflected in the titles of the books they publish. Some of these publishers declared that they started their own businesses because they wanted to be free to publish their own books and/or to give an opportunity to other authors who often struggle to have their writings published. Many of them were concerned that in state-controlled or larger publishing houses, their intellectual production could be at risk of being exploited. A woman publisher who is also a translator of Arabic poetry and religious books openly told me that she became a publisher because she was tired of seeing her translations published under someone else's name.

Many women publishers are, in fact, also translators of foreign – mainly European – languages; therefore they pay a great deal of attention to what is written abroad. Consequently, they are often influenced by foreign sociocultural and literary trends but, as is inevitably the case, still maintain a critical opinion when blending these trends with those within the Iranian social milieu. Women publishers thus show great consideration for local needs, and virtually all of them declare that Iranian society needs a wave of 'new thinking' (*fekr-e now*). According to them, this new movement could be nurtured, for instance, through an innovative approach to historiography, i.e. by giving preference to social history, rather than to the *feuilletton* way of writing history typical of most past Iranian scholarship;[7] or even by going back to some 'vintage' philosophers such as Karl Marx, retrieved from their ban under the Pahlavis and the early revolutionary era. Anecdotally, books on and by Karl Marx were quite numerous on the stalls of the last book fairs from the mid-2000s.

Literature, both foreign and domestic, seems to be the favourite choice of women publishers, though it is also the Ershad's preferred target. In this respect, it is surprising to note how writers such as the Italian Alberto Moravia, who deals explicitly with matters of modern sexuality, have been published in translation without undergoing extensive editing and amendments, while works by the far more prudish Kiran Desai have long been waiting for a publishing permit. Evidently the state is now more than ever concerned about the potential threat contained in politically-engaged literature than worried by some licentious words or images.

Side by side with world celebrity authors, ranging from Danielle Steel to Paulo Coelho, one may find many books written by young Iranian authors, especially women. I enquired of women publishers whether they try to encourage female rather that male authors, but only one of my interviewees told me that she expressly privileges women writers, as well as in general preferring to recruit a female workforce (graphic designers, editors etc). This fact led me to inquire into their general opinion on feminism: the great majority of publishers replied that they are feminist only if the term implies their support for women's rights to be achieved in the framework of an egalitarian society. One added that, if we take this parameter for granted, we may say that all the women in the world are feminists. Another publisher underlined that she does not want to substitute a patriarchy (*mardsalari*) with a matriarchy (*zansalari*). A third one was more specific, explaining that she opposes the radical twist that local (Iranian) feminism has in some cases assumed. Two publishers who share socialist ideas, answered me with an enthusiastic 'Yes, I am feminist'; another three women offered a flat 'No'. However, it is obvious that they do not refute feminism itself, but rather that they object to the political implications – and manipulations – of some feminist struggles in present-day Iran.[8]

Beyond the books

Women publishers are a good indicator of the level of education women have reached and of the subsequent slow but inexorable questioning of traditional roles. For example, some women publishers work with their husbands, but the licence is in *their* name, as they have a university degree that the husband does not posses. I even met a man whose publishing house carries the name of a graphic company run by a female colleague – as *she* has the licence.

The courageous visibility of these women who combine intellectual effort with entrepreneurship offers an insight into the shifting institutional and ideological context and contest between men and women. Until very recently, women needed their husband's authorisation to manage a publishing house, a highly masculinised working place where men would often refuse to work under a woman's command. One publisher told me that the lithographer who 12 years ago refused to collaborate with her has now become her most ardent supportive master-in-chief and has even encouraged his daughter to enter the world of publishing.

There are also critical voices regarding women's entry into the publishing industry, claiming that women are now allowed to venture into this arena in part due to the financial crisis. In other words, as publishing profits have decreased, this cultural business has become less valuable and desirable than before, and therefore it is now suitable for women. Dismal though this attitude may be, there might be some truth in this assertion. Despite this, all of my interviewees asserted that they are literally in love with their work.

It is undeniable that women's access to the publishing business has established and nurtured new political cultures and communities that promote equitable and meaningful intellectual production and productivity.

Women publishers not only demonstrate they are prepared to cultivate potential and actual markets; they also dare to propose innovative subjects to encourage discussion and response from society. The books dealing with women's issues are a case in point: one publisher narrated to me that some years ago, when she was producing her first book carrying the word 'feminism', she received a call from the printing house announcing that the book on 'fominisom'[9] was ready. Nevertheless, while at her first book fair, boys and girls would stop by her stall and giggle over that title, nowadays men and women commonly buy books on these issues. This episode is a telling comment on the rapid changes which are taking place in Iranian society.

Certainly, many features of Iranian culture are still traditionalist. For example, though Persian is a prominent language in the blogosphere, the internet does not yet seem to be a favoured meeting point between publishers and readers when it comes to what has hitherto been solely printed material. All the publishers I interviewed (many of whom did not have a website) agreed on the fact that many Iranian readers like a more traditional, personal way of interacting, hence preferring to be contacted via telephone, letter, or personally. This approach reinforces publishers' interest in participating in book fairs, especially those organised in provincial towns (*shahrestan*), as they are the best opportunity to establish direct contact between publishers and readers.

Iranian traditional gendered roles are also in part responsible for the dilemma most women publishers meet: publishing is a round-the-clock job, but family daily routine still weighs heavily on women's shoulders. Therefore, as in many industries, striking a balance between work and family life can often pose a very great challenge to these women. Yet, this situation is slowly changing and the personal narratives of some of the publishers I met reveal Iranian men's increasing awareness of the unjust and unequal sharing of responsibilities in the family and their attempt at finding a more balanced division of labour within the home.

Women publishers, though experiencing undeniable difficulties, are also trying to build women's capacity to associate and work together. Although both their professional guild and the more recent Kanun-e farhangi have suffered from misunderstandings and divisions, the members of these associations are still working together *as women*, trying to enhance women's publishing and to enforce their image as a cohesive group. In the past years, for example, the members of the *Kanun-e farhangi-e zanan-nasher* have managed to install their booths at the Tehran Fair next to each other, thus presenting themselves as a cooperative alliance.[10] Some of them have high hopes for the establishment of a publishing selling network and even for a common bookstore that could sell books printed by all of them.

Despite the fact that most women publishers declare themselves not to be motivated by any feminist beliefs, they work and exist within a context of heightened gender awareness. While Iranian women publishers strive to avoid the common stereotypes of women's publishing houses and the 'ghettoisation' of women's writing, nevertheless their contribution is crucial to the development of a gendered reading culture.

Some final considerations

The first consideration that comes to the fore is that Iranian women publishers do not seem to feel professionally discriminated because of their sex. Not only have they entered the world of publishing almost unconcernedly detached from gender issues, but some of them show irritation if approached as 'women' publishers and not just as 'publishers'. They advocate their right to be considered as serious professionals regardless of their gender, and refute the suggestion that they are subjected to discrimination on account of their sex. They do not see there to be any structural or institutional barriers affecting women's publishing and affirm that they face the same challenges their male counterparts encounter. Nevertheless, the question of women's access to publishing cannot be detached from that of the development of the struggles on which Iranian women have embarked to expand their intellectual and professional space. Gender discrimination afflicts virtually every society and especially the patriarchal ones – as one could characterise Iran. For instance, a publisher lamented that it is impossible for her to invite a male colleague (either a writer, another publisher or an operator in the publishing industry) for a business lunch, something her male counterparts do all the time. Such a proposal would sound awkward or even provocative to Iranian society, although, of course, there is no written rule against it. Thus, an important social space for relationship building and a crucial part of the common 'business etiquette' is somehow off limits for Iranian businesswomen.

A second issue involves the correlation between women publishers and feminism. As we have seen, the relationship between female publishers and the women's movement is not separated from more general discussions on feminism, which is currently a hotly-debated topic in Iran. It emerges that most women publishers prefer to disentangle themselves from the composite and often internally divided Iranian feminist movement. There are, of course, notable exceptions, such as is Shahla Lahiji, one of the first women publishers in Iran, whose intention to declare her interest in women's issues is stressed even by the name of her publishing house,

Entesharat-e roshangaran va motal'at-e zanan, (Intellectuals and Women Studies Publishing).[11] Another example is that of Noushin Ahmadi Khorasani, the outspoken feminist who is among the promoters and activist of the campaign 'One million signatures' (*Yek miliyon emza*), whose range of activism spans essay writing to publishing.[12]

But many other publishers, consciously or not, try to avoid the idea that they are 'female publishers who would publish female literature', to such an extent that a great majority of them are not primarily devoted to publishing books by/on women. None of the best-selling female authors, for instance, regularly collaborates with a female publisher, and the co-operation between woman publishers and woman authors seems rather occasional and not as a result of a choice based on the consideration of gender issues. Perhaps, on both sides, there is an overall fear of being marginalised or confined into a predominately female enclosure that would keep them far from the mainstream of the publishing world.

Interestingly, however, more than one publisher confessed to prefer professional collaboration with other women, such as authors, graphic artists[13] and all the other staff, such as editors or production editors that are involved in the path to a book's publication.

Another publisher declared that, being deeply involved in the issue of women's rights and fighting for gender equality, she had always strived to give voice to the 'tales, novels, poems and research hidden and suffocated in Iranian women's throats'. However, she added, she was convinced that women's rights and equality could not be reached by struggling against men. Consequently, in her writing she had always avoided any of the stereotypes characteristic of certain female writing that aims to construct men negatively.

They reiterate concern about being subsumed into the (stereo)type of 'women writers' who aspire to substitute patriarchy with matriarchy shows how many politically- and socially-engaged Iranian women do not feel comfortable being placed within a radical feminism paradigm. Yet, women publishers, who are on the frontline that articulates female voices, values and experiences, seem likely to shape a new model of feminism that is indigenous, original and well rooted in the local culture and society.

What's for the future?

Needless to say, women publishers face many challenges and evolving political events can be decisive for their future. Virtually all the independent women publishers established their business under Khatami's presidency, and almost all my interviewees expressed their hope for 'another Khatami' for president. Unfortunately, the June 2009 presidential election and its aftermath disclosed an uncertain and dangerous future for both Iranian publishers and civil society in general, with increased censorship and surveillance since then.

Like other Iranian intellectuals, women publishers are not a monolithic group, each of them having individual aspirations and projects for the future, both of Iranian society and the publishing industry. Nevertheless, all of those to whom I spoke look forward to the resolution of some common problems, such as that of copyright, the absence of which in Iran causes, among others, difficulties with foreign authors and publishers and limits the revenue stream for authors.[14]

It is almost impossible to predict the future for Iranian society in general and for its intellectual component in particular. However, women publishers are alive and well represent the untamed spirit of this unpredictable country.

Notes

1 This was the opinion, among others, of some participants in the debate: 'Women in Iran: An online discussion', conducted in early 2001 as part of the Gulf/2000 project at Columbia University. See the transcripts at: http://gu X000.columbia.edu/. See also the same concern expressed by one of the most active feminists, who is also a writer and a publisher in Iran, Noushin Ahmadi Khorasani, 'Qodrat-e siyasi va zanan dar Iran-e emruz' ('Political power and women in contemporary Iran'), first published in the journal *Fasl-e Sabz*, 3/1999, reprinted in Khorasni's collection of essays: *Zanān zir-e sāye-ye pedarkhāndehā* (*Women under the Patriarchs' Shade*), published by the author's printing house, Touse'e (Tehran, 2001:147–57).

2 The large number of women who joined the massive street protests that followed the June 2009 elections is an example of their social activism and participation in political movements.

3 I want to thank all the publishers I met at the Fair and who were extremely kind and cooperative.

4 The data in this and the following paragraph is inferred from Mansoureh Ettehadieh (2003) 'The art of female publishing', in *Middle Eastern Women on the Move*. Washington DC: Woodrow Wilson Center For Scholars: 23–32, esp. 26 and 27.

5 Among other activities promoted by this Association there were also humanitarian actions organised for the people affected by the 2003 Bam earthquake.

6 As far as I know, there is no research available about the reasons that compelled so many women to abandon their publishing enterprises and in such a short spell of time, but, presumably, the phenomenon can be said to be in part due to a combination of financial constraints and social pressures.

7   I am quoting one of my interviewees' words.
8   See Nahid Tabataba'i's interview 'Ba feminism-e Irani mokhalef-am' ('I am against Iranian feminism'), in the newspaper *E'temad-e Melli*, 22 Farvardin 1388/11 April 2009: 10.
9   This word does not exist in Persian, but in the publishing house they did not know the word 'feminism' and how to pronounce it.
10 At the last book fair this arrangement was not possible, officially for lack of space: see www.ibna.ir/prtgx39w.ak9yu4prra.html.
11 Shahla Lahiji is one of the most famous and active intellectuals and publishers, as proved by her publishing houses' catalogue and also by her social activism. In 2006 she was recognised for her promotion and defence of freedom of expression by the International Publishers Association. See her interview given to the Iranian feminist site *Madrase-ye feminist* (Feminist School) on 24 Ordibehesht 1387/13 May 2008, at www.feministschool.com/spip.php?article604. A long interview in English given on February 2007 is in the daily *Asharq Alaswat* (www.asharq-e.com/news.asp?section=3&id=8835).
12 See note 1. It is also important to add that the space of 'women studies' is also dominated by religious or governmental presses, such as Ketab-e Zanan (Women's Books) whose aim is to promote the Islamic 'official' idea of womanhood.
13 It is interesting to note that a job as a graphic artist or designer is a particularly coveted one by the new generation of women.
14 Some publishers talked about their discomfort in dealing with this issue: they would like to pay the rights to foreign authors, in order not to feel like they were exploiting these authors. However, most Iranian publishing houses, especially those ones owned by women, cannot afford the huge amount of money asked by famous authors' literary agents. The copyright issue affects Iranian authors as well, as their works can be translated abroad but these authors find it very difficult to make sure that they are recompensed.

References

Elmi, ZM (2009) 'Educational attainment in Iran' in *The Iranian Revolution at 30*, Viewpoints Special edition Washington DC: The Middle East Institute (also available at www.mideasti.org): 62–8.

Ettehadieh, M (2003) 'The art of female publishing' in *Middle Eastern Women on the Move*. Washington DC: Woodrow Wilson Center For Scholars: 23–32, esp. 26 and 27.

Kian, A (2009) 'Social change, the women's rights movement and the role of Islam' in *The Iranian Revolution at 30*. Viewpoints Special edition Washington DC: The Middle East Institute (also available at www.mideasti.org): 55–7.

Mehran, G (2003) 'The female educational experience in Iran: The paradox of tradition and modernity' in *Middle Eastern Women on the Move*. Washington DC: Woodrow Wilson Center For Scholars: 69–74.

Moghadam, FE (2009) 'Women and the Islamic Republic: Emancipation or suppression?' in *The Iranian Revolution at 30*, Viewpoints Special edition Washington DC: The Middle East Institute (also available at www.mideasti. org): 49–51.

Vanzan, A (2009) *Figlie di Shahrazàd. Scrittrici iraniane dal secolo XIX secolo ad oggi*. Milan: Bruno Mondadori.

Websites

Iranian Iranian Women Publishers, Center for Women Studies, The University of Tehran, http://cws.ut.ac.ir/Databank/Iranian WomenPublishers.aspx.

Kanun-e farhangi-e zanan-e nasher (Cultural Association of Women Publishers), http://zanan-nasher.blogfa.com/.

PART V

BEYOND BORDERS

CHAPTER 16

THE OTHER SHORE

Iranians in the United Arab Emirates Between Visibility and Invisibility

Amin Moghadam

While exchanges around the Persian Gulf are pursued through trade – whether legal or illegal – between a network of countries to the north and south, the considerable Iranian presence in the United Arab Emirates bears witness to new migratory trends in the Gulf region, in turn reflecting a broader process of globalisation and the growth of the urban metropolis.

Over 500,000 Iranians live and work in the United Arab Emirates (UAE), the total population of which is around 4 million.[1] It is widely recognised that Dubai's development owes a great deal to migrant workers from all corners of the world. But while the majority of Dubai's immigrants come from southern Asia and indeed one in every two inhabitants is from India, the longstanding Iranian presence remains significant, with 80 per cent of Emirates-based Iranians living in Dubai.

As in any city where migrants play a major role, Dubai-based Iranians are divided and channelled into different sectors of activity. The heterogeneity of the Iranian presence has made it hard to fully identify the sectors in which migrants are active and also seems to have precluded the development of new community ties, especially between the older generation and the new, more recently-migrated one.

This heterogeneity reflects the diverse origins of Iranian migratory flows into the Emirates, each with its own moral and political economy. Nevertheless, the general trend is towards increasingly highly-qualified migrants who are thus able to meet the demands of a society in search of ultra-modernity.

My aim here is to outline the role of Iranian migration in the development and 'metropolisation' of Dubai. But this is complicated by the fact that the Iranian presence in the Emirates today takes various forms, more or less visible, whether emerging from regional communities or individual moves from the Iran's major urban centres. Over the past century or so, we have witnessed a trend away from ancient migratory patterns based on shared values and a sense of community towards a more recent migratory pattern, which is characterised by a process of individuation. This echoes the political and social evolution of both the home and host societies, i.e. Iran and the UAE. The move towards new migratory patterns has not, however, been to the detriment of the former, based on communities' ties between the two shores of the Gulf, even if the Emirates' determination to create a knowledge-based society begs the question as to how long a community-centred, peripheral economy will be able to survive.

A reversal of migratory flows linked to geo-political conditions

The flow of people back and forth between the Arabian and Persian shores of the Gulf has been a feature of everyday life in the cities concerned for centuries. Iranian-Arabs and some of the Iranian non-Arab Sunni communities have bound relations with the southern coast of the Gulf and continue to benefit from their 'double belonging' status and contribute to a regional economy that characterises the southern territories of Iran and the Gulf islands. Before the establishment of the Arab Gulf states in the 1970s, these exchanges were limited to areas along the Gulf and in the eastern region until Baluchistan and even reaching toward the centre of the Iranian land mass, including some towns such as Lar, Bastak, Evaz and their populations in Fars province and near Shiraz, due to their common obedience to Sunni Islam. The Gulf played the role of a geographical interface in this regional-level migration, supplying the needs of the local economies of towns and villages on both sides. The resulting transnational community often reflected religious and linguistic ties between the inhabitants of the south of Iran and the southern Gulf countries on one hand and, on the other, historical events affecting countries on each coast, which accelerated or hindered migratory flows in either direction.

The development of the port of Siraf in Iran in the ninth century and the expansion of trade in the Indian Ocean, from the distant cities of the far east to those of the Persian Gulf, made Siraf and its nearby towns both reachable and attractive to merchants (Priestman, 2008). From Bushehr to Bandar Abbas on the coast and over the mountains which separate the coast from the main plateau where are located towns like Bastak, Galehdar and Lar, they all have been attracted by the exchanges through the Gulf. Therefore as Abdullah states (1978: 221) 'the Gulf has never been a barrier but a link strengthening the social and economic ties between both sides'. The constitution of a strong, Persian- and Shia-centred nation-state in the fifteenth century, under the reign of the Safavids, saw some of these Sunni Arabs, who had settled in the south of Iran, ejected by the local governors. At the beginning of the eighteenth century and following the fall of the Safavid dynasty and their reducing control power on the coastal region, a wave of migration of Arabs to the Persian shore took place (Abdullah, 1978: 221). Mostly Sunnis, as reported by Niebhur (Niebuhr, 1772) a German traveller in the eighteenth century, and Lorimer (1970) at the beginning of the twentieth century, Matârish tribes migrated from Oman and became rulers of Bushehr while Qawasim, the actual rulers of Sharjah in the UAE, became the rulers of Bandar Lengeh. Sunni Arabs, they sealed alliances with the inhabitants of these cities especially with the Persian Sunnis who probably felt more affinities for the Arab Sunnis than for their Shia compatriots. As quoted by Muhammad (1978: 222), 'cultural and religious relations continued between both sides of the Gulf, since some of the religious teachers in the Trucial states were educated on the Persian side in schools by the wealthy Sunni merchants, notably at Lingah'.[2] These regions became somehow semi-independent until the time when the Qâjâr dynasty (1796–1926) started expanding its power from its new capital of Tehran to the Gulf coast and islands. Although these tribes resisted the central power, Persia's fight against the settled Arab tribes consolidated the authority of the strong central government of Tehran (Abdullah, 1978).

Following the extension of Persian authority through the appointment of the governors for the coastal cities from Tehran as well as the support of Western powers to the government of Tehran (notably the arrival of two German warships, *Persepolis* and *Susa*, in 1887) and finally the imprisonment of the Qasimi ruler of Lengah, some Arab inhabitants commenced in 1899 a new wave of migration to the Arab shores announcing a reversal of migratory trends. This trend was prompted in 1910, as a sizable merchant community, in many cases Arabic and Persian-speaking Sunnis, left the shores of Iran for the south coast of the Gulf, as a result of customs barriers that had been set up in 1902 by Belgian representatives empowered by the central government of Tehran. The introduction of very high customs duties on all merchandise imported and exported through Iran's ports favoured the development of Dubai, which progressively replaced Bandar

Lengeh, the dominant port until that date. As quoted by Muhammad Morsy Abdullah (1978: 232):

> The merchants of Lingah and other Persian ports found their interests directly threatened and their goods subjected to heavy duties. At last some heading merchants, mainly Sunni Persians, found no alternative but to close down their stores in protest and emigrate to Dubai. There they began to establish agencies and ordered their big ships to come from India direct, by-passing Lingah.

According to Heard-Bey (1982) the population that had moved from the Iranian shoreline to the port of Dubai had maintained their ties to the Persian coast and arranged for goods to arrive in Persia while evading customs duties. When Reza Shah (Shah of Iran 1925–41) came to power in Iran in 1925, he established a strong central government for which access to the Gulf was very important. To prevent foreign interference, he refused to ask for external loans; instead he raised the taxation on local products, such as tea and sugar, using them for financing a huge network of infrastructures. These measures again affected the inhabitants of southern Iran whose revenues relied on the imports of these goods through the Gulf ports. Therefore not only was migration towards the Arabian littorals reinforced, but the smuggling that until that date was on a small scale, became the main resource of local families despite the attempt of Reza Shah in building a navy in 1930 for ending this activity. Adding to these measures, the enforced unveiling that was imposed on women by Reza Shah in 1936, following his Westernisation policy, precipitated the waves of emigration of Sunni inhabitants (Arabs and Persians) who considered these new rules as heretical (Abdullah, 1978: 247).

The contemporary mass migration of Iranians to the Emirates is, for the larger part, a result of the geo-political context and relations between the Gulf Arab nations and Iran. The political and economic changes in both Iran and the Gulf Arab countries led to a new wave of migration expanding the transnational ties from the small towns of southern Iran to the major Persian culture-dominated metropolises toward the southern shores of the Gulf; particularly in the UAE and Dubai where the traditionally positive immigration policies toward Iranian nationals stands out from the rest of Gulf States significantly (at least until very recently). This movement started with the discovery of oil on the southern shore of the Gulf, increasing the demand for labour, and it was reinforced after the Iranian revolution of 1979, during the Iran–Iraq war, and with the strong economic liberalisation in Dubai. The rise of the real estate sector and the appetite of Iranians to invest in it, the rise of sanctions against Iran transforming Dubai into a re-export platform followed by the economic growth of service sectors less than ten years ago around the activities of media, art market, green growth etc, transformed Dubai into the best platform for a various range of activities for Iranians.

Nowadays, Dubai, whose current situation in the Gulf opposite the Islamic Republic of Iran might be compared to that of Hong Kong in the Pearl River delta, close to communist China, is facilitating Iran's circumvention of the international embargo: 'Curiously, Dubai plays the role of both Switzerland and Hong Kong for Iran: Shelter for mullah's capital and starting point for smuggling that enables Iran to operate in spite of embargo and internal rigidity' (Lavergne, 2009: 43).

Since the discovery of oil (1958 in Abu Dhabi, 1966 in Dubai) and during less than three decades, the neighbouring emirate developed rapidly and the city of Dubai was quickly dubbed a 'city-state' (Gibert, Maraut and Telle, 2005) and elevated to the rank of global city. It became a consumer and financial paradise. Dubai took full advantage of its competitive edge over the Iranian coast: highly-developed infrastructure, an efficient airport, port installations, credit payment and foreign exchange facilities and the presence of foreign banks. Every year, Iranian investors in large numbers leave their country with significant capital and invest it in Dubai. The economic and political changes in Iran have had direct effects on Dubai's markets notably after the election of President Ahmadinejad and the rise of conflict regarding the Iranian nuclear programme (Fathi, 2005, Coville, 2006). A good example of this was seen in September 2005, after the International Atomic Energy Agency's resolution referring Iran to the United Nations Security Council for violating its nuclear obligations. While stock prices in Tehran fell, the Dubai stock market and real estate saw a surge of Iranian capital (Gholipour Fereidouni and Namdar, 2011). Fariba Adelkhah (2001: 41) wonders if Dubai has not become 'the true economic capital of the Islamic Republic', as it has also become the centre for the re-export of goods, especially US products, into Iran since the embargo. Also, Dubai hosts some of the so-called front companies, which are originally governmental, allowing them to circumvent the sanctions.

Although the rise in trade and increasing interdependence have strengthened ties between the two sides, bilateral relations between Iran and the Gulf's Arab nations are marked by mutual wariness. The alliance with the Western powers and especially with the Americans before the Iranian revolution had transformed Iran into 'General of the Gulf' which gave it the legitimacy to intervene in the territories of the Gulf without considering its Arabs counterparts who were still under the British protectorate. In Iran,

Pahlavi's (1925–79) policy tended to promote greater Persian culture in the country despite the existing cultural and linguistic diversity (only 50 per cent of the population is Persian). The Shiraz art festival in Persepolis glorified pre-Islamic and ancient Persia. 'The monarchy in Iran represented a cultural nationalism closure corresponding to a particular time of this ideology in the world and very classically based on the exclusion or denial of cultural identities' (Fariba Adelkah, 1996: 86).

Following the Iranian revolution (1979), the leaders of the Arab nations were considered by Imam Khomeini to be 'infidels' and traitors to Islam on account of their ties to the USA. Conflict between the UAE and Iran over the control of three Gulf islands (Abu Musa, Greater and Lesser Tumbs) has bubbled up regularly in debates for more than 30 years. With Imam Khomeini's death, Iran embarked on a new pro-Arab policy with the Gulf Cooperation Council (GCC) countries. Aware of their economic, geographical and cultural interdependencies, Iran's foreign policy attempted to pacify its relations with these states (despite some tensions with the UAE in 1992 regarding the sovereignty on the islands), but it was the tendency to export its model of the Islamic revolution, particularly through its influence on the Shia communities in Arab countries, that resulted in a constant mistrust in their mutual relations. With the mandates of the pragmatic Rafsanjani (1989–97), followed by the reformist Khatami (1997–2005), the concerns Arab states had regarding Iran's willingness to spread its model in the region were subdued for a short period. During this time, Iranian leaders had tried to show their good will and some conferences took place between Iranian intellectuals and Arab thinkers in order to detect the origins of Arab–Iranian antagonism. The Doha conference in 1995 with the participation of all Arab nations and Iran, as well as the publication of the book *Arab-Iranian Relations* is one such example (Haseeb, 1998). But the nuclear ambitions of Iran and the political radicalisation with the presidency of Mahmoud Ahmadinejad since 2005 have gradually eroded efforts made in the 1990s.

Tensions between the two sides have always impacted upon the Iranian communities in Arab states. As Nadjmabadi (2010: 30) observes,

> Iranian migrants consider that their treatment in the Arab states is not simply a matter of individual behaviours but often one of interstate relations. For example, those who had lived in the Arab states during the 1960s, when Nasserist Pan-Arabism was sweeping the region, explained that Iranians became scapegoats during this period, suffering maltreatment as a result. Similarly, political events within Iran influence how the Arabs treat the Iranian migrants.

The independence of the Arab Gulf States in the 1970s, the Islamic revolution of Iran in 1979 and the Iran–Iraq war (1980–8), contributed to socioeconomic imbalances between the two coasts, which have forced the transnational families to change their strategies regarding their identity in the Gulf, which previously enjoyed a greater fluidity. Following the recent tensions between Iran and the Arab Gulf countries as well as US pressure on the UAE to control Iranian activities, it is manifest in communications by authorities that they play down the contribution of Iranians to their development and the immigrants themselves often attempt to cover up their Iranian origins. My assumption consists in saying that the evolution of economic sectors in Dubai as well as that of Iranian civil society is recomposing the Iranian presence in the UAE and particularly in Dubai. I was able to test these assertions via surveys and interviews carried out during assignments to the UAE in 2007, 2008, 2010 and 2011, in addition to research carried out along the Iranian coast and on Iranian islands in the Gulf in 2006.[3]

Iran's past influence on Dubai visible in Dubai today

Despite Dubai's futuristic landscape of skyscrapers and motorways, the city's present still has roots in the past. The Dubai Creek, Al-Khor, which separates the Deira district in the east from Burdubai in the west, is still home to many traditional yachts, called *dhow* in Arabic or *lenj* in Persian, which are sailing under the Emirates flag but manned by Persian, Jazirati (a dialect of the islands in the Gulf) or Pashto (Afghani) speakers. The mainstays of the Gulf economy of yore are today relegated to a role on the sidelines, contributing to the regional trade 'from the bottom' (Tarrius, 2002), transporting a wide range of goods bought duty-free from Dubai to Qeshm, Bandar Abbas and Kish in Iran, where they are much-sought-after for their bargain prices.

Dubai Creek is still a meeting place for the protagonists of the grey economy. Yachts and rowing boats congregate nightly and travel the Straits of Ormuz, to be met on the Iranian side by a fleet of SUVs driven along back roads and cart tracks, or even 'parachute women'.[4] This trafficking, involving networks of families, friendships and longstanding alliances, is little-known and impossible to evaluate. It also includes the transport, via Iran, of illegal Iranian or Afghan immigrants supplying casual labour for low-qualified jobs. Their existence in the Gulf is acknowledged but the number and spread of them is difficult to assess. The traders of Dubai, often called smugglers on the Iranian side, cross borders that in many cases they refuse to recognise. This is to ensure the survival of the circulatory territories of the Persian Gulf, which struggle to keep up with developments in Dubai and its rapid evolution towards a knowledge economy.

The veiled or unveiled importance of a new generation of Iranians

In the race towards a 'knowledge society' as defined by Philippe Cadène (2008) and characterised by its emphasis on qualified labour, the Iranian population is evolving to adapt to the demands of this 'cross-border coastal conurbation' (Dumortier, 2007) as it seeks its place in the global trend. Whether visibly or invisibly, the new Iranians of the UAE have participated for over a decade in a broad range of activities responding to developments in the predominant economic sectors. Statistics supplied by the Emirates Chamber of Commerce and Industry only take into account activities carried out officially by Iranians with Iranian nationality. However, Iranians in the Emirates are not always Iranian from the administration's point of view, for two reasons.

The first Iranian immigrants arriving in the Arab principalities at the beginning of the last century often sought to 'arabianise' (or re-arabianise) themselves and their Persian family names in order to better integrate into local society based on their ethnic, religious and linguistic affinities. At the time of independence of the UAE in 1971, the members of this community, established well before the discovery of oil, fulfilled the conditions for obtaining the enviable status of full national citizenship in the same way as the local Arab tribes. This process of assimilation even went so far as the denial of Iranian origins, as witnessed by their refusal to speak Persian, transmitted down through the family, or to mix with other Iranians in public. These behaviours result not only from the geopolitical tensions between Iran and the Gulf Arab countries, but also because of the establishment of an allocative state (Davidson, 2005), in the Arab Gulf countries, notably in the UAE, which attributes a large number of privileges to the nationals, creating new socioeconomic barriers between those who have been naturalised in the 1970s and others who are still Iranian nationals, or *bidoons*.[5] Meanwhile, the constitution of a national identity for the young nation of the UAE requires that some of the multi-belonging communities abandon the ambiguity of their identity, at least in their discourse, for the benefit of a national UAE identity in order to participate in a common national history. The degree of their transnational characteristics being variable, these families are the most representative of the fluidity of the Gulf identity. Shahnaz Najmabadi's (2010: 21) study of transnational families in the Gulf reached the same conclusion:

> The Iranian migrants [those of south of Iran] living and working in Arab countries do not perceive the Arab environment as a competing or different frame of reference. Given the historical entanglement of the two regions, these migrants actually feel less marginalised in Arab countries than when travelling to places in the interior of Iran.

However, consternation at state level regarding increasing Shi'a power, tensions resulting from Iranian nuclear ambition and territorial conflicts might weaken the centuries' old interchange of transnational families.

Another group of Iranians comprises those who have lived for a long time in Europe or the USA, often since the Iranian revolution, and obtained nationality in their adoptive countries. The economic opportunities available in the cities of the Emirates have encouraged them to develop businesses in Dubai or Ras Al Khaimah, returning to the vicinity of their native land while remaining in a more stable, liberal environment. Iranians who have lived in the West, while not showing up in the UAE's official statistics as Iranian nationals, are keen to develop relations with the younger generation of immigrants who have arrived from Iran's major cities since the end of the 1980s, who in their case come to seek a better quality of life than in Iran, where they see the current situation as holding out little promise. To these may be added some 11,500 (Minoui, 2007) tertiary students, most of whom follow courses in practical subjects in English. The Iranian government also has its own Persian-speaking primary and high schools in Dubai and in Sharjah (seven for the two cities), which adopt the national Iranian educational programme. The majority of students of these high schools pursue their studies in Iranian governmental universities of Dubai, such as Azad University or Shahid Beheshti university. However, according to one the professors of the Azad University, the majority of this university's students are Iranians for the following reasons. It is very difficult to pass the very selective Iranian examination to university, *concours*, while students do not need to pass this test in Dubai to enter Iranian UAE-based universities. The scholarships fees are lower than in other private universities in Dubai and some students living with their parents in the UAE's cities prefer to go to these universities. According to my interviews, some of these students, mostly the second generation of Iranians from the south of Iran who migrated to the UAE more than two decades ago, do not have the appropriate level of English for pursuing their studies in English-speaking universities. Therefore, even though the language of all the courses is officially English, they prefer to study in a Persian environment where the English requirement is less important. Similarly, starting at the age of 18, especially for the male members of the family, these students will need either to seek employment or get student status in order to renew their residency. As some of them grew up in the UAE with their whole family and friends, if they are not able to find a job, they extend their studies at university. Iranian universities, aware of the visa problems of some these students, have adopted a flexible structure allowing them to subscribe in different fields for several years, bringing economic benefits to these universities.

Despite the shortcomings of the Dubai Chamber of Commerce and Industry's statistics on the Iranian population, some general figures give an idea of the importance of their presence. In 2006, 400,000 were living in Dubai (25 per cent of the approximately 2 million people of Dubai) and have moved up to $200 billion of capital into Dubai (Rahman, 2005). 20 per cent of recorded foreign investment in Dubai's commercial centres was made by Iranians. At the same time, 7,000 companies were registered at the Chamber of Commerce as being of 'Iranian nationality'. However, only 3,000 or 4,000 of these companies are believed to be active, with the rest considered to be empty shells by the Iranian consulate's economic aide. Some firms are registered solely for tax purposes, using Dubai as a springboard to export Iranian goods to other countries

Concerning trade and exchange between the two countries, the total value of non-petroleum trade in 2008 was $11.7 billion, of which $9.2 billion represented export and re-export flows from the UAE to Iran. In 2010 the UAE exported or re-exported over $9 billion worth of goods to Iran, and only imported $1.12 billion worth. Iran's trade deficit with the UAE is its largest (Sadjadpour, 2011). In addition, according to a contact at the Iranian consulate in Dubai, who asked for his full name to be withheld, 40 per cent of Iran's petrol (gasoline) imports are from the Emirates, a figure not included in those supplied, which exclude crude oil. The most important export (and re-export) trade for Dubai (and for the UAE after India) is with Iran, whereas the latter is not among the UAE's principal suppliers, occupying 27th place. The significant level of re-export is a result, on the one hand, of international sanctions, and on the other of the non-competitive nature of Iran's port facilities. Following sanctions, some of the main economic partners of Iran, such as China whose commercial relations with Iran are about $15 billion, prefer to conduct their bilateral relations through the Emirates.

Similarly, the level of investments in the Emirates rose by 50 per cent from 2005 to 2006. The biggest growth was in the real estate sector, which increased from $200 billion to $300 billion. During the same period, Iranians were estimated to be behind 10 per cent to 30 per cent of transactions in the real estate sector (*Iran Daily*, 2006). In 2006, Iranians were, behind the UK and the US, in terms of the most important buyers of pre-construction products in Dubai (Thomas, 2006). The REIDIN report in 2010 still shows the importance of Iranian transactions in the real estate sectors, coming, in order, after Indian, UK and Pakistani actors with 11 billions UAE Dirhams (REIDIN, 2010).[6] These investments reflect the ongoing process of coastal urban sprawl, as a near-megalopolis stretches along the entire shoreline from Ras Al Khaimah in the north to Abu Dhabi in the south, via the Ajman-Sharjah-Dubai conurbation. The activities of the Oriental Real Estate agency are an eloquent illustration of this. Mr Touraj Bakhtiar, founder and director of the company, boasts about his Iranian origins. In an interview with the local press and CNBC TV, he declared: 'I am 100 per cent Iranian and oriental blood flows through my veins', even though he has lived in the UK and France since the age of five. Today his agency contributes to sales of property from Dubai to Ajman and Ras Al Khaimah. A law enacted in 2006 allowing foreigners to own property without time limits, as well as to hold 99-year leases, boosted the development of the agency, which was founded that same year. A large proportion of the company's employees are Iranian. With agencies located in Dubai's malls and shopping centres, Oriental Real Estate's sales staff are skilled in attracting a wealthy Iranian clientele on the lookout for new investments in the Emirates and, if necessary, they are able to speak Persian to facilitate communication. Although there are no statistics available on the number of Iranians who left the UAE after the economic crisis in 2008, some newspapers (*Mohit Joshi*, 2009) as well as some the members of the Iranian business council of Dubai reported that about 30 per cent of Iranian businessmen have withdrawn their activities in Dubai and returned to Iran after the Dubai property bubble burst and the knock-on effects of the global economic crisis hit the Gulf. Added to the crisis, it is important to mention the UAE's policy deciding, under US pressure, to follow, moderately of course, the international sanctions against Iran as, according to my personal interviews with Iranians inhabitants and press articles (Farah Stockman, 2008), it is today nearly impossible to obtain residency for Iranians arriving in the UAE or to open a new bank account, get the credit letters in any Emirate-based bank for business activity owned by Iranian nationals. It seems, moreover, that Iranian investments in real estate, following a logic of speculation, has declined. However, it is not uncommon still to see Iranians continue to buy an apartment or a studio in the new real estate development project in Dubai, because of their low prices compared to some of the same towers in Tehran and, by so doing, to take advantage of the more liberal and free environment that Dubai offers, particularly in its new quarters. Also, as Gholipour Fereidouni and Namdar (2011) suggest from their recent study, the relative economic growth and returns from stock market variables are not statistically significant, meaning that this factor is not the main concern of Iranian investors in regard to real estate investment decisions in Dubai.

While in some cases Iranian origins are accepted, affirmed or even publicised in the media, elsewhere they may be 'veiled'. Ras Al Khaimah, in the northern tip of the Emirates, now benefits economically from an express highway linking it to Dubai in one hour. The new motorway is incontestably one of the main reasons for the concentration of companies and services in this 260,000-inhabitant emirate. An integral participant in the process of coastal metropolisation, Ras Al Khaimah is today attempting to make the most of its location by extending a hand towards both the other emirates in the federation and their neighbouring countries. Saqr Port, the main harbour and the closest to its Iranian counterpart, Bandar Abbas, has traditionally kept up ties with the Iranian coast and Gulf islands via the transport of farm produce and passengers. Two other ports are under construction and will help intensify relations with both the rest of the country and its neighbours.

According to interviews I conducted in 2007 during my trip to the north of the Emirates, a large proportion of companies registered in Ras Al Khaimah are domiciled locally but have little actual activity. The fees paid to the Ras Al Khaimah authorities to register or renew trading licences ensure permanent official status without obliging firms to locate their headquarters there. An added bonus is the opening up of access to the other emirates through these licences. Faced with both their own restrictive national legislation and international sanctions, Iranians have jumped at the chance to make use of these facilities. For example, a curtain-making firm of Iranian origin is based in Ras Al Khaimah, but it holds its business meetings in the hotels of Dubai, the city that provides most of its customers. Most UAE-based Iranian companies also use Ras Al Khaimah as a base for banking, trade and the re-export of goods to Iran.

Some Iranians returning from the West, and from Europe in particular, have nevertheless succeeded in officially establishing their presence in local production. Shares in a major company, RAK Petropak, whose activities are centred on packaging and plastics in collaboration with the country's most important cement maker, RAKCC, are 50 per cent owned by Iranians and 50 per cent by the local government. Nevertheless, the authorities play down or even cover up Iranian participation in Ras Al Khaimah-based projects, though they do not hesitate to solicit Iranians to build up further links with the opposite shore.

A new scene: The Iranian presence in Dubai marked by art activities

While in the neighbourhood of Deira, located in old Dubai along the Creek, Persian signs are more numerous than in other parts of the city, they are not the only marks of the Iranian presence. Added to the lively concentration of Iranian merchants, evidence of a longstanding presence that continues to exist thanks to the nearby sailboat traffic, is the bustle of hotels full of Iranians sallying out to descend on Dubai's *souks* and shopping centres, or spending a night in transit for Abu Dhabi and the US embassy in the hopes of obtaining a visa. The visibility of the Iranian presence in this neighbourhood is no longer representative of its true economic impact. Yet just a few yards further on, in the heart of the newly-refurbished alleyways of the 'Heritage Village' and in contrast with the neo-orientalist, Hollywood-style *medinas* rising out of the surrounding desert, the Iranian presence is undeniable. This district is now the showcase for many Iranian artists, thanks to cultural events such as the 'Bastakia Art fair' and the presence of a number of galleries that display the works of the most sought-after Iranian artists, for example the photography of Abbas Kiarostami or Bahman Jalali, who are widely known and recognised in the world art scene. This phenomenon, although partly confined to the so-called historic quarters of Dubai, plays a supporting role in the new ambitions of the emerging metropolis of culturalisation of the economy (Moghadam, 2012). The quest for globalisation and a creative city compels the city fathers to project a new image of Dubai, not only one of skyscrapers and express highways, but also through creating cultural complexes of which Bastakia, revamped to serve both history and contemporary art, is not the only example. These new policies have paved the way for the emergence of new players and spaces in which Iranians play a very active role. They participate in a network of cultural places from Bastakia, through DFC center and Al Quoz area where some of the most dynamic galleries are situated, and finally the Maddinat Jumeira, which hosts every year the fair of contemporary art of Dubai, Art Dubai, which is one of the most important in the world.

Most of those galleries have been thriving thanks to the development of contemporary Iranian art. Its development first started in 2000 in the outlying industrial area of Al Quoz. Gallery owners are mostly of European or Middle Eastern origin and they, for the major part, started off their businesses in the past decade. Independent of public cultural institutions, the private and commercial sector has a strong impact on the cultural and artistic scene, especially in Dubai, where companies of cultural management, cultural foundations, local cultural centres, galleries, fairs and auction companies are at the root of artistic dynamics of the emirate, while splitting the activity in time and space. In this regard, the Art and Culture Department of the Dubai International Financial Center, which was founded in 2007, has become a leading institution, which lends to groups of artists huge exhibition spaces and serves as intermediary between artists and buyers. It has sheltered, since the end of 2008, about ten galleries and coordinates big projects. It also sponsors the Art Dubai annual fair. Among the galleries of this financial centre, one stands as an exception: the gallery of the collection Farjam (the Farjam Collection), which has non-commercial activities. Farhad Farjam, an Iranian who runs a company specialising in pharmaceutical products, has gathered an important collection of Islamic, mainly Persian, works of art such as manuscripts, carpets as well as ceramics and miniatures, which are displayed in his gallery. This Iranian art collector is the first to have set up a private Art Foundation in the UAE where collections are displayed to testify of the brilliance of the Iranian culture. The Iranian presence in the field of the arts in Dubai is characterised by such pioneer initiatives.

In the Al Quoz district, most of the galleries are located in warehouses and boast vast spaces with high white walls. Dariush Zandi, an Iranian architect, was the first gallery owner to be established in the district. He is the director of a complex designed and built by him. The gallery specialises in traditional and Middle Eastern arts and crafts and aims to discover and expose new artists, as well as enrich the cultural heritage of the UAE. He left Iran when he was 19 to study in the USA and he graduated as an architect. He joined Dubai Municipality, where he was senior architect and town planner from 1981 to 1994. He was the first person, in 1997–8, to erect a block of several buildings in the hitherto deserted district of Al Quoz, in the wake of the culturisation policy of the city. The very first gallery specialized in Iranian contemporary art; then another gallery was dedicated to the contemporary art of the Middle East. Two other galleries specialising in Iranian art also opened in 2005 next to this block. These dynamics also brought some Iranian artists to live in the city. Ramin and Rokni Haerizadeh, whose works are displayed in one of these galleries, are two brothers who left Iran in late 2008 for political reasons related to their controversial work. After a raid on a party in Tehran at a house where one of the paintings (considered as 'immoral' from a religious point of view) was displayed, they were forced to move to Dubai. With the help of a European gallery owner who gave them a studio, they managed to obtain the legal papers necessary to stay there. Today, their works are exhibited in Dubai, Paris, Berlin, London and New York and command a premium in art auctions. London's Saatchi Gallery has purchased a large number of Haerizadeh works. The brothers' residence in Dubai and recent political events in Iran have influenced their work. In this respect, it is interesting to note that since 2009 and after the electoral crisis in Iran, Dubai has begun to play the role of 'country of exile' for Iranians who have had to leave their country, even if these Iranians are not considered to be refugees, but freelance workers or employees.

From the merchant city, which was organised around the Creek and its nascent activities, to the industrial city which was made possible thanks to oil revenues and then on to a post-oil city of services, the Iranian presence has always been strong and sometimes engraved on the urban landscape of Dubai. Today, the demand of a creative city has drawn new forms of migratory flows from the urban centres in Iran or from Iranian communities elsewhere in the world and they are playing an active role in the culturisation of Dubai economy.

Changes to the laws of residence and labour could ensure more stability for migrants and could give rise to the establishment of an Iranian diaspora, made up of artists, intellectuals traders or business people, who may include political opponents. Nevertheless, the Emirate of Dubai, an old friend of the various Iranian governments since the revolution of 1979, may preclude the development of a 'land of exile' scenario, which could be detrimental to economic and political relations with Iran, as the role of the state continues to be eminent in transnational relations. Dubai's severe control of political demonstrations after the election crisis and the ban on certain anti-regime works of art are a reflection of such a trend. At the same time, as mentioned above, the UAE is severely controlling the Iranian presence in its territory following international sanctions against Iran. The future of this somehow paradoxical policy will certainly affect the Iranian presence in the UAE.

Conclusion: A bittersweet dream

In the 2006 film *Café Setareh*, by Iranian director Saman Moghadam, a young Iranian girl called Saloumeh, building on the promises made by her suitor,

Ebi, dreams of moving with him to one of Dubai's artificial islands to escape from the poverty and misery of her condition. She draws a picture of the island, with her neighbourhood mosque in the south of Tehran and a luxurious mansion where her handicapped grandmother, her future husband and she will live in peace and prosperity. Ebi's vain attempts to emigrate to the UAE lead him into illegal activities and he ends up in jail. With tears in her eyes, Saloumeh hangs the dream vision of her Dubai island above her bed and awaits the return of her loved one.

Many young Iranians share the girl's longing, but the dream of Dubai leaves a bitter taste on Iranians' palates. This bitterness stems from the spectacular growth of the Emirates, which has left Iran behind. Popular and official opinion reflects this communal Iranian resentment towards the rapid development of the south coast of the Gulf, which has been fuelled in part by the historical presence of a dynamic Iranian community in the region. These sentiments – or resentments – also affect the views of political players. The frontier location of Iranian free zones such as the islands of Qeshm and Kish, just inside Iran's territorial waters, encourages comparisons of respective public policies. If they are seen as lagging behind, this is put down to competition from the Emirates' free zones seducing clientele away from Iranian companies, rather than being viewed as the adverse effects of Iran's own politico-economic model on the design and management of the country's free zones. Similarly, Tehran shared Dubai's ambitions for a long time. In the 1970s, Tehran's Mehrabad International Airport and Iran Air were designed to become what Dubai's airport and the Emirates Airline are today. Dubai's success and its place in the global network of world metropolises sheds its light on Iranian public policy, all the more so since a series of Iranian players of various socioeconomic classes travelling regularly between the two countries report Dubai's rapid ascension. These elements contribute to the fabrication of an image, idyllic no doubt, of Dubai in Iran. But until Iran emerges from its current politico-economic stalemate, Saloumeh, the impoverished girl in Samam Moghadam's film, will continue to nurture her dreams of her beloved's return and their eventual prosperity in Dubai.

Notes

1 While it is impossible to determine an exact number of Iranians in the UAE for various reasons that I will explain in this article, the mentioned number has been confirmed by the economic section of the Iranian consulate in Dubai in 2007 and in some articles in newspapers to which I have referred. In addition, from 2006 to

2010, the UAE population has grown with a growth of 64.5 per cent according to the National Bureau of Statistics in 2011.
2   Before 1971, the UAE was known as the Trucial States or Trucial Oman, in reference to a nineteenth-century truce between the UK and several Arab sheikhs.
3   The first surveys in 2007 and 2008 were part of the Gulf component of the CITADAIN programme ('Comparison of the degrees of integration of territories and the adaptation of law in the Arab and Indian world') financed by France's national research agency, ANR. The latest surveys in 2011 are part of the Gulf component of the SYSREMO programme financed by France's national research agency, ANR. This programme will be going on up to 2013. The results of my personal research have been presented in the Annual Gulf Conference Exeter 2010 under the title 'New identity roles for new development programs in the Gulf: the case of Qeshm'.
4   These are women whose role is to transport luxury goods from Iran's free trade areas into the interior. 'Parachute women' is the colloquial term used in these free areas. See Moghadam, A (2006) *La Zone Franche: Implications Economiques et Territoriales du Projet de 'Qeshm Free Area' dans le Sud Iranien*, Masters dissertation in urbanism and urban planning, Paris IV-Sorbonne university.
5   Stateless populations in the UAE who are represented by two major groups – Arabs (from neighboring countries) and non-Arabs (mainly from Iran and the Indian subcontinent) whose families settled in the Gulf generations ago as merchants or workers but have not been naturalized as Emirati.
6   REIDIN.com is the leading real estate information company focusing on emerging markets.

References

Abdullah, MM (1978) *The UAE: A Modern History*. London: Croom Helm.
Adelkhah, F (2001) 'Dubai, capitale économique de l'Iran?' in Marchal, R (ed.) *Dubai, Cité Globale*. Paris: CNRS, Espaces et Milieux collection.
Cadène, P (2008) 'Société de la connaissance et developpement aux Emirats Arabes Unis'. *Mondialisation et société de la connaissance aux Emirats arabes unis, Maghreb Machrek* 195.
Coville, T (2005–6) 'L'Economie iranienne, rupture ou continuité?'. *Géoéconomie* 36: 97–107.
Davidson, C (2005) *The UAE, A Study in Survival*. Boulder: Lynne Rienner Publishers.
Dumourtier, B (2007) 'Dubai' in *Images Economiques du Monde*. SEDES.
Fathi, N (2005) 'Iran's stocks plunge after vote for U.N. review of nuclear program'. *The New York Times*, 9 October.

Gibert, B, Maraut, A, Telle, B (2005) *Et Après La Pétrole? Risques et Enjeux Géopolitiques-Financiers pour les Emirats Arabes Unis*. Paris: L'Harmattan, Entreprises et Management collection.

Gholipour Fereidouni, H and Namdar, M (2011) 'Determinants of Iranian investment in Dubai's real estate sector'. *The Middle-East Journal of Business* 6, 2.

Haseeb, Kh (1998) *Arab-Iranian Relations*. Beirut, British Academic Press.

Heard-Bey, F (1982) *From Trucial States to UAE*. London: Longman ELT Publishers.

Iran Daily (2006) 'Capital flight to Dubai worrisome'. 8 March.

Joshi, M (2009) 'Dubai loses gilded status for business-minded Iranians'. *UAE Top News.in* (www.topnews.in/dubai-loses-gilded-status-businessminded-iranians-2168351).

Lavergne, M (2009) 'Dubaï, utile ou futile? Portrait d'une ville rêvée à l'heure de la crise'. *Hérodote* 133.

Lorimer, JG (1970) *Gazetter of the Persian Gulf, Oman and Central Asia*. Calcutta 1908 and 1915, 6 vols, republished by Gregg International Westmead, England.

Minoui, D (2007) 'Depuis Dubaï, l'Amérique surveille l'Iran'. *Le Figaro*, 19 January.

Moghadam, A (2012) '"L'art est mon métier": émergence et professionalisation du marché de l'art à Dubaï'. ['"Art is my job": emergence and professionalization of the art market in Dubai'] *Transcontinentales*, no. 12/13 (http://transcontinentales.revues.org/1339).

Nadjmabadi, S (2010) 'Cross-border networks labour migration from Iran to the Arab countries of the Persian Gulf'. *Anthropology of the Middle East*, Vol. 5, no. 1.

Niebhur, C (1772) *Description de l'Arabie*, 2 vols. Copenhagen.

Priestman, SMN (2008) 'The rise of Siraf: Long-term development of trade emporia within the Persian Gulf'. *International Congress of Siraf Port*. Bushehr, Iran.

Rahman, S (2005) 'Iranian investors pump Dh730b into UAE ventures', Gulfnews, 20 August (http://archive.gulfnews.com/articles/05/08/20/178061.html).

REIDIN (2010) 'Emerging markets real estate information' (http://dubaifocus.reidin.com/ (last accessed 4 July 2010)).

Sadjadpour, K (2011) 'The battle of Dubai: The UAE and the U.S.–Iran cold war Carnegie Paper' (http://carnegieendowment.org/2011/07/27/battle-of-dubai-united-arab-emirates-and-us-iran-cold-war/4a44).

Stockman, F (2008) 'U.S. sanctions hit Iranian entrepreneurs in Dubai'. *The New York Times*, 16 September.

Tarrius, A (2002) *La Mondialisation par le Bas. Les Nouveaux Nomades de l'Economie Souterraine*. Paris: Balland.

Thomas, J (2006) 'The dynamics of globalization and the uncertain future of Iran: an examination of Iranians in Dubai'. *Al Nakhlah*, Autumn.

LIST OF CONTRIBUTORS

Liliane Anjo has a first degree in philosophy from the University of Brussels, Belgium (Université Libre de Bruxelles) and a master's degree in political science at the School for Advanced Studies in Social Sciences, Paris (Ecole des Hautes Etudes en Sciences Sociales).

She is currently a doctoral student at the Ecole des Hautes Etudes en Sciences Sociales, where her PhD thesis focuses on the cultural policy of, and artistic practices in, the Islamic Republic of Iran, from the perspective of contemporary theatre. Since 2009, she has been the holder of an *AFR* PhD grant from the National Fund Research Luxembourg (Fonds National de la Recherche Luxembourg).

Mahmoud Arghavan obtained a B.S. in Physics in Iran. He then undertook graduate studies in the newly established interdisciplinary program of American Studies at the University of Tehran, receiving an MA in 2008 with a thesis on 'Representations of American Identity in Hollywood Bestsellers.' Since October 2009, he has been a PhD candidate in American Studies at the John F. Kennedy Institute at the Free University Berlin, Germany. His thesis is entitled 'Iranian-American Literature: From Collective Memory to Cultural Identity'.

Alice Bombardier is Research Associate at CADIS (Centre for Sociological Analysis and Intervention, EHESS–CNRS Paris), specialising in modern and contemporary Iranian painting. In 2012 she completed both a PhD in sociology at the Ecole des Hautes Etudes en Sciences Sociales (EHESS) in Paris and a PhD in Middle East studies at the University of Geneva. Her thesis was entitled Iranian Painting in the 20th century (1911–2009): History, Artistic Trends and Artists' Voices.

She has published on Iranian revolutionary painting, including 'Peinture de guerre et représentations anthropomorphiques dans un lieu de prière musulman en Iran', *Asiatische Studien*, 3, 2012: 565–98; and 'War painting and pilgrimage in Iran', in *Visual Anthropology*, 25, 2012: 148–66.

Katja Föllmer is a teaching and research assistant at the Institute of Iranian Studies of the University of Göttingen. Her PhD in Iranian studies focussed on contemporary Iranian press satire, published as *Satire in Iran von 1990–2000*, Wiesbaden: Harrassowitz, 2008. She has also translated *Farid ud-Din Attar: Die Konferenz der Vögel*, Wiesbaden: Marix, 2008. Currently she is working on religious and national aspects of public communication in Pahlavi Iran.

Mehri Honarbin-Holliday is the author of Becoming Visible in Iran: Women in Contemporary Iranian *Society* (London: I.B.Tauris, 2013) and Masculinities in Urban Iran: Men in Contemporary Iranian *Society*, forthcoming. She is a Fellow at the Centre for Gender Studies and affiliated to the London Middle East Institute at the School of Oriental and African Studies, University of London.

Mehri is also a practising artist and has exhibited her fired clay and video installations in Iran, Britain, and Mexico.

Azadeh Kian is Professor of Sociology and Director of the Centre for Gender and Feminist Studies and Research at the University of Paris 7-Diderot; Co-Director of the National Federation of Research on Gender in France (RING); and a member of the Scientific Council of French Research Institutes in Turkey, Russia, Iran and Central Asia.

Her recent publications include *L'Iran : Un Mouvement Sans Révolution ? La Vague Verte Face au Pouvoir Mercanto-Militariste*, Paris: Michalon, 2011; *Le Moyen-Orient en movement,* éditions Kimé, 2012 (edited with S. Dayan); 'Gender, ethnicity and identity in Iran: surrender without consent among Baluchi women in changing contexts', in Leif Stenberg and Eric Hooglund (eds), *Navigating Contemporary Iran. Challenging Economic, Political and Social Perceptions*, London and New York: Routledge, 2012; 'Gendering Shi'ism in post-revolutionary Iran', in Roksana Bahramitash and Eric Hooglund (eds), *Gender in Contemporary Islam: Pushing the Boundaries*, London, Routledge 2011.

Pardis Mahdavi is Associate Professor and Chair of Anthropology at Pomona College. Her books include *Passionate Uprisings: Iran's Sexual Revolution*, Stanford University Press, 2008; and *Gridlock: Labor, Migration and 'Human Trafficking' in Dubai*, Stanford University Press, 2011.

Her current research focuses on the nexus of race, class, gender, sexuality, labour and migration and she is completing a manuscript entitled *Trafficking and Terror: Interrogating the Construction of a Paradigm*. She is also working on a project looking at migrant parents and how their status as parents makes them vulnerable to detention-type situations.

Amin Moghadam majored in anthropology (University of Paris V) and has a double masters degree in urban development and geography from the University of Paris IV- the Sorbonne and the Ecole Nationale des Ponts et Chaussées. He has a PhD in geography and urban studies from Lyon 2 University. His work investigated the characteristics of various waves of Iranian migrants to Dubai.

He is currently a lecturer and the academic co-ordinator of MPA (Master of Public Affairs) at Sciences-Po Paris. He is a member of the SYSREMO (Middle East Regional System) research programme within France's National Research Agency.

Parmis Mozafari studied Persian classical music in Iran and completed her PhD in ethnomusicology at the University of Leeds. Her current research is focused on female performers in modern and pre-modern Iran and the transformation of gender roles in contemporary Iranian music culture. She has taught Iranian classical music, music in Islam, Iran's regional music, and the changing patterns of performing religious music in Iran and the UK. She has published on female singers in post-revolution Iran and is currently working on her monograph on female musicians in contemporary Iran.

Bronwen Robertson graduated with a PhD in ethnomusicology from the University of Melbourne in 2010. From July 2007 – July 2008 she lived in Tehran, performing with unofficial rock musicians and gathering data for her PhD thesis on identity and expression in the unofficial rock music scene, now published as *Reverberations of Dissent*, Continuum, 2012. She is currently the Director of Operations for London-based Small Media.

Naghmeh Samini holds an MA in cinema and a PhD in drama and mythology from the University of Tehran, where she teaches. She is an award-winning playwright and more than 15 of her plays have been staged in Iran, France, India and Germany including *The Spell of Burnt Temple* (2001), *Sleeping in an Empty Cup* (2003), *Death and the Poet* (2006), *The Home* (2009) and *Born in 1982* (2010). She has also written several screenplays including *Main Line, Three Women* and *Heiran*.

Nahid Siamdoust is completing her doctoral degree in modern Middle Eastern studies at St Antony's College, University of Oxford, examining music as politics in post-revolutionary Iran. She teaches history and politics of the Modern Middle East and Modern Iran at Oxford. Before returning to academia, Nahid worked as a full-time journalist for *Time* magazine, the *Los Angeles Times* and Al Jazeera English TV.

Vít Šisler is an Assistant Professor at Charles University in Prague. He is the founder and editor-in-chief of Digital *Islam* (www.digitalislam.eu/), a research project on Islam, the Middle East and digital media. He is also editor of *CyberOrient* (www.cyberorient.net/), an American Anthropological Association journal.

Annabelle Sreberny is Professor of Global Media and Communication in the Centre for Media and Film Studies, SOAS, University of London and was the first chair of the Centre for Iranian Studies, SOAS. She is immediate past president of the International Association of Media and Communication Research (IAMCR) 2008–12.

Her books on Iran include *Small Media, Big Revolution* (with A Mohammadi), University of Minnesota, 1995 and *Blogistan* (with G Khiabany), I.B.Tauris, 2010. She is currently completing (with M Torfeh) a book on the history of BBC Persian broadcasting to Iran and Afghanistan to be published by I.B.Tauris, in 2013.

Massoumeh Torfeh is UNAMA's Director of Strategic Communication and Spokespersons Unit in Kabul. She is a former senior producer at the BBC World Service (1986–98 and 2000–2) specialising in the politics and media of Afghanistan, Iran and Central Asia. She holds a PhD in political science from LSE. She has worked as a spokesperson and Chief Public Information Officer for the UN Mission of Observers in Tajikistan (1998–2000); as a public information consultant in the office of President Hamid Karzai (2002–4); and as the Director of the Tajik Service and the Editor of the Asia Desk at the Central Newsroom of Radio Free Europe in Prague. Between 2008 and 2011, she was a research associate in the Centre for Media and Film Studies, SOAS, and commented on the politics and media of Afghanistan and Iran for the *Guardian, Christian Science Monitor*, BBC, Al Jazeera English, amongst others.

She is co-author (with A Sreberny) of a book on the history of BBC Persian broadcasts to Iran and Afghanistan to be published by I.B.Tauris, 2013; and has a chapter on Iran's role in Afghanistan in *Partners for Stability* published by the German Council on Foreign Relations (DGAP) Berlin, 2012.

List of Contributors

Anna Vanzan holds a degree in oriental languages and cultures (University Of Ca' Foscari, Venice) and a PhD in Near Eastern studies (New York University). She works on gender studies in the MENA, particularly; Iran, Central Asia, Pakistan, Afghanistan and Muslim India. She teaches Arabic culture at the University of Milan and is Visiting Lecturer at the European Master MIM Ca' Foscari University where she teaches gender and Islamic thought. She is Editor of the Italian journal *Afriche&Orienti*.

Her book, *La storia velata: le donne dell'islam nell'immaginario italiano*, 2006 is a history of the image of Muslim women in Italian culture from the Middle Ages; *Figlie di Shahrazad, scrittrici iraniane dal XIX secolo a oggi*, 2009, focuses on Iranian women's literature; *Le donne di Allah, viaggio nei femminismi islamici*, 2010, examines the emergence of Islamic feminisms, while her last book, *Che genere di islam, omosessuali, transessuali e queer tra shari'a e nuove interpretazioni* (with J Guardi, 2012) considers the multifaceted relationship between Islam and homosexuality.

Recent articles in English include 'The women of Allah: a personal journey through Islamic Feminisms', in *Alam-e niswan* 19, 1, 2012; 'Posht-e pardeh, Behind the painting: Women as art gallery managers in contemporary Iran', in www.persiangendernetwork.org/; 'Covering Iran', in *Archivi Indo Mediterranei:* www.archivindomed.altervista.org/pagina-43177.html, 2011.

Saeed Zeydabadi-Nejad studied anthropology at the University of Queensland, Australia, before completing a PhD in media studies at the Centre for Media and Film Studies, SOAS, University of London. He teaches media and film studies at SOAS and the Institute of Ismaili Studies.

He is the author of *The Politics of Iranian Cinema: Films and Society in the Islamic Republic*, Routledge, 2010. Based on groundbreaking ethnographic research in Iran on practices of regulation and reception of films, the book explores major aspects of Iranian cultural politics. His research interests include the Middle Eastern media's relationship with culture, religion and politics as well as diasporic media.

INDEX

Page references to illustrations are in *italics*, references to notes are shown by n.

127 (rock band) 140, 143–6, 147
2009 election 5–6, 87–8, 125, 154, 163, 241
   and protests 13, 14, 16, 75
   and women 43, 53, 54

Abadan 112, 233
Abbas 2–3
Abol-Qasem Aref Qazvini *see* Aref
Abtahi, Mohammad Ali 201
Abu Dhabi 257, 259
Abu Musa 252
actors 113
actresses 6, 113
advertising 72–4
Afarid, Gord 63
Age of Pahlevans (*Asr-e Pahlevanan*) (video game) *182,* 183, 185, 187–8
Aghebati, Mohammad 87
Ahang-Kowsar, Nik 199
Ahangaran, Sadeq 160
Ahmadi-Khorasani, Noushin 51
Ahmadinejad, Mahmoud 28, 62, 152, 199, 251, 252
   and the arts 91
   and caricature 200
   and conservatism 3
   and economics 162
   and morality 17
   and women 52–3, 54
   see also 2009 election
Ahura Mazda 72
Akbari, Mina 110
alcohol 37, 87
Ali Ebn Abi Taleb 63–4, 71
Alizadeh, Hossein 156
Alizadeh, Javad 200
Alizadeh, Qazaleh 52
Allah-o Akbar ('God is great') 162, 163–4
allegory:
   and film 112, 119, 120, 123
   and satire 202, 203
   and songs 153, 154
America's Army (video game) 174
An eye and one hundred tears (*Yek cheshmi o sad nam*) (song) 161
Anahita 211
anarchism 139
animation 200
Ansar Hizbullah 124
anthems 136
anti-feminists 52, 53
anti-monarchism 20
anti-Westernism 2, 7, 28
Arabs 62, 248, 249
Ardebili, Ayatollah 137
Aref 152, 153, 154–5, 165n.4

Armenians 62
Army of the Savior of Times, get ready! (*Ey Lashgar-e Saheb-Zaman Amade Bash!*) (song) 160
arson 112, 119
art 6, 8, 259–61
Art Dubai 259, 260
artists 2, 8, 72, 259–61
Arts Centre 204
Ashura ceremonies 29, 36, 64, 70, 71, 218
Assault on Iran (video game) 174, 178, 180
Attar 84, 85
audience, the 81, 86, 91, 101
and jokes 214, 215
Audioflows 135
authorisation of public staging 82, 87, 91, 104–5, 139, 204
autonomy 22, 45, 59, 81, 84
Azad University 14, 19, 225, 255
Azeris 62
Azimi, Bahram 200

Bahar, Malek o-Sho'ara 6, 153, 154, 155, 165n.5–6
Bahram 152, 162
Bakhtiar, Touraj 257
Baluchis 62
Baluchistan 248
Bam 185
Bandar Abbas 249, 253, 258
Bandar Lengeh 249–50
Bani-Etemad, Rakhshan 52, 110, 125
Basiji forces 8, 46, 65
Bastak 248, 249
Bastakia art fair 259
Battle of Karbala *see* Ashura ceremonies
BBC Persian Service 4, 6, 7, 159, 201
Beheshti, Sattar 7
Behrouzi, Maryam 53
Beyzaei, Bahram 204
billboards 72–3
billiard clubs 33

Bioshock (video game) 171
Bird of dawn (*Morgh-e Sahar*) (song) 151–2, 153–4, 155–6
birth rates 47, 61
Black Friday 156
black market 100, 205
blasphemy 82
bloggers 2, 7, 53
Blood Wedding (Lorca) 90
body, the 59, 64–5, 66–7, 70, 72–3, 75
and dance 102
Bollywood 100
books *see* literature; publishing
Born in 1983 (*motevaled-e 1361*) (play) 91
boys 36–8
Breakin' (film) 100
Brick and the Mirror, The (film) 111
bricolage 31–2, 33, 34, 36, 39
Britain *see* Great Britain
British Embassy (Tehran) 8
Bushehr 249

Café Setareh (film) 261–2
Call of Duty 4 (video game) 172
Campaign Against Stoning and all Forms of Violence against Women 53
caricaturists 197–8, 199, 200–1, 206, 218
cartoonists 5, 197, 199, 200
Censoring an Iranian Love Story (novel) 5
censorship 1, 2–3, 8, 59, 66, 199, 206
and film 111, 113–14, 124, 204
and internet 134
and music 136–8
and publishing 4–5, 234, 235
and theatre 81, 82, 91, 92
and video games 172
Centre of Thought and Islamic Art 218–19, 220
Chaharshanbeh Soori 38, 40, 101
Charmshir, Mohammad 87, 90
Chavosh Culture and Arts Society 156–7, 158, 160

Cheshmeh 5
children 3, 43, 44, 102
   and publishing 235
   and video games 179
China 256–7
choreographers 103, 105
cinema *see* film
Civil Code 49
civil rights 14, 62
classical literature 59, 63, 64, 194
   and sexuality 210–11
clothing *see* dress codes; fashion
codes 6, 7, 31, 89, 90
Coelho, Paulo 236
coffee shops 33, 36, 62, 66
cohabitation 36
colour 90, 222
comedy 202, 203, 206
comics 200, 206
Committee to Protect Journalists (2011) 7
communication technology 28, 30, 32, 46, 215
communicative codes 31
comportment 3, 14, 15–16, 17, 19, 20, 21
computers 28, 172; *see also* internet
concerts 100, 101, 142, 158, 160, 166n.15
confusion 95–6
consumerism 15, 72–3
contraception 43, 47
Convention of the Elimination of All Forms of Discrimination Against Women (CEDAW) 50, 52, 53
conversation culture 211
copyright 9, 172, 180, 185, 242n.14
corruption 162
cosmetic surgery *see* plastic surgery
cosmopolitanism 33–4, 59, 61–3, 75
Council of Music 139
Council of Poetry 139
counterculture 21, 22
Cow, The (film) 111

Croesus' Treasure (film) 110–11
Cultural Association of Women Publishers 233–4, 238
cultural flows 30
Cultural Guild of Women Publishers 233

Dabbagh, Marzieh Hadidchi 46
Dadgar, Puya 179, 180, 184, 185, 186
Damavand Publishing *(Entesharat-e Damavand)* 233
Dance 5, 68, 137
   as art form 101–5, 106–7
   banning of 99–101
   historical 97–9
   learning of 105–6
Daneshvar, Simin 52
Dashti, Ali Asghar 85
dating 32, 33, 37, 38
Davis, Fred 31
Dawn (Sepideh) (song) 158
defa (defence) 178
Dehkordi, Payam 91
democracy 50, 62
depression 144
Derakhshandeh, Pouran 52
Derambakhsh, Kambiz 200
Desai, Kiran 236
diaspora 8, 60, 174, 201, 261
digital media 5, 183
discrimination 50, 53–4, 110, 196, 232, 234, 239
disobedience 7, 14, 23, 24, 25, 81
divorce 50, 55n.1, 115
Do Kalame Harf-e Hesab (satirical column) 193, 194, 195, 196–8
documentaries 111, 112
Doha conference (1995) 252
Dome of the Rock (Jerusalem) 221, 222, 227
Donya-ye Sokham (magazine) 193, 198
Dramatic Arts Centre 83, 91
dress codes 3, 19, 27, 39, 95, 96
   and counterculture 22, 23, 25
   and dance 105

and film 116, 126n.6–7
and men 65, 141
and migration 250
and theatre 89
see also fashion
drugs 17, 23, 26n.1, 39–40
Dubai 8, 247, 248, 249–51
  and culture 259–61
  and dance 100
  and education 255–6
  and real estate 257–8
  and resentment 262
  and trade 253–4, 256–7

Earth and the Universe, The (play) 85
Ebadi, Shirin 49
economics 9, 44, 62, 234, 250–1, 256–7
education 17, 33, 44, 61
  and murals 225
  and United Arab Emirates 255–6
  and women 3, 43, 44, 52, 115, 232, 237
Ehterami, Manuchehr 201
Ejei, Gholam Hossein Mohsen 7
elections 8, 50; *see also* 2009 election
embassies 8, 104, 107n.6, 144, 259
Emirates Chamber of Commerce and Industry 254
employment 44, 47, 52, 60–1
enjoyment 37–8
entertainment 96, 99
  and satire 195, 196, 203
equality 14, 22, 23, 48, 49, 240
Ershad *see* Ministry of Culture and Islamic Guidance (MCIG)
Etemad (newspaper) 119
ethnic minorities 44, 55, 62
etiquette 202, 239
Ettela'at (newspaper) 193, 194, 195, 197
Evaz 248

Facebook 7, 142
Factory of Martyrs, The (documentary) 219

Faculty of Decorative Arts (Tehran) 218
Faculty of Fine Arts (Tehran) 218, 219
Fajr International Film Festival 119
Fajr International Theatre Festival 82, 85, 86, 92n.2
Fajr Music Festival 158
family 32, 35, 36, 38, 60–1, 178
  and women 44, 45, 46
  and work balance 238
Family Protection bill (2007) 54
Family Protection Law (1967) 55n.1, 115
Fanafzar 181, 182, 183
Farhad Mehrad 153
Farhadi, Askhar 4
Farjam Collection 260
Farmanara, Bahman 114
Farrokhi, Hossein 86
Farrokhzad, Forough 112, 115
Fars News Agency 159
Fars province 248
Farsi One 6
Farzaneh (magazine) 48, 49
fashion 7, 15, 16, 19, 20, 22, 25
  and boys 37
  and girls 39
  and men 66–7
  and morality 66
  Western 29
  and youth 31, 35–6, 40
fatwas 5
feminism 53, 110, 232
  and publishing 236–7, 238, 239–40, 242n.9
Ferdowsi 63, 68, 84, 194
fertility rates 43
Festival of University Theatre 83
film 1, 6, 110–116
  and censorship 3, 4
  and dance 102
  and music 147
  and satire 193, 203–5, 206
  Western 28, 29

and women 46, 52, 53
film critics 111, 120
film directors 2, 4, 7, 204
  female 6, 52, 109–10, 112, 115–16, 122, 124–6
film-farsi 110, 111, 112, 116
Floor, Willem 89, 91
Flying Shams (play) 84
folk music 144
Foroozand, Afrooz 87
Foundation of Martyrs 220, 221, 222, 223–4
Fox Hunting (Shekar-e roubah) (play) 90
Free Keys 142
freedom of expression 53, 59, 62, 67
freedom of thought 4, 7
fusion music 160

Gaffary, Farrokh 111
Galehdar 249
'game nets' 172
Gandbazi 7
Garshasp (video game) 171, 181–3, 188
Gerami, Mazdasht 163
Ghaderinejad, Nilufar 219
Ghadyanlu, Mehdi 224–5
Ghobadi, Bahman 141
girls 38–9
Give me my gun (Tofangam ra bede) (song) 157–8
globalisation 28, 30, 32, 61, 259
God of War (video game) 188
Gol-Agha (magazine) 193, 195, 197–8, 199, 200, 203
Gol-Agha Institute 199, 200, 203
Golestan, Ebrahim 111
Gorgani, Ayatollah 137
graffiti 218
Grand Theft Auto: San Andreas (video game) 172
Great Britain 8, 23–4
Greater Tumbs 252
Green Days (film) 125

Green Movement 13–14, 15, 16, 20, 23, 24–5, 125
  and music 154, 163
grooming 67
Guardian Council 50, 53
Gulf Cooperation Council (GCC) 252

Habibi, Mohammad Nabi 200
Haerizadeh brothers 260–1
Hafez 160, 161, 166n.15
Haghshenas, Rasoul 86
hair 7, 19, 22, 34, 38, 67, 68
hajw 194, 195, 196
Hala Hekayat-e Mast (satirical column) 198
Hall, Stuart 21, 30–1
Hamas 222
hangings 8
happiness 96
harassment 2, 67
Hashempoor, Narges 87
hazl 194, 195, 196
Hazrat-e Khadijeh Association 49
healthcare 44
Hebdige, Dick 21, 22, 31
Hedda Gabler (Ibsen) 91
Hejazi, Mohammad 119
Hekmat, Manijeh 52, 110, 125, 126; *see also Women's Prison*
hero concept 183–4, 187
Hezbollah 125, 171
  and video games 174, 176, 178
Hichkas 6, 152, 162
Hidden Half (film) 124–5
High Council of Cultural Revolution 47
High Walls (film) 116
higher education *see* universities
hijab 3, 16, 20, 95, 96, 115, 126n.6
  and theatre 82
Hoghough-e Zanan (magazine) 49
Hollywood 109
'Holy Defence' Theatre Festival 86
homo-eroticism 64
Hossein Ebn Ali 63–4, 71, 73–4, 160

House is Black, The (film) 112
House of Artists (Khaneh
  Honarmandan) 8
House of Caricatures, The 200
human rights 4, 7, 53, 62, 75
humour *see* jokes; satire
Hypernova (rock band) 139
hypocrisy 152, 161, 164

Ibsen, Henrik 88, 91
identity formation 31–2, 39
  male 59, 63
  and men 67
  and migration 254–5
  and video games 172, 173, 179, 186, 187
illegal immigrants 253
Imam Ali (film) 102
immigration *see* illegal immigrants; migration
Indian Ocean 248
individualism 33, 35, 62
inequality 43, 45, 46, 47, 50, 51, 122
inflation 44, 135
Intellectuals and Women Studies Publishing 240
intercultural communications 30
International Atomic Energy Agency 251
International Book Fair (Tehran) 234–5, 238
International Cartoon Biennial 200
International Festival of Ritual and Traditional Theatres of Iran 107
internet 3, 6, 28, 30, 199
  and music 134, 138, 147, 161, 163
  and satire 193, 200, 201, 206
  and students 62, 63
  and women 53
Iran:
  and Arab nations 251, 252
  and trade 256–7
  and video games 174–5, 179–80, 187

Irancartoon (magazine) 200
Iranian identity 140, 142–3, 144, 146
Iranian News Agency 184
Iranian Student Union 174
Iran–Iraq war 45–7, 61, 91, 96, 114
  and Arab nations 253
  and martyrdom 217, 220, 227
  and migration 250
  and music 153, 160
  and satire 193, 194, 197, 198, 205
  and theatre 85–6, 89
  and video games 175, 178
Isfahan 62, 98, 119
Isfahan Symphony Orchestra 7
Islam 163–4
  and Arab nations 252
  and video games 175, 178
  and women 48, 49, 53, 54
  see also Shi'a Islam; Sunni Islam
Islamic Coalition Party 53
Islamic discourse 33, 37, 39
Islamic law 43, 45, 46, 47, 49; *see also* sharia law
Islamic Propaganda Organisation 175, 220
Islamic Republic 1, 2, 9
  and the body 65
  and film 112, 113–15
  and media 33
  and murals 219
  and music 152, 156, 158, 159–60, 164
  and publishing 234, 236
  and rock music 134–5, 136–8, 140, 146
  and satire 194, 195, 197, 201
  and sexuality 210, 211, 212
  and social activities 17
  and theatre 81, 82, 89, 91, 92
  and video games 171, 172–3, 178–9, 184, 186–7
  and women 45, 46, 47, 51
  and youth 18, 23, 25, 39–40

INDEX 279

Islamic Republic of Iran Broadcasting (IRIB) 1, 158, 218
Islamic Revolution (1979) 13, 14, 16, 91, 96
 and Arab nations 253
 and film 112
 and migration 250
 and murals 218, 219
 and music 154, 155
 and theatre 85–6
Islamic Sims (video game) 178
Islamic Vice Squad *(Entezamat)* 101
Isolated Libertine, The (Rend-e khalvatneshin) (play) 84
Israel 217, 221, 222, 223, 227
 and video games 171, 176, 177, 178

Jackson, Michael 100
Jafari, Arash 182, 183, 185
Jalali, Bahman 259
Jamalzadeh, Mohammad-Ali 197
Jame'e (newspaper) 193, 198
Jang-e narm ('soft war') 7
Jannaati, Ayatollah 137
Jayeze-ye Bozorg (The Grand Prize) (TV show) 202
Jens-e Dovvom (magazine) 51
Jihad 46
jokes 209, 210, 211–15
Jonbesh-e Sabz see Green Movement
journalists 2, 7, 8, 62
 female 48–50
judiciary 50, 91

Kaboli, Farzaneh 103, 104
Kadivar, Jamileh 51
Kalameh 162
Kamali-Deghan 4–5
Kar, Mehrangiz 49
Karaj 62
Karbaschi, Gholam-Hossein 200
Karimi, Nikki 52, 110
Kasesaz, Habibollah 124
Kayhan (newspaper) 5, 159

keffiyeh scarf 221
Kerman 62, 185
Ketab-e Cheragh (The Light Books) 232–3
Keyhan-e Karikatur (magazine) 198, 199
Khal Punk (album) 144
Khaleqi, Ruhollah 152–3
Khamenei, Ayatollah Ali 5, 7, 114, 152, 194
 and murals 221, 222
Khatami, Mohammad 16, 45, 62
 and Arab nations 252
 and the arts 83–4, 91
 and film 113, 114
 and music 160
 and publishing 233, 235, 240–1
 and reforms 3, 28, 193, 195
 and satire 198, 200
 and women 50–1
Khomeini, Ayatollah Ruhollah 19, 114, 115, 194
 and Arab nations 252
 and film 112–13
 and martyrs 220
 and murals 218, 219, 221, 222
 and music 136–7, 158
 and women 46
Khorasani, Noushin Ahmadi 240
Khordadian, Mohammad 100, 105
Khosrojerdi, Hosein 218, 219
Kiarostami, Abbas 259
Kimiai, Masoud 204
'King Raam' 139–40
Kiosk 6, 151–2
Kiss You and Tears (Miboosamet va ashk) (play) 87, 88
Komeil prayer 37
Koohestani, Amir Reza 87–8
Koskhol (song) 133, 142
Kowsar, Nikohang 5
Kuban, Sima 232–3
Kurds 62

Lahiji, Shahla 239–40, 242n.11

Language of fire, The (Zaban-e Atash) (song) 159
Lar 248, 249
Larijani, Ali 158
Lauzen, Martha 109
Law (Qanun) (song) 161–2
Lebanon 125, 174, 178
Leili is With Me (Leili Ba Man Ast) (film) 205
leisure 6, 83, 171
Lesser Tunbs 252
Let's not muddy the water (Nakonim ab ra gel) (song) 162
Letter to the president, A (Nameh-i be rais jomhur) (song) 162
literacy rates 43, 44, 63, 232
literature 3, 4–5, 236
 and women 52, 53, 231
 see also classical literature; poetry
Lizard, The (film) 205
Lodgers, The (film) 204–5
London International Film Festival 7
Lorca, Federico García 88, 90
Lors 62
Los Angeles 100, 105
Lotfali Khan Zand (video game) 180, *181*, 188
Lotfi, Mohammad Reza 156–7
lower classes 36, 44
lyrics 139, 140, 142–6, 153, 155–9, 161, 163

Mahmoody, Betty 143
makeup 17, 19, 38
Makhmalbaf, Hana 125
Makhmalbaf, Mohsen 125, 204
Makhmalbaf, Samira 52, 110
'Man Kiyam' (song) 144, 145–6
Mandanipour, Shahriar 5
Manoto TV 6
Mansurimaneh, Akram 51
Mard-e Hezar Chehreh (Man of a Thousand Faces) (TV show) 202–3
marginal functions 209–10

Mariam and Mani (film) 115
Marjan (film) 115
marriage 36, 38
 age of 43, 44, 50, 55n.1
 see also divorce
martyrdom 46, 63–4, 65, 75
 and mural painting 217, 219, 220, 223, 226, 227
 and music 160
 and video games 175
Marx, Karl 236
Marxism 219
Marzban, Hadi 103
Marzolph, Ulrich 220, 221
masculinity 60, 75
Mashad 15, 62
Mashayekhi, Jamshid 113
Matârish tribes 249
media 34, 114, 159–60
 and satire 193, 194
 see also press, the
Mehrjui, Dariush 204
Memorable Battles (Nabardehaye Manadekar) (video game) 175, 178
men 60, 102
 and the body 59, 63–4, 64–5, 66–7, 70, 72–3, 75
 and family 44, 45
 see also boys; patriarchal order
Meshkatian, Parviz 156
Meshkini, Marziyeh 52
middle classes 36, 37, 44
 and dance 97, 105–6
 and women 48, 51, 55
migration 61, 254–5
 and Persian Gulf 248–50
 and United Arab Emirates 247–8, 251, 252
 see also diaspora
Milani, Tahmineh 52, 110, 114, 124–5
military service 68, 135
Ministry of Culture and Islamic Guidance (MCIG) 4, 5, 82, 87, 89, 91, 139

and dance 101, 102
and film 113, 119, 123, 124, 204
and music 146, 160
and publishing 232, 233, 234, 235, 236
and satire 196, 206
and video games 172, 173, 184
Ministry of Intelligence 143, 144
Mir-Bagheri, Davoud 102, 205
Mir Mahna (video game) 188
Mirtamasb, Morteza 7
mixed-gender parties 32, 36, 38, 40, 137
mobile phones 28, 33, 209; *see also* SMS text messaging
Modiri, Mehran 202–3, 206
Moghadam, Saman 261, 262
Mohajerani, Ayatollah 5, 114, 115
Mohammad Reza Shah 13, 14, 20, 55n.1, 98–9, 136, 218
Mohandespour, Farhad 83
Moharram 37
Moheb-Ali, Mahsa 52
monopolism 210–11
morality 15, 17, 18–19, 25, 65–6
    and film 112
    and music 162
    and satire 197, 198
    and theatre 82, 89
    and video games 183–4
Moravia, Alberto 236
Morgh e Sahar (song) 6
Moshiri, Fereydun 159
Mourning for Siavash (play) 84
Mousavi, Mir-Hossein 13, 156
Mowlana Jalal-al-Din Mohammad Balkhi *see* Rumi
Mrs Abu's Husband (film) 111
murals 1–2
    development of 217–24
    new genres 224–7
Museum of Martyrs 220
music 5, 8, 16, 96, 97, 101
    and censorship 136–8

and criticism 151–7, 161–2
and politics 158–60, 163–4
state-sponsored 160
traditional 157, 158
Western 28
see also rap music; rock music; underground music
music videos 100, 105
musicians 2, 105, 137–8, 156
Muslim Women's Olympics 104
Myspace 136, 142
mythology 63, 171
    and sexuality 211
    and video games 180–3, 187

Nabavi, Ebrahim 198–9, 201
Naderi, Amir 204
Naderlu, Mustafa 224
naghali 63
Naghi 5
Najafi, Mohammad Ali 102
Namjoo, Mohsen 8, 151–2, 153, 160–1
namus 160, 165n.14
National Foundation of Computer Games (NFCG) 172, 173, 184, 185, 188
nature 225–6
Nayestani, Mana 5
Nazeri, Shahram 158
Nazr 36
New Wave cinema 110, 111–12
Neydavud, Morteza 153
Neyestani, Touka 200
Night of the Hunchback (film) 111
Night on the Wet Cobblestone, The (play) 103
Nights of Barareh (Shabha-ye Barareh) (play) 202
No-one knows about Persian Cats (film) 6, 141
Noghtechin (Dots) (TV show) 202, 203
non-conformism 35–40
Norouz (video game) 179–80

nuclear weapons 251, 252, 255
Nuri 'Ala, Partou 233

O-Hum (rock band) 160
Obaash 141, 143
Obama, Barack 210
Oblivion (video game) 171, 188
Office for Rhythmic Movements 103
Office of Beautification 224, 227
Office of Theatre 103
Office of Women's Affairs 47
oil 61, 250, 251, 256, 261
Oman 249
One Million Signatures Campaign 53, 55, 240
openness 3, 5
Oriental Real Estate agency 257

Pahlavi era 1, 45, 95, 157, 195, 252; see also Mohammad Reza Shah; Reza Shah
Pahlevan concept 183
Palestine 217, 221–2, 223, 227
Panahi, Jafar 4, 7, 148n.11
paper 234
pardeh khani 63, 72
parks 19, 35, 37, 62, 101
parliament 45, 50, 51–2, 53–4
Parrot's Feather (Tooti Par) (play) 85
Parsai, Hossein 83
Parsipour, Shahrnoush 52
Pasdaran (Revolutionary Guards) 46, 100, 136, 171
patriarchal order 43, 45, 59, 87, 110
Pavarchin (On Tiptoes) (TV show) 202, 203
Payam-e Hajjar (magazine) 48
Payam-e Zan (magazine) 48
performance art 69–70
period of reconstruction 45, 47, 50, 61
Persepolis 252
Persian Gulf 247, 248–50, 252, 262
and trafficking 253–4
Persian heritage 84–5, 157, 158

Persian language 140, 144, 238
pets 36
Pezeshk, Mohammad Hassan 119, 124
photography 7, 8, 13, 72, 200
piercings 67
piracy 9, 172
Pirzad, Zoya 52
plastic surgery 15, 67–8
playwrights 84, 89
poetry 5, 6, 64, 68, 160, 161
political 153–4, 155, 156
police 18, 25, 65–6
and dance 101
and dress codes 39
and satire 203
and youth 37
polygamy 48, 52, 115
population growth 44, 47, 61
posters 1, 73–4
power elite 47, 48
prayers 37, 38
press, the 1, 3
and satire 193, 195, 197–9
Prince of Persia (video game) 180
prisons 116–19, 122, 123
privacy 33, 67, 95, 96
and dance 99–100
and rock music 135
procedural rhetoric 173–4, 175–8, 188
propaganda 89, 137, 143, 220
prostitutes 98
public affection 3, 17, 19
public life 96, 115–16
public space 70–1, 95, 96
and dance 99, 101, 104
and neutrality 219–20
public transport 62
publishing 1, 4–5
and women 231–41
punishment 18
puppetry 102
purification 113

Qajar dynasty 249

Qawasim 249
Qazvin 203
Qom 48, 62
Quest for Persia (video game) 179, 180, 184, 185, 187, 188, 189n.3
Qur'an, the 5, 161
  and music 136
  and women 48, 49

Rabena prayer 159, 165n.12
Rad, Saeed 113
Radi, Akbar 103
radif 157, 160
radio 1, 156
Rafii, Ali 90
Rafsanjani, Ali-Akbar Hashemi 47, 194, 200, 252
Rahbani, Vahid 91
RAK Petropak 258–9
Ramadan 36, 38, 159
Raminfar, Monir 233
rap music 5, 6, 152, 161–2
Ras Al Khaimah 255, 257, 258–9
Ravanipour, Monirou 52
real estate 257, 258
religion 1, 18
  and dance 99–100
  and film 116
  and hypocrisy 161, 164
  and men 70–1
  and migration 248, 249
  and women 46, 47, 48
  and youth 36–8, 39, 40
  see also Islam; Zoroastrianism
repression 28, 52, 54, 152
Resalat (newspaper) 202
Resaneh (magazine) 196
Resistance (*Moqavamat*) (video game) 171, 175–6, 177, 178–9
restaurants 36, 62
Revolutionary Guards *see* Pasdaran
Rex Cinema (Abadan) 112
Reza Shah 95, 153, 157, 202, 250
Rezana Afzar Sharif Company 183, 185

Rezayi, Babk 158
Rhythmic Movement *(Harakat-e Mozoon)* 102–3, 107n.4
Riyahi, Shahla 115
rock music 133–6, 138, 139–40, 141, 141–7, 160
Rostam and Esfandiar (play) 84
Rostam's Seven Labours (play) 84
Roustaie, Hamid 175, 178, 183, 187
Rudaki Hall (Tehran) 103
Rumi 64, 68, 84, 85, 194
rural areas 44, 55, 61
Rushdie, Salman 5

Saanei, Ayatollah 137–8
Saberi Fumani, Kioumars 194, 195, 197–8, 199
Saberi, Pari 84–5, 103
Sabri, Zahra 85
Sadeghi, Qotbedin 107
Sa'di 194
Sadr, Roya 201, 204, 205
Sa'edi, Gholam-Hossein 111
Safavids 98, 249
Saidi, Korba 115
Sakharov Prize 4, 7
Salahi, Omran 198, 199
Salman (art movement) 218
Samimi, Farshad 179–80
Samini, Naghmeh 91
sanctions 251, 256–8, 261
Saqr Port 258
Sarbedaran (film) 102
Satanic Verses, The 5
satire 1, 193, 194–6, 205–6
  and caricature 199–201
  and film 203–5
  and the internet 201
  and the press 197–9
  and SMS 211
  and television 202–3
SAVAK 1
Saving Harbor (*Najat-e Bandar*) (video game) 175, 178

scenic language 89–90
Season of wine (*Hengam-e mey*) (song) 154–5
secularism 33, 36, 37
  and dance 99
  and women 49–50, 51, 54
Sepah (Army of the Guardians of the Islamic Revolution) 178, 187
Separation, The (film) 4
Seven Labours of Rostam, The (*Haft Khan-e Rostam*) (play) 103
sexual revolution 14, 15, 16–19, 22–3, 24
sexuality 2, 7, 37, 62, 65, 67
  and dance 102
  and film 110, 111–12
  and jokes 210, 211, 212
  and literature 52
  and video games 172
Shafiei, Morteza 7
Shafi'i-Kadkani, Mohammad Reza 154
Shahabi, Mahmood 33–4
Shahid Beheshti University 20, 255
Shahnameh (Ferdowsi) 63, 76n.4, 84
Shajarian, Mohammad 8, 157–60, 164, 165n.12
  and *Bird of Dawn* 151, 152, 153, 155–6
Shakespeare, William 1
Shamloo 68
Shamlou, Sepideh 52
Shargh (newspaper) 5, 202
shari'a law 47, 114
Sharjah 249, 255
Shay, Anthony 102, 105
Shi'a Islam 46, 59, 63–4, 178, 184
  and film 112
  and the Persian Gulf 249, 252, 255
  and pilgrimage 36
Shiraz 15, 62, 203, 248
Shojaei, Zahra 51
shopping centres 36, 37
Sigh of Peace, A (*Ahi-ye sefid*) (play) 86
signs 31–2

Sims, The (video game) 171
singers 2, 105
  English language 140, 144
  female 3, 82
Siraf 248–9
Sistani, Ayatollah 137
Sizdah be Dar 101
slogans 14, 218, 221–2
SMS text messaging 209–10, 211–15
smuggling 250, 253–4
Snowman, The (film) 204, 205
Sobhani, Arash 152
social justice 14, 22, 23–4
software studios 178–9
Sohrab's message (*Neday-e Sohrab*) (song) 163
Soltan, Neda Agha 43, 46, 163
Something Happened in the Year 2000 (*Dar Sal-e 79 Ettefagh Oftadeh*) (book) 199–200
Songbird (*Morgh-e Khoshkhan*) (album) 160
songs:
  and criticism 151–7, 161–2
  and politics 157–60, 163–4
sorud 157, 165n.10
Sotoudeh, Nasrin 4, 7
Sotun-e Panjom (satirical column) 198
South of The City (film) 111
Soviet Union 23, 219
Special Force (video game) 174, 176, 177
Special Operation (*Amaliyat-e Vizhe*) (video game) 174–5
spirituality 64
sports stadiums 33
stage design 90
state, the *see* Islamic Republic
Steel, Danielle 236
Step Up (film) 100
stereotypes 143, 202, 239, 240
street demonstrations 6, 13, 14, 20, 87, 163
  and women 241n.2
street theatre 86

students 3, 13, 20, 23
  and activism 14
  female 43
  and the internet 62
  and United Arab Emirates 255–6
subcultures 21–2, 30–1
Sufi traditions 64, 84, 85
suicide 87
Sunni Islam 44, 248, 249, 250
surveillance 1, 6, 66, 92
symbolism:
  Islamic 164
  and murals 224, 226, 227
  and theatre 86, 90
  and women 210
Symphony of Awareness (play) 86

taboos:
  and feminism 53
  and film 205, 206
  and satire 197, 200
  and jokes 210, 211, 212, 213
Tabriz 62
Tabrizi, Kamal 205, 206
Tahlil Garan Tadbir 179
Tale of a Woman's Play Reading (play) 85
Taleghani, Ayatollah Mahmoud 48
Taleghani, Azam 48
tanz 194, 195, 196, 202
Tanz-o-Karikatur (magazine) 198, 199, 200
Taraqi, Goli 52
tasnifs 152–3, 155, 156, 157, 159, 160, 164
ta'ziyeh (passion plays) 64, 71, 85, 90, 93n.5
Tebyan Cultural and Informative Institute 175–6, 178, 183, 187, 188
Tehran 1, 15, 37, 60–1, 249, 262
  and bricolage 32
  and education 62
  and mural paintings 218, 220, 221, 223, 224, 227
  and publishing 233
  and rock music 134, 138, 139, 140, 141, 147
  and sexual revolution 17
  and theatre 92
  and Western influences 29
  and youth 34–5
Tehran City Theatre 87
Tehran University 20, 218, 219
television 1, 6, 17, 204
  satellite 28, 29, 30
  and satire 193, 202–3, 206
  and women 46
text messaging *see* SMS text messaging
theatre 4, 5
  and censorship 82, 91, 92
  and dance 102
  design 90
  and disobedience 81
  and Persian heritage 84–5
  political 85–8
  and the West 88–9
  and women 53
  and the young 82–4
  see also street theatre
theatre directors 84–5, 89–91, 103
This is Not a Film (film) 4, 7
Three Women (film) 116
Torabi, Morshed 63
Towfigh (newspaper) 195, 197
trade 248–9, 250, 251, 256–7, 258–9
trafficking 253–4
transnationalism 255
travel 6, 35, 36, 100
  and rock musicians 135
  and women 55n.3
Turkey 100
Two Women (film) 114

underground economy 44
underground music 6, 17, 135, 138–40, 160
unemployment 16, 135
United Arab Emirates (UAE) 247–8, 250, 252, 253, 254–5, 257

and culture 260
see also Dubai; Ras Al Khaimah
United Nations 251
United States of America (USA) 35, 251, 252
   and Arab nations 253, 257
   and counterculture 22–3, 24
   and embargoes 172, 186
   and video games 174, 176, 177–8, 180, 181
Universal Declaration of Human Rights 49
universities 1, 16, 20, 23, 61, 62, 66
   and United Arab Emirates 255–6
   and women 232, 235
University of Art (Tehran) 224
Unwritten Whispers (Najvaha-ye naneveshteh) (play) 87, 88
upper classes 35, 37
urbanisation 43–4, 61

Vafi, Fariba 52
Vahdat Hall (Tehran) 86
Valentine's Day 29–30, 37, 38, 40
Valfajr 8 (video game) 171, 175, *177*, 178
Vaziri, Qamar ol-Moluk 153
veil, the *see* hijab
video games 171–3
   and censorship 184
   and Islam 175
   and Persian mythology 180–3
   and procedural rhetoric 173–4, 175–8, 188
   production of 178–80, 185–6, 187
violence 3, 172, 183

war:
   martyrs 1, 65
   and music 160
   and theatre 86
   and video games 174
   see also Iran–Iraq war
Westernisation 32–3, 34, 111, 157

and dance 100
and Reza Shah 95
and theatre 88–9
Westoxification 20, 136, 147n.2
Where Were You on January 8th? (play) 87–8
White Scarves Campaign against Sex Segregation in Stadiums 53
winged deities 72
women 3, 5, 60, 75
   and dance 102, 103, 104
   and dress 20, 33, 95
   and film 6, 111–12, 114, 116
   and journalism 48–50, 51
   and murals 223
   and protest 43, 47
   and public life 115–16
   and publishing 231–41
   and rock music 134
   and sexuality 210, 212
   and society 44–6
   and sports clubs 105–6
   and theatre 82, 87, 88, 89
   see also girls
women's movements 13–14, 48, 49, 51, 55, 109–10, 125
Women's Prison (film) 110, 116–24, 126
women's rights 52–3, 54, 55, 125, 236–7, 240
Worker's Union (Tehran) 219
World Cup 101
writers 5
   female 52, 231, 236, 240
   see also playwrights

Yasemi 110
Yasin, Sheikh Ahmad 222
Yazd 62
Yellow Dogs 133, *134*, 140, 141–3, 147
youth 6, 7, 144, 146
   and activism 15–19, 20–6
   and demonstrations 13, 14
   distinctive 35–6, 37
   and education 63

and theatre 82–4, 86, 92n.2
and video games 171–2, 173
and Western influences 28–30,
    32–4, 39
see also boys; children; girls
YouTube 137, 163

Zabetian, Zahra 49
Zabul 185

Zahedan 62
Zan (magazine) 48
Zanan (magazine) 48, 49, 52
Zandi, Dariush 260
Zands 98
Zardosht, Djamshid-e 220–1
Zeynab Association 53
Zoroastrianism 72, 184, 211

www.ingramcontent.com/pod-product-compliance
Lightning Source LLC
Chambersburg PA
CBHW050337230426

43663CB00010B/1899